For Bernard Ashmole

Contents

Illustrations

(between pages 140 and 141)

The author and publishers would like to thank the following for permission to reproduce photographs: Plates 1, 2, 3, 4, 5, 6, 7, 9, 12, Trinity College, Dublin; 8, Kilmainham Gaol; 10, Trustees of the Imperial War Museum, London; 11, 14, 15, Illustrated London News Picture Library; 13, 16, Hulton Deutsch Collection.

Preface

A word about the origin and purpose of this book.

In an idle moment several summers ago I found an old friend with whom to pass some time. It was a favourite from childhood, *The Riddle of the Sands*. Reading the novel afresh, I was struck again by the qualities that make it almost the first and arguably the best of all thrillers: the action and the adventure, the mystery unfolded with drama and pace, the winding screw of tension, the marvellously managed climax. Yet there was also its charm, subtlety, humour, its refreshing ethical delicacy, and the extraordinary sense of time and place. I wondered about the novel's author. That he was an ardent patriot was clear enough from the book. I had read somewhere that he had fought in South Africa, had been decorated for his service in the Great War. But was there not a far odder story, that he had somehow involved himself in the civil war in Ireland, was subsequently shot for his trouble? I vaguely thought there was. I wanted to know more.

So began an adventure in itself, one that took me from Childers' childhood home in Ireland to his English school; from his 'beloved and lovely Baltic' to the eerie region of the Frisians; from his early homes in Chelsea to the House of Commons where he worked; from Boston where he was married to the Belfast of the Ulster Covenant; from his last home in Dublin to the Wicklow mountains where he was captured; and from there to the bleak square in Dublin where he died.

Whether this has all been worthwhile, the reader alone must judge. There have been, after all, other books about Erskine Childers. In his last months, Childers' character was so traduced that he willed his voluminous private papers to be embargoed until well after his death. He knew what his enemies could make of them. In 1971, when they were about to be released, the journalist Michael McInerney wrote an excellent call to action to biographers by way of his sketch, *The Riddle of Erskine Childers.* This stimulated two contrasting American biographies, a scholar's work from Tom Cox, a novelist's from Burke Wilkinson; there was also the late Andrew Boyle's authorized study of 1977. Boyle was distracted in composition by his discovery of the identity of Anthony Blunt as the Fourth Man, and his book does neither himself nor his subject quite the justice they deserve. Subsequently, Hugh and Diana Popham made a fascinating collection of Childers' nautical writings, and Maldwin Drummond produced in 1985 a dual study of Childers' sailing exploits and the historical background to the invasion story of the novel.

In preparing a fresh portrait of Childers I have had the immeasurable benefit of these books by my side; I hope, though, not merely to have summarised their arguments. Since Andrew Boyle was at work, a number of private papers and publications variously relating to Childers have come into the public domain, and these I have used. My starting-point was the novel, and as a key to his character I have accordingly employed Childers' own writings to a considerable extent. The present mood of reconciliation in Ireland casts a fresh light on those who last seriously attempted to resolve the question of that land. Finally, I have found particularly fruitful Tom Cox's hint of the remarkable counterpoints and parallels between the careers of Childers and that greatest of all Englishmen, Winston Spencer Churchill. Hence this book, which is above all an attempt to provide, for a new generation, a coherent psychological portrait of an intriguing man.

On the Irish aspects of Childers' story, two points must be stressed. First, that so tangled were the years of the 'troubles', and so important Childers' role at the time, that a book might be devoted to this subject alone. A work of such a nature would include a fresh scholarly assessment of Childers' work as a propagandist, and of his precise role in the treaty negotiations that created the Irish Free State. As a general biography, however, this has no such pretensions. Secondly, not being especially Irish myself, I have been obliged in preparing this book to climb (with Roger Casement) the stairs of Irish history. In some senses this ignorance is a handicap, perhaps a crippling one, yet I can at least say that it means I was in no way predisposed to Republicanism or Unionism, the Scylla and Charybdis of Irish politics, even in their moderate forms. Given the divisions of Ireland and its civil war, the consequences of which remain all too plainly apparent, this seems at least a point in the case for the defence: in other ways I must acknowledge the natural disadvantages of an English birth, background and education. Leaving aside such perspectives and prejudices as are perhaps inevitable, they may have led me to try to explain for an English audience what to an Irish one is a commonplace, and vice versa. In this I seek the reader's patience.

Childers took a less accommodating line. Of mixed English and Irish parentage, he declared himself to be by birth, domicile and inclination an Irishman and, more than seventy years ago, sacrificed everything to the Irish cause. Quite how the man who had once been among the Empire's staunchest advocates and defenders came to such an end is a curious and dramatic story, heavily laced with romance. In short, it is itself a thriller. 'No revolution', said John Buchan, 'ever produced a nobler or purer spirit.' Buchan was right.

Burnham Overy Staithe, 1996

Acknowledgements

As is usual with a book of this nature, there are more people to be thanked for their help in its preparation than space permits. Besides the various established authorities, I have talked to many people who, sometimes for the most surprising of reasons, in the least predictable of circumstances, have provided an insight into Childers and his times. To list all would be impracticable, to highlight only some discourteous; yet I must express particular gratitude to a few.

My starting-point was Childers' family. I was able to meet the widow of Childers' eldest son in Dublin, her stepson in Chicago. Dr Rory Childers is a distinguished cardiologist who takes a considerable and informed interest in his grandfather. I also met Childers' surviving son, Robert, at Glendalough. Mrs Diana Stewart, Robert's daughter, was present at that meeting, and was subsequently good enough to show me the various sites in Boston associated with her paternal grandmother, Erskine Childers' wife Molly. Without her friendly interest and help, the book would scarcely have been worthwhile. I am especially grateful to both Mrs Stewart and Rory Childers for giving me access to private family papers.

Childers' personality seems to have been moulded by his earliest years, but his schooling was also significant in the development of his character. Haileybury treasures the memory of its sons (now daughters, too), and I must thank Alistair Macpherson, the school archivist, for his help. He also drew my attention to the fragment of Childers' boat *Vixen*, which is to be seen in the school library.

W. R. McKay performs, at a more senior level, the role discharged by Childers for many years at the House of Commons. He pointed me to his biographical list of the Clerks, and was also able to add valuable anecdotal material about his predecessor.

Maldwin Drummond and John N. Young have written, respectively, about Erskine Childers and about his elder son. Both were generous enough to provide me with pointers to Childers' early years in London. Mr Young has also deposited in Trinity College, Dublin the opening chapters of his own planned biography of Erskine Childers, which should be consulted by any serious student.

For an English biographer, the real challenge of Childers' story lies in the Irish connections and, later, the Irish years. Maldwin Drummond eschewed these matters in his study, *The Riddle*; he may well have been wise to do so. I, more foolhardy, must above all thank the family of Colonel Paddy Flynn, for introducing me to the charm, the idiosyncrasies and the complexities of Irish life. Without this help, such understanding as I have of Ireland and the Irish would be negligible. Of the Irish it was, I think, Asquith who said: 'Aren't they a remarkable people? And the folly of thinking we can ever understand, let alone govern them!'

Ireland, as someone else has said, is a land where not everything known is written down; nevertheless, a book about a writer is of necessity heavily dependent on his writings, and this gives anyone interested in Childers the perfect pretext for spending a few days in the Wren Library at Trinity College, Cambridge. I am grateful to the Master and Fellows of the College for their permission to quote from the Childers papers kept there.

Rather longer will be spent in Trinity College, Dublin. The bulk of Childers' papers are there, and bulk is the operative word. Dr Bernard Meehan and his staff have been helpful in providing frequent access to these valuable papers, and I must also thank the Board of the College for permission to quote from this evocative and expressive material.

Childers' War Diary was presented to the Imperial War Museum in London by Robert Childers in 1987. I am grateful to the Museum for permission both to consult the diary and to reproduce some of its contents.

Although there is little academic interest in Childers as an imaginative writer, there is much in his activities as a politician: Professor Roy Foster and his graduate students at Hertford College, Oxford, here constituted more than a convenient beginning. I am also particularly appreciative of conversations with Dr David Fitzpatrick of Trinity

College, Dublin; Dr Tom Garvin of University College, Dublin; Dr Brian Caul of the University of Ulster; Dr Richard English of Queen's University, Belfast; and Commandant Peter Young, in charge of the archives of the Irish Army. Lord Longford also added some personal notes to the remarkable scholarship of his seminal study of the Anglo-Irish Treaty negotiations, and Dr Michael Dockrill of King's College, London made a significant contribution to the chapters on the Great War.

Finally, a number of people have had the patience to read and comment upon the manuscript in its various stages. I should thank first my mother, Dr Stella Ring, for her faith in the merit of the book. May I also thank my brother Christopher Ring, Dr Ann Ockwell, Lieutenant-Colonel Colman Goggin, Mary Stokes, Clive Jenkins, John Johnson, and Matthew Uffindell? All have helped me to bring into focus disparate material and incoherent opinion. Likewise, Dr Brian Murphy made some particularly imaginative suggestions about the last five chapters of the book, Dr Rory Childers about the text as a whole. The most tried of all has of course been my editor at John Murray, Gail Pirkis. She has been outstandingly patient and invariably constructive.

I owe thanks to all these people, and to many others besides. All have given most generously both of their insights and of their time, and without their help the book would have been more flawed than it remains. Nevertheless, as Jan Morris observed of one of her works, 'The faults of this book are patently my own.'

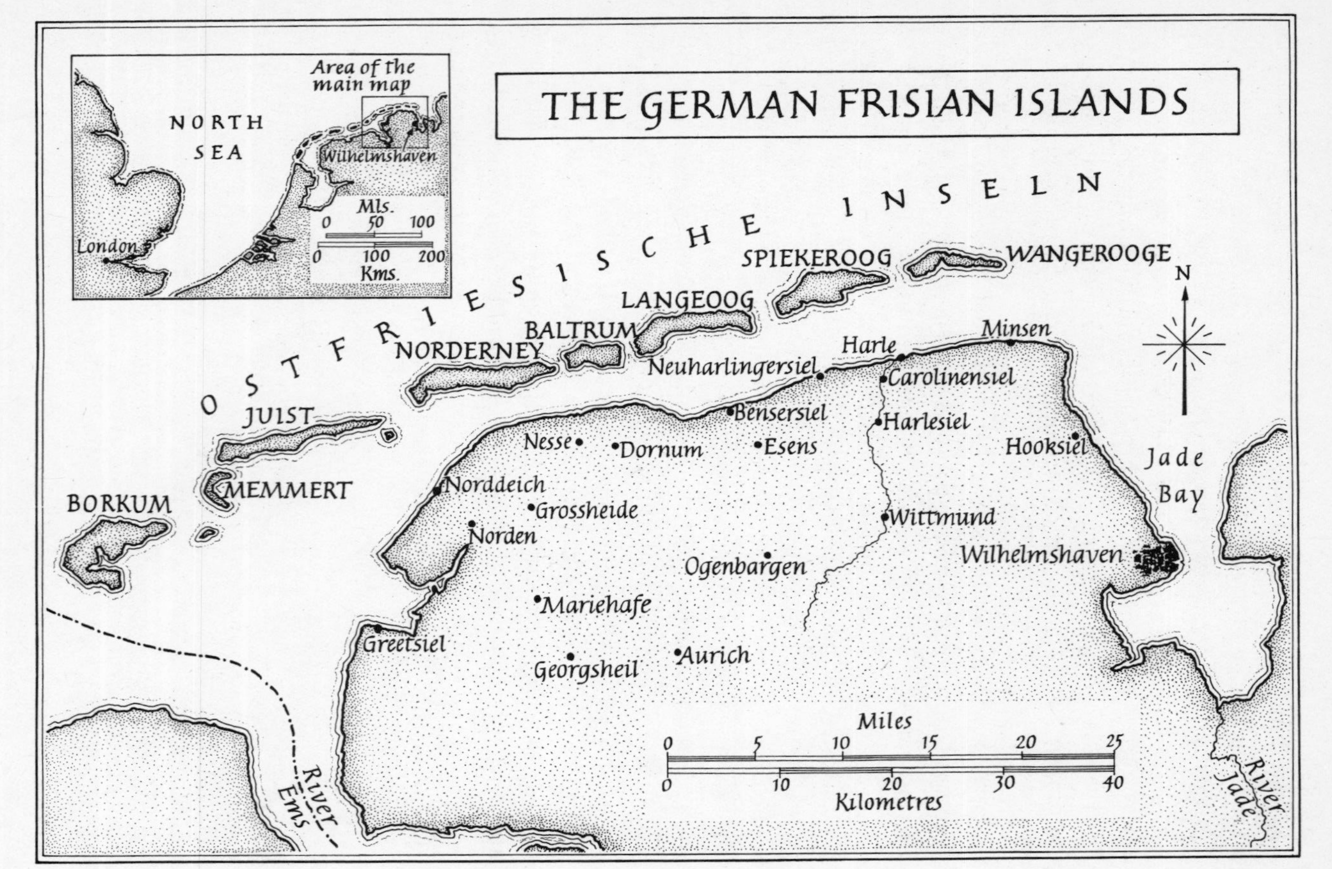
THE GERMAN FRISIAN ISLANDS
Area of the main map
NORTH SEA
London
Wilhelmshaven
Mls.
0 50 100
0 100 200
Kms.
OSTFRIESISCHE INSELN
BORKUM
MEMMERT
JUIST
NORDERNEY
BALTRUM
LANGEOOG
SPIEKEROOG
WANGEROOGE
N
Minsen
Harle
Neuharlingersiel
Carolinensiel
Bensersiel
Harlesiel
Nesse
Dornum
Esens
Hooksiel
Jade Bay
Norddeich
Grossheide
Norden
Wittmund
Ogenbargen
Wilhelmshaven
Mariehafe
Greetsiel
Georgsheil
Aurich
Miles
0 5 10 15 20 25
0 10 20 30 40
Kilometres
River Ems
River Jade

IRELAND AT THE TIME
OF THE EASTER RISING, 1916
N
Londonderry
ULSTER
Belfast
Portadown
Sligo
IRISH
CONNAUGHT
Athlone
Dublin
Howth
Galway
LEINSTER
SEA
Glendalough
Limerick
Wexford
Waterford
Tralee
MUNSTER
Cork
Bandon
Miles
0
25
50
75
0
40
80
120
Kilometres

Erskine Childers and the Breaking of Nations

Only a man harrowing clods
In a slow silent walk
With an old horse that stumbles and nods
Half asleep as they stalk.

Only thin smoke without flame
From the heaps of couch-grass;
Yet this will go onward the same
Though Dynasties pass.

Yonder a maid and her wight
Come whispering by:
War's annals will cloud into night
Ere their story die.

Thomas Hardy, 'In Time of "The Breaking of Nations"'

PART ONE

His Chance

'In our talk about policy and strategy we were Bismarcks and Rodneys, wielding nations and navies; and, indeed, I have no doubt that our fancy took extravagant flights sometimes. In plain fact we were merely two young gentlemen in a seven-ton pleasure boat, with a taste for amateur hydrography and police duty combined. Not that Davies ever doubted. Once set on the road he gripped his purpose with childlike faith and tenacity. It was his "chance".'

The Riddle of the Sands

1
The Gathering Storm

'The mightiest and most beneficent Empire ever known in the history of mankind.'

The Times, June 1897

On 27 May 1903 there was published a book of such a character as quite to define the spirit of the times, of such force and graphic power as to transport the author to immediate fame, and of such abiding popularity as to lend immortality to a man subsequently shot for what amounted to treason. It was a book beguilingly subtitled *A Record of Secret Service Recently Achieved*, otherwise known as *The Riddle of the Sands*.

The Great Britain of that happy age is scarcely our own, for the turn of the twentieth century was the zenith of a century of national triumph. Largely untroubled by war, the country had successfully managed the transition to a democratic society without the violence that seemed perpetually to deface Continental Europe. She had created out of the industrial revolution a country which, with reason, called itself the workshop of the world, which provided in the Pound Sterling the basis for the world's economy, and in her Grand Fleet 'the ultimate arbiter of the world's affairs'.[1] Her Empire since Queen Victoria's accession had grown tenfold; a quarter of the world's map was attractively shaded red, and a third of its population – some 370 million people – was held under the Queen's equable and condescending sway. Even so partisan an observer as *Le Figaro* was obliged to concede that 'Rome itself had been equalled, if not surpassed, by the Power . . . which in Canada, Australia, India, in the China seas, in Egypt, Central and

Southern Africa, in the Atlantic and in the Mediterranean rules the peoples and governs their interests.'[2]

It was an age in England of great feats, great discoveries, great challenges, and great men. There were the engineers – men like the Stephensons, Joseph Locke, and Isambard Kingdom Brunel – who paved the country with the iron road, and shrunk the oceans with great steamships like the *Great Britain*, and the giant *Great Eastern*, some six times the size of anything then afloat. There was the inventor Wheatstone, who devised the telegraph, a fundamental instrument of modern communications. There were great clerics like Cardinal Newman and Cardinal Manning; their foes the iconoclasts Charles Darwin and J. G. Frazier, who were largely to recast Western religious thought. There were the remarkable explorers Livingstone, Stanley and Speke, who 'withdrew the veil from the immemorial secrecy of the Dark Continent';[3] and then Palmerston, Gladstone and Disraeli, bestriding like giants the European political stage. In the arts, Elgar was the finest English composer for two hundred years, Kipling the Empire's quintessential chronicler and celebrant, and Tennyson the last Poet Laureate to enjoy genuinely popular readership and acclaim. There were Imperialists like Rhodes and George Taubman Goldie, who personally brought under the British flag an area in Africa exceeding that of France and Germany combined; and like Gordon, who made the supreme sacrifice at the siege of Khartoum. And then of course there were the seers – Ruskin, Carlyle, Morris and Arnold – who in incomparable prose deplored it all.

It would certainly be absurd to paint an unshaded picture of an era in which much of the country's wealth rested on a labour force which was by modern standards grossly ill-rewarded and grossly overworked, whose industrial cities were bywords for poverty and vice, whose countryside since the mid 'seventies had been ravaged by agricultural depression, and which was deplorably neglectful of human rights. As late as 1895 Oscar Wilde had been imprisoned for homosexual offences, while the Queen herself said of the nascent suffragist movement that she was 'most anxious to enlist everyone who can speak or write to join in checking this mad folly of "women's rights" with all its attendant horrors.'[4] Yet national prestige and individual achievement were in many respects matched by improvements to the common lot. A myriad factors, particularly a growing understanding of the transmission of disease, had led to a doubling of the population in the years since the Queen had come to the throne. The extension of the education acts had given even the poor the basics of learning, and the broadening of the franchise was gradually devolving power downwards in society. Even the wealth of the nation, if not spread everywhere, was – like the Empire – being ever more widely spread. If it was demonstrably not the age of the common man or woman, it was undoubtedly a period of transition which was to usher in such an age.

It was perhaps, to the modern eye, most strikingly an age of national self-confidence. 'We don't want to fight,' declared the music hall song, 'but by jingo if we do, we've got the ships, we've got the guns, we've got the money too.' And when Arthur Balfour tactlessly ventured to draw the Queen's attention to disagreeable developments in the Boer War – Stormberg, Magersfontein, Colenso, Ladysmith – she of course interrupted: 'Please understand that there is no one depressed in *this* house; we are not interested in the possibilities of defeat; they do not exist.'[5]

So it was by no means difficult, in the glorious morning of that other age, to feel that God was in His Heaven and all was right with the world. Yet, as the early days of the new century passed, there were some to whom that confidence seemed misplaced.

In the agnostic world that is late twentieth-century England it is difficult to appreciate both the extent to which religion was the corner-stone of the Victorian age, and the consequent impact on the national psyche of a growing fundamental doubt. Consciously or otherwise, Evangelism pervaded mid-Victorian England in word, thought and deed: the extent to which it governed the daily lives and actions of our great-grandparents is remarkable. Here it is enough to note that when Sidney Herbert declared he was 'more and more convinced every day that in politics, as in everything else, nothing can be right which is not in accordance with the spirit of the Gospel',[6] his words were those of simple faith, divorced from rhetoric. In such circumstances the broadside of the freethinking movement, spearheaded during the 'sixties and 'seventies by Matthew Arnold and Darwin's disciple T. H. Huxley, was shattering. How could it be otherwise when, more profoundly in the West than ever before, man's place in the order of creation, his very *raison d'être*, was being radically questioned? Arnold, a favourite of Erskine Childers, had set the matter in lapidary form:

> The Sea of Faith
> Was once, too, at the full, and round earth's shore
> Lay like the folds of a bright girdle furl'd;
> But now I only hear
> Its melancholy, long, withdrawing roar,
> Retreating to the breath
> Of the night-wind down the vast edges drear
> And naked shingles of the world.[7]

If by the turn of the century, then, the tenure of God seemed uncertain, so too was that of the woman whom many quite literally regarded as His prime instrument on earth. The Queen had reigned since 1837, when she was just eighteen, presiding over a period which had seen the final stage of transformation of the country from an agricultural to an industrial state, from a country ruled by the few for the few to one in which the creators of wealth were beginning to have a significant say in the governing of its affairs. She had seen Britain grow from being merely one of the victorious Powers that had defeated Napoleon to the pre-eminent Power, the richest and most powerful nation, the world very grudgingly at her feet. At the end of the Queen's reign she was idolized by her subjects, the vast majority of whom had never known another monarch. Now she had proved mortal. To her people, her death in 1901 seemed 'some monstrous reversal of the course of nature'.[8] While welcoming the accession of King Edward VII, the author of *A Record of Secret Service* commented: 'I have a superstitious feeling that her death closes our greatest epoch as her crowning certainly began it.'[9]

That the same fate, dissolution and death, should befall the Empire on which – for geophysical reasons – the sun never set, seemed a hundred years ago hardly imaginable. Yet there were those who were beginning to imagine it.

It was the South African war during the final two years of Victoria's reign that raised the alarm, the war that began when two small farmers' republics flourishing under her 'suzerainity' had the temerity to challenge the Queen's authority; indeed, to impose horrifying and entirely unexpected reverses on the greatest empire the world had ever known. It was true that the rising was in due course suppressed, by superiority of numbers, of organization, of military skill and above all of courage, which the British people naturally expected; but not before some disturbingly equivocal signs had been broadcast to Great Britain and to the world beyond, regarding her military power and even regarding the wisdom and morality of the Imperial progress.

Were these things really open to question? To the Irish, ruled by the English from Dublin Castle, undoubtedly they were. Since the eighteen-nineties Ireland had been presciently twinned with the Boer lands as the imperial colonies most likely to rise against their creator; it was the most dangerous place in the British Isles; and it was the country which had first focused attention on the moral – and the practical – issues of Imperialism. For some it raised greater matters still. The *Edinburgh Review* once declared that the real Irish Home Rule question was whether Imperial Britain was to continue the dominant nation in the world.[10] Much later, the author of *The Riddle of the Sands* was to urge: 'This Irish war, small as it may seem now, if it is persisted in, will corrupt and eventually ruin not only your Army, but your nation and your Empire as well.'[11]

Still, when *A Record of Secret Service Recently Achieved* was published in May 1903, the problems of Ireland had begun to pale into insignificance beside those presented by the new King's nephew, Kaiser Wilhelm II, and his bright cuirass of a country that was Germany. That very relationship between the sovereigns, coupled with a longstanding belief in the perfidy of France, was among the things lulling the British into a false sense of security regarding a country with painfully clear colonial ambitions, and with an industrial and commercial base increasingly threatening to Britain's supremacy. The Kruger telegram of 1896, in which the Kaiser signalled to the Transvaal President his support for Boer independence, had shattered fond belief in Germany's harmlessness – leaving the English disillusioned, furious and suspicious. 'Germany's a thundering great nation', remarks 'Arthur H. Davies' in *The Riddle of the Sands*; 'I wonder if we shall ever fight her.'[12] Far more than Ireland, this was the question of the hour, a question highlighted by the Kaiser's construction of the Kiel canal between the landlocked Baltic and the North Sea, and his assertive programme for the building of capital ships – his challenge to what was simultaneously the Empire's shield and its most resonant symbol, the Grand Fleet.

On the splendid occasion of the Queen's Diamond Jubilee in 1897, when *The Times*, then a paper of unimpeachable authority, talked of 'the mightiest and most beneficent Empire ever known in the history of mankind',[13] such heresies were almost unthought-of. But soon would come the allusive and disquieting presentiments of Kipling's poem *Recessional*, the Queen's death, and then the 'clarion warning'[14] of *A Record of Secret Service Recently Achieved*, whose author, Erskine Childers, was to play such a strange part in the future of what was then the dominant nation in the world.

2
The Golden Morning

1903

'I am so tremendously happy, old chap.'
Erskine Childers, November 1903

I

Anyone who met Erskine Childers in the early summer of 1903 – at 'Morven Lodge', or with 'the Catesbys in Kent' or his 'people in Aix' – was unlikely to have identified him as a harbinger of Imperial doom. A slight, limping, bespectacled figure with the facial hair – a moustache – that the new King had done so much to popularize, and an almost pedantic turn of speech, he had something of the remoteness of a don.

He was diffident, self-possessed and unassuming, his background not particularly remarkable. His late father had been the Orientalist Professor Robert Caesar Childers, a pioneer of Western linguistic studies of Buddhism; Hugh Culling Eardley Childers, his father's cousin, had served prominently in a series of Gladstone's cabinets, and was so far-sighted as to have introduced the telephone to Whitehall; a distant ancestor, Thomas Erskine, had been a distinguished Lord Chancellor. The death of his father at the age of thirty-eight, followed by that of his mother six years later, had left his upbringing in the hands of Anglo-Irish kin. Charles and Agnes Barton had provided a prosperous upper-middle class home for Childers himself, his elder brother Henry, and their three younger sisters, Dulcibella, Constance and Sybil. Childers was schooled initially by a governess, then prep school was followed by Haileybury, an institution very much of Imperialist hue. Here he eventually distinguished himself, rather than positively excelling. Trinity College, Cambridge, followed, where he at first read Classics. There he was a leading light of the debating society, and collected some agreeable cronies, most notable among them the man who was to become Winston Churchill's long-serving private secretary, Edward Marsh. A switch to law for his Finals, and a period at a crammer's in London, saw Childers passing out third in the Civil Service examinations of 1894 – and into a Clerkship in the House of Commons. Seamless if unspectacular progress was arrested in 1899 by the Boer War, in which Childers, with his irreproachably conventional Imperialist views, volunteered. As the driver of a mobile battery he saw only a little action, but the publication of his letters home revealed a writer of personal charm with a talent for immediacy, and brought him a brief popular vogue.

So: an administrator – but not so able as to have been asked to join the likes of John Buchan in Lord Milner's precocious 'kindergarten', busily reconstructing South Africa; a writer – but without obvious aspirations to greatness; well-educated – but without serious pretensions to scholarship. At thirty-three he was single and, somehow, remote – a man yet to discover his métier. Yet, that year, the publication of a new book and his meeting with the woman who was to become his wife were to set him irrevocably on the passage to both martyrdom and immortality.

II

The modest success of his South African war book, *In the Ranks of the CIV* (City of London Imperial Volunteers), encouraged Childers to seek a larger canvas. Perhaps he would write a novel, but one which would reflect his personal experience of Great Britain as a country in many respects disturbingly ill-prepared for war. Even before the reviews of the volume of letters appeared, he had the basic idea for a novel set in the Baltic and the Frisian islands, both of which he had explored in 1897. Perhaps it might concern a secret German plan for the seaborne invasion of the east coast of England. In January 1901 he wrote to a distant relative, Flora Priestley: 'I have not begun that book yet. I forgot before coming away to get the diary of that cruise from the flat. An idea has struck me that a story, of which I have the germ, might be worked into it as a setting.'[1] Mrs Priestley, a close friend of the painter John Singer Sargent, took an interest in the young man's artistic ambitions; her response was encouraging. But to Childers, the creative task was unfamiliar. He was as practised a correspondent as the communications of the age demanded, and from his days at Haileybury it had been his habit to entertain in particular his three younger sisters with accounts of his doings, this culminating in the letters that had formed the basis of the South African book. Yet such a direct rendering of experience requires rather different talents from the imaginative creation of events, situations, characters and circumstances in which the author has not been personally involved. Childers was an enthusiastic reader, both of the Classics in which he had been educated and of rather more contemporary literature, Thackeray, Stevenson and Tennyson being particular favourites. Yet such examples, in their relative perfection, can overawe the novice. Four months later Childers wrote again to Flora Priestley, in some uncertainty: 'I have not begun the Baltic book yet. I fear it would be no good without pictures. I also fear the story is beyond me.'[2]

Even when the book was finally begun, at the end of 1901, Childers found the going far from good. Naturally enough, by now the idea had crystallised into rather more concrete form. To Basil Williams, his closest friend in the clerks' office at the House of Commons, and former comrade-in-arms in the Boer War, the author wrote in June 1902: 'It's a yachting story, with a purpose, suggested by a cruise I once took in German waters. I discover a scheme of invasion directed against England.' The problem in the first instance lay in the unfolding of that purpose, for on what drama was the story to hinge? The crucial revelation in such a plot obviously lies in the discovery of the invasion plan itself. So how was tension and dramatic interest to be maintained until this point, especially as to Childers the plausibility of the tale was paramount? 'I find it horribly difficult', he continued, 'as being in the nature of a detective story, there is no sensation, only what is meant to be convincing fact.'[3] Then there was the romantic interest. As originally planned, the plot of the book was to be driven solely by the story of an enquiry by solicitor-cum-yachtsman 'Arthur H. Davies' and his holiday companion 'Carruthers'. The central question posed at the beginning of the book, and which it set out to answer, was simple: why had the enigmatic Herr Dollmann attempted to wreck the inoffensive Davies on the sands of the German Frisian islands? Hitherto, it has been thought that the book's publisher Reginald Smith insisted on the incorporation of romance, introduced by way of Davies' involvement with the antagonist's daughter, Fräulein Dollmann;[4] yet it may rather have been the inspiration of Childers' sister Dulcibella. This sub-plot, which actually enlivens and complements the basic theme, merely meant trouble to Childers at the time. 'I was weak enough to "spatchcock" a girl into it,' he recounted to Williams, 'and now find her a horrible nuisance. I have not approached Reginald yet.'[5]

The book was finished to the author's satisfaction at the end of 1902, but was returned to him by Smith with demands for what Childers described as 'drastic revision'. The publisher asked for a series of changes, the principal ones seemingly concerning the extensive and detailed descriptions of the management and sailing of the book's real heroine, Davies' yacht *Dulcibella*. Childers, who had just spent a pleasant month indulging in the newly fashionable winter sports with his sisters in St Moritz, was much put out. 'In some points he was right,' Childers wrote to Williams, 'but in others I held wrong, and I have concocted a compromise which I think he will swallow.'[6]

As the book went to press in the early spring of 1903, there were two final checks. The first was when some of that very complacency in matters of national defence which the novel attacked was countered by a number of measures introduced by Arthur Balfour's Conservative government, including the establishment of a National Defence Committee, the selection of a site for a North Sea naval base in the Firth of Forth, and the creation of a North Sea Fleet. To avoid the appearance of preaching a panegyric over an empty coffin, Childers hastily drafted a postscript to the book welcoming these moves, in the vein of decisions excellent if tardy. Then Smith himself attempted, in Childers' view, to 'wreck' the book, 'by promoting it as a novel'. Given the author's intention that the book should be taken seriously as a 'clarion warning', and his consequent wish to make the story appear as plausible as possible, his view was understandable. From the beginning the idea had been to use the literary convention of presenting the narrative not as fiction but as fact. In the end, the novel was duly billed in the advertisements that appeared in weeklies like *The Spectator* – and on its spine – as *A Record of Secret Service Recently Achieved*, EDITED by Erskine Childers. 'By quiet persistent opposition', Childers went on, 'I have managed to effect a good deal.'[7] It was thus on 27 May 1903 that *The Riddle of the Sands* was finally published.

III

The circumstances of the writing of the book had inevitably lowered the expectations of both author and publisher as to its likely success. For Childers, scribbling corrections in his Chelsea rooms late at night after a long day in the Commons was hardly a pleasure. For Smith, cajoling a reluctant author to revise his work was equally onerous. To both the novel, as produced, represented a somewhat painful compromise. The initial print-run was a modest twelve hundred and fifty.

Yet on publication their labours were rewarded. Even if Childers did not wake up to find himself famous, the book was an immediate triumph in terms of its sales, its critical reception, and the manner in which it discharged its author from obscurity. It made Childers' name.

Before 1903 was out, Smith had had the happy task of returning to his printer twice to order further impressions of the book, admitting, in the words of Childers' authorized biographer Andrew Boyle, 'that he had misjudged both the flair of the writer and the subtlety of the handiwork'.[8] To slip outside chronology: the book was reprinted twice in 1904 in hard covers, and sold sufficiently in the years up until the First War to demand impressions in 1907, 1908, 1910 and 1913. The war itself engendered a new, highly successful cheap edition; 1915 saw its publication for the first time in the United States, 1917 in France. Between the wars interest was sustained sufficiently for the book never to be out of print, and by 1938 there had been no fewer than seventeen editions in Britain alone.[9] Since then editions have proliferated on both sides of the Atlantic, in paperback form as well as in more elaborate and illustrated editions, and it has been estimated that in all rather more than two million copies of the book have been sold. These include those German translations that may be discovered today in the bookshops of that remote Frisian island, that 'cluster of sandhills surmounting a long slope of weedy sand'[10] that is Norderney.

The book was as warmly welcomed by the reviewers, most of whom responded to Childers' insistence upon the novel's presentation as fact rather than fiction by puzzling over how it was to be treated. 'One hesitates to class it in the category of fiction,' declared *The Scotsman*, some six weeks after publication. The *Courier* found it similarly 'difficult to say how much of Mr Childers' present work is fiction and how much fact.' The means by which this verisimilitude was achieved were widely applauded. The *Northern Whig* remarked that 'Mr Childers writes with restraint and vraisemblance that almost compels the belief in his narrative as a statement of cold fact'. Another review at first notes the 'minuteness of detail with which the narrative is loaded, the apparent familiarity with the scene of the incidents described – a familiarity intimate and confident to the last degree.' Continuing, the writer declares, 'But if it be fiction, the author must be credited with an ability amounting in the minutia of his art only to Defoe, and in the resources and fertility of his imagination only to Robert Louis Stevenson.' Although to a few, notably the *St James's Gazette*, the book was primarily a 'breezy and thoroughly entertaining romance', most took it as the 'story with a purpose' the author intended. The *Daily Chronicle* in August observed that Childers' intention was 'to point out to his fellow countrymen a peril to England which lurks in the shallow estuaries and river mouths, masked effectively by any number of small islands, on that portion of the German coast washed by the North Sea.' Caveats were few, although several reviewers noted a weakness in the portrayal of Fräulein Dollmann: 'We regret that Mr Childers has so far surrendered to the demands of novel readers as to insert the usual conventional "love-interest". It was not wanted here a bit.' *The Times* declared it to be scarcely very plausible that the Germans, 'a practical people', would 'permit a professional traitor to drag a pretty daughter through his muddy courses.'[11] Overall, however, the book's critical reception both during the course of that summer and in later years was overwhelmingly favourable. The last word is best left to John Buchan, who shared with Childers a passion for both the world of letters and the world of action. 'It is a tale of the puzzling out of a mystery which only gradually reveals itself, and not till the very end reaches its true magnificence; but its excitement begins on the first page, and there is a steady crescendo of interest.' Of the characters, he observed: 'I think they are the most truly realised of any adventure story that I have met, and the atmosphere of grey Northern skies and miles of yeasty water and wet sands is as masterfully reproduced as in any story of Conrad's.' It was, he concluded, 'the best adventure story published in the last quarter of a century.'[12]

Appreciation of his literary skills was not, however, Childers' main objective. Rather, he sought *The Times*' response, that 'the contents may be highly important, and the revelation may be useful to Admiralty and the War Office.' It is a testimony to the timeliness and plausibility of the tale that not only should the paper have thought this, but that the Admiralty did indeed take note. On 27 April 1904 Lord Selborne, First Lord of the Admiralty, wrote to no less a person than Prince Louis Battenberg, the Director of Naval Intelligence:

> I have several times spoken to you about a book called *The Riddle of the Sands*, and I think you told me that, although you had not read it yourself, it had been examined in your Department. I have no more than merely glanced at it and therefore do not profess to have any opinion on it, but it is very remarkable how many people have been struck by it and who constantly come to me about it . . . I do not know which of your officers examined the book for you or whether his examination was cursory or thorough. Unless the book was examined by an officer in whom you have complete confidence and in a very complete manner, I shall be greatly obliged if you will again have it examined most thoroughly and by an officer in whose judgement you can absolutely rely.[13]

It was this sort of end, rather than mere literary acclaim, to which Childers aspired; and had he known of the Admiralty's interest he would have been delighted. For, as he had hoped, it was by acting as a catalyst for concerns about Germany that the book played a part in ensuring that Britain was prepared for the Great War; and indeed it may fairly be said that 1903 marked the beginning of a re-orientation of national perceptions, from regarding France as the primary enemy, to so regarding Germany.

More immediate, though, was the impact on Childers' reputation. Not hitherto particularly distinguished by his connections, nor was he by outstanding talents or endeavour – for which his job as a responsible if junior civil servant in the House of Commons was arguably a just reward. Now the flame that had briefly burned with the publication of his first book was rekindled far more brightly. It was certainly flattering to be buttonholed by Lord Rosebery, a man doubly distinguished, by reason of his short premiership in the 1890s, and by the Derby wins of his horses Ladas and Sir Visto in successive years. 'He wanted to know how much was fact,' Childers wrote to Williams, 'and talked delightfully on the various subjects suggested by the book, urged me to write again and was most kind and encouraging.'[14] Socially, too, there were advantages. *In the Ranks of the CIV* had led to a pleasant acquaintance with the Earl of Denbigh and Desmond, Commanding Officer of the City of London Imperial Volunteers' parent battalion, the Honourable Artillery Company. With talk of his new book on everyone's lips that summer of 1903, Childers began to live the social life, if not of Riley, then at least of 'Carruthers', as so engagingly portrayed by him in the opening chapter of the novel. Although he was too modest a man to be unduly susceptible to lionization, it was still pleasant to spend the season enjoying the factual counterparts of 'Morven Lodge' and 'the Catesbys in Kent'. Finally that summer, and thanks to the Earl of Denbigh and Desmond, came the journey which led to the second critical event of that year.

IV

The HAC had been asked to Boston to return a visit paid in 1896 by its 'cousin', the Ancient and Honourable Artillery Company of Massachusetts. This would represent rather more than a straightforward if fearsomely convivial reunion: it would be the first social visit by a British military unit since the Declaration of Independence in 1776 and its painful aftermath; or, in Childers' own words, 'the first time armed Britishers have marched through American streets since the Revolution.'[15] Moreover, it was to be made to the city that was the very cradle of independence, and in the immediate context of the

Company's recent Imperialist involvement in South Africa. In the light of its own former struggle for independence from Britain, there was much sympathy in America for the Boer cause, and much of it very publicly expressed. It was thus by no means certain how the Company would be received.

In such circumstances, it was clearly of the first importance that the HAC's most recent chronicler should be present. Childers, writing to Williams, showed initial reluctance: 'I dismissed the notion of going myself as I dread the round of drinking and feasting, especially as I am a teetotaller.' In the end, though, he relented. There was a wanderlust in his character which, in days when international travel was far from commonplace, had already taken him to the West Indies as well as South Africa, and in very small boats across the Channel, and across the North Sea as far as the Baltic. He was also placed under a certain amount of personal pressure from Lord Denbigh. 'I am less averse to it now,' he wrote, 'as I find Herbert is going, and Budworth and the Colonel are strongly in favour of it, and are trying to get the right men to go.'[16]

It was a visit during which the formalities were in the main very much observed. The party of 173 boarded the liner *Mayflower* on 23 September 1903, taking with them the good wishes of their Colonel-in-Chief, the King. They whiled away the voyage with squad drills and sword exercises; a sermon from the Chaplain, the Revd Dr Leighton Parks, appropriately took as its theme 'The Miracle of the Anglo-Saxon Race'. On the last night a fancy-dress ball was held, at which Lord Denbigh appeared as Father Neptune, Lady Denbigh as Britannia.[17]

In Boston the King's farewell prediction of 'a most gratifying reception in the United States' was proved a happy one. The Company was treated more as conquering heroes than as ambassadors. As the *Mayflower* steamed towards Boston's Charlestown dock, waiting to welcome them was a delegation from the Massachusetts 'Ancients' themselves, the United States cruiser *Chicago* and, from Halifax in Nova Scotia, HMS *Retribution*. The guns of Fort Warren boomed a twenty-one gun salute, from the Bunker Hill Monument the Stars and Stripes and Union Jack streamed in the wind together, and 'every ship large or small joined in the reception with display of bunting . . . with screech of siren or toot of whistle.'[18] No sooner had the Company disembarked than there was assembled as great a parade as the city had seen: every military unit in the area had come to welcome and march with them. Childers himself related that 'From the moment we arrived we have been fêted and raved over – whenever we turn out the whole town turns out and cheers, men, women and children, and our march after landing on October 2nd in some ways surpassed the City Imperial Volunteers Day in London'. It was a moving experience after the months of scrappy fighting on the veldt which had left ten CIVs dead, and one which led Childers to reflect on Britain's Imperial role: 'It came on me with a flash that there's a good deal more than I thought in the "union of hearts" phrase, and in the excitement of the time one can set no limits to the possibilities of an alliance of English-speaking races.'

As well as marching, there was relaxation. A select number of Bostonians, 'The Ten of Us', had each put up the then very considerable sum of $1,000, for the better entertainment of their guests at a dinner. The consequences of this generosity were perhaps predictable. Continuing his letter to Williams, Childers remarked: 'As to behaviour, I believe we have got through without open scandal – mercifully, for the primitive instincts of the HAC are set towards tipsy debauchery, and when champagne is perpetually flowing like water the descent to the Averno is abnormally easy, especially as our escort, a hundred members of the Boston Company . . . aren't noted for sobriety.' Two weeks of this sort of thing was enough for the habitually sober Childers, but though he had always intended to take the opportunity of the visit to see something of New England, he watched the regiment's departure with mixed feelings: 'I am alone in America with a visit or two to make but nothing particular to do – and not feeling very keen.'[19]

This was disingenuous of the normally punctiliously truthful Childers. For he had just formed an attachment that was to change his life.

V

Dr Hamilton Osgood, a prominent Bostonian and one of the leading physicians in North America, was the father of two daughters, the elder of whom was married to a man whom Childers later described as 'an impassioned anti-Imperialist who spends quantities on the cause'.[20] Dr Osgood himself was similarly inclined, and kept open house to supporters of Irish independence. His younger daughter Mary Alden, usually known as Molly, was twenty-five. Crippled at the age of three in a skating accident, she had spent the remainder of her childhood in a basket which doubled as her bed, until an operation at the age of thirteen largely but not completely restored the use of her legs. The experience had endowed her equally with stoicism, and considerable strength of will; she was highly intelligent and, as a consequence perhaps of her long invalidism, very well-read. A contemporary photograph shows a delicate face, a contemplative air, and considerable beauty.

Dr Osgood's brother-in-law Sumner Pearmain had been an acquaintance of the late Robert Caesar Childers, and to him the professor's son sent a letter of introduction on his arrival in Boston. He was invited to dinner, and there sat next to Pearmain's niece Molly. Childers, eight years her senior, author, soldier, and employed at the very hub of the Empire, must have been possessed of a glamour that was belied by his appearance and his unassuming manner. Moreover, his sensitivity and kindliness were manifest. Here was an exceptional man. Molly's beauty was incontrovertible, but for Childers her appeal lay more in a warmth, charm and force of personality which quite countered the effects of her miserable childhood. In both, too, there was innocence, unworldliness, and something of the idealism of a happier age. Within a very short time they had fallen in love.

With no series of successful liaisons behind him to engender self-confidence, alone and far from home, Childers felt himself very much the supplicant. Yet would he forgive himself if he let slip this chance? With a life and a job awaiting his return, three thousand miles away, he could not idle interminably in Massachusetts. Just three weeks after the couple first met, he made his decision. On 30 October 1903 he took Molly in a canoe onto the still waters of the lake at Harvard known as Bare Hill Pond. There, tremulously and with great diffidence, he proposed: 'I would like to ask you to be with me for ever.'[21] Molly's acceptance was immediate. To Childers' aunt Agnes Barton she wrote simply, 'I cannot find words with which to tell you what Erskine means to me.'[22]

With Dr Osgood's blessing, and with similar celerity, the wedding was arranged for just nine weeks later, 5 January 1904. Childers then sat down to the happy task of informing his relatives and friends, to whom, characteristically, he had so far said nothing at all. 'I am engaged to be married to Miss Mary Osgood of this city,' he wrote a little stiffly to Williams. Then, suddenly unbending: 'I am so tremendously happy, old chap.'[23]

For Childers it was the end of what had every appearance of having been a miraculous year: 1903 had transformed the retiring civil servant into a famous author on the brink of what was to prove an enduringly happy marriage. Only with hindsight is it possible to regard this year as the one which held in it the genesis of his legend, and of his final tragedy.

3
Native Impulses, Stucco Crusts

1870–1894

> 'What a mystery the growth of one's personality is. It is well nigh hopeless to distinguish native impulses from stucco crusts imposed by environment . . .'
>
> Erskine Childers, 1903

I

Robert Erskine Childers was born on 25 June 1870 to Robert Caesar Childers and Anna Henrietta Barton.

The Bartons were a family peculiarly representative of certain aspects of Irish history. As far back as they may usefully be called 'English', the English had interested themselves in Ireland, which from the twelfth century was more or less a Crown possession. Apart from simple land-lust, the English occupation had defence as its aim, since the island provided a convenient staging-post for any attack by England's European rivals, notably the Spanish and the French. This was a threat of which England was all too vividly aware, and which long dictated her Irish policy. One of the natural consequences of the English presence was the domination of the Gaelic masses by a small group of Anglo-Normans, a domination in due course exacerbated by Henry VIII's break with Rome, which left the Catholic majority ruled by a Protestant minority, later known as the Ascendancy. Ireland thus became divided both by religion and by race. Under Ascendancy rule at its most iniquitous, it was illegal for Catholics to own, rent or inherit land, the indigenous inhabitants thereby being deprived of what might be supposed to be their birthright. A famous Lord Chancellor could even declare that 'the law does not presume any such person to exist as an Irish Roman Catholic'.[1] As a result a native tradition of rebellion was early established, and from time to time the country was governed, either metaphorically or actually, under martial law. In 1801 the situation was to an extent regularized by the legal union of the two countries, with MPs elected in Ireland sitting in Westminster. As the Irish contingent often held the balance of power, this came to have a mischievous effect on English politics, yet at the same time rarely a positive one for Ireland. Then arose various attempts, constitutional and otherwise, to repudiate the Union. Fuelled by the great famine in which more than a million people died, at the time of Childers' birth these were on the point of being channelled by Charles Stewart Parnell into the great nationalist upsurge which so nearly gave Ireland her freedom. In the meantime, the country continued to be ruled under an English Viceroy in Dublin Castle – known simply as The Castle.

By reputation, Thomas Barton of Norwich was one of the followers of the Earl of Essex's chaotic Irish venture of 1599, but abandoned the campaign to settle in County Fermanagh. He became one of the first burgesses of Inneskillen, and the family subsequently made its fortune through trade with France; a branch even acquired a château and vineyard in Bordeaux. Like many such families it was traditionally Protestant, retained the mores and manners of the English, and kept a certain distance from the native Gaels. Soon the family had established itself in several other parts of Ireland, as well as in France; Thomas Johnston Barton was the first to venture south, in the 1830s, and settled at Glendalough, an estate of some two thousand acres between Dublin and Wicklow. Barton, a gentleman farmer, became Deputy Lieutenant, and a JP. The Bartons, in short, typified the Ascendancy in their long but somewhat equivocal relationship with the land which they ruled.

To the respectability of the Bartons, Thomas Erskine added the distinction of a remarkable Lord Chancellorship. Born in Edinburgh in 1750, he was the youngest son of the tenth Earl of Buchan. A 'quick, idle and frolicsome boy', he spent his early years abroad, first in the army and then in the navy. When he eventually returned to England, he encountered Samuel Johnson, as recorded by James Boswell: 'On

Monday, 6th April 1772 I dined . . . at Sir Alexander MacDonald's where was a young officer [Erskine] in the regimental of the Scots Royal, who talked with a vivacity, fluency and precision so uncommon that he attracted particular attention.' Erskine published a pamphlet on *Abuses in the Army*, began to interest himself in the law, and in 1778 was called to the Bar. Then he had a stroke of fortune. A chance meeting with the defendant in a case of criminal libel brought by Lord Sandwich led to Erskine taking on what was regarded as an impossible case. 'Finding courage', as he said, 'by thinking that his children were plucking at his gown, and crying that now was the time to get them bread,' he carried the day by sheer force of rhetoric, an observer remarking that in the middle of the speech 'he found the court, judges and all in a trance of amazement.' Erskine's name was made; he found himself almost at once in the enjoyment of a large legal practice. This led to absolute fame with his successful defence of Horne Tooke and other rather too active English friends of the French Revolution in October 1794. 'His portraits and busts were sold all over the country, tokens were struck bearing his effigy, and he was presented with the freedom of numerous corporations.' Although dismissed from his post of Attorney-General to the Prince of Wales for accepting a retainer from Thomas Paine, by 1802 he had been forgiven and was appointed Chancellor to the Duchy of Cornwall. In 1806 he became Lord Chancellor. He was, we read, 'always attached to animals and had many pets, a dog which he introduced at consultations, a goose, and even two leeches'; and he had privately printed a pamphlet entitled *An Appeal in favour of the Agricultural Service of Rooks*.[2]

Erskine's granddaughter, Frances Morris, married Thomas Johnston Barton, of Glendalough; to them in 1840 was born a daughter, Anna Henrietta, who married Robert Caesar Childers; and it was in honour of the Lord Chancellor that these two named their second son Robert Erskine.

The Childerses were a family accomplished in rather different ways from the Bartons, but of very much the same class. Like the Bartons they had removed themselves from East Anglia in the sixteenth century, to settle some hundred miles north in Yorkshire's West Riding. Hugh Childers was a successful banker who became Mayor of Doncaster in

1604, but it was his grandson Leonard who brought the family name to national prominence when his part Arab hunter Flying Childers became one of the country's first famous racehorses. (The descendants of Flying Childers have been Grand National winners in generation after generation.) Leonard's grandson, Colonel John Walbanke Childers, was a successful professional soldier, sensible enough to marry the granddaughter of one of the founders of what eventually became the London Stock Exchange. His tastes included literature; and though no author himself, he had printed the narrative of a voyage made in 1774 by Lord Orford, around the as yet undrained East Anglian fens. This delightful book has some passages of a charm worthy of the Colonel's great-grandson, Erskine: 'Hippopotamus, who, though a Sea horse loved grass and ease as well as any land horse whatever, being taken out of an adjoining meadow and brought to the fleet, hung down his head, and looked very melancholy, as if, like some foreigners, he did not like his own Country best.'[3]

The Reverend Canon Charles Childers, one of Colonel John's five sons and father of the Robert who was to marry Anna Henrietta Barton, was a clergyman of the school of Samuel Butler, inclined to take his duties lightly. Although he was as an undergraduate a close friend of William Gladstone, it was his nephew who kept the Childers name in the public eye in the latter years of Queen Victoria's reign. Hugh Culling Eardley Childers, a graduate of Trinity College, Cambridge, took the Pontefract seat for the Liberals in 1860. His qualities were such that he duly became Secretary of State for War, First Lord of the Admiralty, Chancellor of the Exchequer and finally, in 1886, Home Secretary. While he was at the Admiralty, Hugh Childers was obliged to deal with the Queen's correspondence concerning a proposal that men in the Navy might be permitted to sport beards. 'Has Mr Childers ascertained anything on the subject of the beards?' the Queen inquired. 'Her own personal feeling would be for the beards without the moustaches, as the latter have rather a soldierlike appearance; but then the object in view would not be obtained, viz., to prevent the necessity of shaving.' Later she wrote, 'to make one additional observation respecting the beards, viz., that on no account should moustaches be allowed without beards. That', she declared, 'must be clearly understood.'[4] Plainly a diplomat to have been able to deal satisfactorily with this delicate matter, Hugh Childers shared with his uncle Charles a close association with Gladstone, whose line on Ireland he supported. In the early 1890s he headed the Childers Commission, which established how severely Ireland was overtaxed, and with his leader was one of the earliest English advocates of the devolution of power to Ireland that came to be known as Home Rule.

Robert Caesar Childers, born in 1838, seems to have been rather a contrast to the somewhat self-indulgent Reverend Charles. He had a conventional upbringing and education, took a degree in Hebrew at Wadham College, Oxford, then followed the increasingly well-beaten path of young Englishmen sent out to govern those whom Kipling later described as the 'lesser breeds without the law'.[5] In Robert's case the path led him to coffee-rich Ceylon, to which he was posted in 1860 as private secretary to Sir Charles McCarthy, the Governor.

The immediate aftermath of the Indian Mutiny was no easy time for the Empire or for Imperialists. The great colonial expansion of the 'scramble for Africa' was yet to come, and the old notion of the quiet acquiescence of native populations in their social, moral and religious betterment had been cast into doubt. In the consequent cooling of relations between governors and governed, even Benjamin Disraeli talked of 'these wretched colonies' as a 'millstone round our necks'.[6] Against this background, Robert Caesar became fascinated by the culture and especially the language of the ancient Buddhist stronghold of Ceylon, devoting his leisure to pursuit of his interest and studying under Yatramulle Unnanse, a 'Buddhist scholar of great learning, and of peculiar modesty and dignity'. Like many before him, Childers fell victim to the tropical climate, and after four years returned home an invalid, to dedicate his life to scholarship. At that time of Darwin, Huxley, and the most fervent religious debate, none of the Buddhist sacred books had appeared in print, least of all in a Western language. In 1869 Robert published his translation of one such text, *Khuddaka Patha*, to be followed by what became the keystone to studies of Buddhism, his dictionary of the Pali language. This was 'not only the most valuable contribution that had yet been made to the study of the language, but was the indispensable means by which further progress could be made.'[7]

It was Robert's marriage that forged the first links between the Barton and Childers families. Anna Henrietta Barton was a beautiful and high-spirited girl, much taken by the scholar, whom she met after his return from Ceylon. The attraction was mutual, and on 1 January 1867 the couple were married. It was a happy conjunction of two eminently respectable families: high-minded, public-spirited, politically conventional yet mildly forward-looking. Comfortably off by virtue of their joint private means, the couple lived for two years in New Barnet, on the outskirts of London, before their growing prosperity permitted a move to Mount Street in Mayfair. Their first son, named Henry Caesar in deference to family tradition, was born in 1868. Two years later, in 1870, Robert Erskine Childers followed.

II

As their social standing demanded and their income permitted, the Childerses kept a housekeeper, cook and parlourmaid, and a nanny who relieved Anna of some the burden of bringing up two small children. Yet this was essentially the home of a scholar; Robert was fond of his family, and it was his habit and pleasure to busy himself in his book-lined study at home rather than work elsewhere. Professionally he prospered. The publication of the first volume of the Pali dictionary in 1872 brought its author a sub-librarianship at the India Office, followed, more importantly, by the Chair of Pali and Buddhist Studies at University College, London, a post created for the purpose of honouring its first incumbent. The second and larger part of the dictionary appeared in 1875, to considerable acclaim, winning the Volney Prize in 1876 for the best philological work of the year. The family also grew, as two sons were followed by three daughters: Sybil, Dulcibella, and Constance. The bond between the Barton and Childers families was further strengthened by a romance between Anna's brother Charles – son of Thomas Johnston Barton and heir to Glendalough – and Robert's younger sister, Agnes. In 1876 they were married.

Robert's and Anna's pleasure in this event was marred only by

Robert's illness. His constitution had never been robust, and a weak chest was exacerbated by his spell in Ceylon; in married life he began to suffer from coughing fits, perhaps brought on by the intensity of his studies; in due course he was diagnosed as having tuberculosis, which in the last century carried some of the horror that cancer does today. The process of its transmission and progress were little understood; it was incurable, and almost invariably fatal. This diagnosis Anna concealed from the larger family, for the medical practice of the time would have consigned the sufferer to isolation in a sanatorium, remote from his work, his wife, his children – in effect, from life. Anna's decision was both generous and courageous, and became more so as the disease progressed. Shortly after his sister's wedding in January 1876, Robert caught a cold which then developed into the most virulent form of tuberculosis, the likely outcome of which must soon have become apparent to both husband and wife. On 25 June Robert struggled downstairs from his bedroom to celebrate his son Erskine's sixth birthday. Then, just a month later, he slipped away from his home, to a Weybridge hotel, where he died in his sleep on 25 July, quite alone. Selflessly, he had wished to spare his family a lengthy death-bed scene.

If Anna had simply died soon of the same disease, the outcome would have been less painful in some ways. As it was, she had to face, alone, the reactions of those kept in ignorance of Robert's disease. The family regarded her as having been grossly irresponsible in failing to protect both herself and her children from her husband's infection; for them – and it would have been the opinion of most other families at that time – there was no alternative: Anna must be separated from her children, and consigned (for as long as she might live) to a home for incurables. And so she was. For practical purposes, this left five young children orphaned. As members of a large and prosperous family they were not of course friendless, and indeed the arrangement whereby they were to live in Ireland with their aunt Agnes and uncle Charles at Glendalough was perhaps the happiest that could have been contrived. Nevertheless, as Charles' and Agnes' eldest son Robert wrote many years later of the parting of mother and children,

> It was a tragically poignant incident . . . the goodbye to five small children was for ever, and she could not even hug them as they left for Ireland and the guardianship of their uncle and aunt . . . imagine what it must have been for the children, but still more to the doubly stricken mother. She was going herself soon; her late husband had opened the door first; yet already it was closing on her little brood, none of whom she would see again. Could anything be more heart-rending?[8]

Erskine Childers was then six, and so it was very early in life that circumstance began to impose itself on what he later described as his 'native impulses'.[9] He was already regarded as a sensitive and imaginative child, and was perhaps at the worst age for such a thing to happen: old enough to understand what had occurred, but too young to comprehend the reason why. Like many children in such circumstances, he seems at first to have become withdrawn, then subsequently developed a strong sense of intellectual and emotional independence. By adolescence he had become an enthusiast for Emerson, in particular his essay 'Self-Reliance'. 'Trust thyself: every heart vibrates to that iron string',[10] the philosopher had written, and since Childers had been deprived of those closest to him, what could make more sense? However, his later outpourings – no other term will do – on the occasion of his marriage suggest an ardent and highly passionate man, longing for close relationships with others but out of necessity obliged to restrain the more expressive and emotional side of his character.

III

If it had not been for the circumstances, the removal to Ireland must in some respects have constituted a pleasant change for the young Childers. His home in Mount Street, for all its social cachet, was a small house in the centre of what was then the world's largest city, the dirty, bustling, crime-ridden, fog-stricken London of Sherlock Holmes. Glendalough, known in the family as 'Glan', could scarcely have provided a greater contrast. Some thirty miles south of Dublin, the house and surrounding estate took their name from the valley of Glendalough, where some picturesque ruins were all that remained of what had once been an important educational and ecclesiastical centre founded by St Kevin. The valley was one of the most beautiful in the country, the more traditional guidebooks declaring that it abounded 'with the most picturesque and romantic scenery'. The house itself dated back to the seventeenth century, but Thomas Johnston Barton and his bride Frances Morris had in the 1840s made various additions. It was now a pleasantly rambling and substantial country house, its mullioned stone façade lending it a faintly military air. It was also, both literally and metaphorically, 'the big house', for as well as the five Childers children there were soon five of the Bartons' own, together with sixteen or seventeen servants. With the stables, hundreds of acres of lush farmland, and boating and fishing on Lough Dan and the lakes of Glendalough, this was a life of privilege, much divorced from the poverty of rural Ireland that in the 1870s surrounded the estate. In due course Glendalough came to represent to Childers the security of which he had been so abruptly deprived. His wife recorded that he 'loved Glan passionately'.[11]

Charles and Agnes Barton evidently made the Childers children feel as much at home as possible. The house was extended for their benefit, they were allocated their own day-room, and various governesses were provided for their education. It was a distinctly late-Victorian upbringing. The Bartons' eldest son Robert reminds us that 'In the 'eighties, children were kept very much in the background and did not mix with their elders except for short prescribed periods. [His two brothers] had a nursery governess and were always confined when in the house to the night and day nurseries . . . the girls got their tuition in the schoolroom with the three Childers girls.'[12]

The two Childers boys remained at Glendalough until they were old enough to be sent to England to complete their education, returning of course for the holidays. Henry was despatched to prep school in 1878, his younger brother two years later to Bengeo, on the outskirts of Hertford, where he was to prepare for Haileybury. Although at the time such arrangements were commonplace, Childers found the experience daunting. Indeed, it was perhaps his experience at school that led him, towards the end of his life, to remark to the journalist Robert Brennan 'that he was terribly afraid as a youth, until he realised that apart from its demoralising effects, fear was unworthy of a man, and he [had to be] determined to conquer it'.[13] Quite apart from what amounted to exile, and the loneliness inherent in such a situation, the choice of Haileybury for a boy such as Erskine seems mildly idiosyncratic. Haileybury was a new foundation, part of the renaissance of public schools led by Dr Thomas Arnold of Rugby, and intended for the education of potential Servants of Empire. It and others like it have been well described as 'spartan institutions where the sons of the rich were hardened and purified for lives of service and self-deprivation. They set out to inculcate certain virtues and qualities in their pupils, amongst which the most prominent were courage, self-assurance, honesty, self-sacrifice and loyalty.'[14] Such a regime was perhaps not the best for a child of some sensitivity, who at the time might well have continued his education at home. On the other hand, of the older foundations the Bartons would have considered, Harrow, which harboured Henry and was soon to accept the young Winston Churchill, would have been no better; and at Eton the age of the infamous Keate was scarcely past. There, 'hundreds of boys, herded together in miscellaneous boarding-houses, or in that grim Long Chamber, at whose name in after years statesmen and warriors would turn pale, lived, badgered and overawed by the furious incursions of an irascible little old man carrying a bundle of birch-twigs, a life in which licensed barbarism was mingled with the daily and hourly study of the niceties of Ovidian verse.'[15] As Churchill himself later wrote, 'I am all for public-schools, but I do not want to go there again.'[16]

Childers' courage was in any case severely tested by the long-expected death of his mother from tuberculosis, shortly after his entry to Haileybury in 1883. He was assailed by religious doubts. How could a Christian God, who had His children in His care, deprive a boy first of his father, then his mother? It was a time when parents and children became estranged over religious differences, that being the experience of, among others, Edmund Gosse, Samuel Butler and Robert Louis Stevenson. Long after his death, Childers' wife wrote:

> When Erskine was about twelve he began to have religious doubts that gave him intense mental suffering. His family was orthodox. To them, religious doubt was sin. They became aware of his state and showed him grief – and prayed for him. Because they loved him – and who

> could not help loving him – they were harder in admonishment. But the sorrow was like a mountain-load to him, and constituted more fear than they realised – the fear that he might be sinning . . . Subsequently he became silent about religious matters, wishing to spare them pain.[17]

In the circumstances, it is scarcely surprising that Childers' initial progress at Haileybury was slow. The boy had no wish to be noticed. When his form master asked the class to name the Chancellor of the Exchequer, no one answered. When Childers himself was asked, his conscience obliged him to reply, 'My cousin, Mr Hugh Childers'.[18] He wished merely to fit in, and this he did. His position in class, and on the sports-field that was becoming such an admirable part of the public school ethos, was at first distinctly middling.

In due course Childers began to adapt himself to the Haileybury regime. In 1885 he was in his House Rugby XV, in 1887 he was appointed a school prefect, and in 1889, his last year, he was Head of House. Academically, too, he gradually outstripped his brother's leisurely performance at Harrow and showed himself more obviously his father's son, towards the end of his time winning prizes in Latin, Greek and English. He was beginning to develop his taste for English literature in particular; he enjoyed the staple fare of Arnold and Dickens, and later grew positively to love Thackeray, Stevenson and Tennyson. From his father he also seems to have inherited considerable powers of concentration, an ability to focus on an intellectual task to the exclusion of all distractions, much noted by his contemporaries. Gradually, too, he seems to have become more at ease with himself. His sense of humour earned him the family nickname 'Perk' – the use of his first name, Robert, having been dropped in favour of Erskine – and his letters home displayed a personality superficially more confident and mature. At eighteen he wrote to his sister Sybil: 'The prefectorial staff of Trevelyan House is grouped around the fire in various attitudes of repose or deep study, their noble Head is wrapped in dignified silence as he pens this epistle to his youngest sister, alas how unworthy a recipient; there is a general sleepiness beginning to pervade everything – Ah! there's eleven striking. Time all decent citizens were in bed, and as I count myself amongst the latter class – and as, however, I cannot go to bed while I am writing a letter, of necessity I must say goodnight.'[19]

Of his deeper development we can be less sure. Hints are to be found in an important figure in Childers' adolescence. This was the Reverend Edward Hardress Waller, an Etonian and graduate of Trinity College, Dublin, who became Rector of Derralossary, near Glendalough, in 1885 – and who forty years later was to attend Childers on the day before his execution. Both Waller and his new young wife took to the youngster from Glendalough. The two men would spend hours tramping the Wicklow hills, thrashing out everything from ancient philosophy to contemporary politics, where Parnell had been so successful in unifying the Irish members at Westminster that he seemed on the verge of delivering to Ireland the 'promised land' of domestic autonomy known since 1870 as Home Rule. Inevitably this was a matter for some dismay among the Ascendancy, committed to the Union with England as they generally were. Robert Barton recalled that 'Edward and his wife were very good friends of "Perk's", in spite of the disparity of their views on religion and politics. Both being good-natured men, they agreed to disagree and seldom argued hotly . . . Perk's views being more liberal than those held by Waller.'[20] Here was a passion concealed under an exterior that had become superficially more urbane. Similarly, while his status at school indicated someone at long last largely in harmony with his surroundings, his singular independence and self-sufficiency remained remarkable to his contemporaries: 'We all liked him and thought him absolutely fair. As a matter of fact I don't think he fraternized with anyone, though he was friendly to all. He was unusual in liking to go for long runs by himself. We were a little daunted by his extreme conscientiousness, to which we hardly dared aspire.'[21]

Evidently Childers in the end made a fair success of Haileybury, crowned in the early summer of 1889 by an Exhibition to read Classics at Trinity College, Cambridge. Trinity was Hugh Childers' suggestion, and an altogether more fitting choice than Haileybury. Founded by Henry VIII in 1546, it was the largest, richest and most prestigious of the Cambridge colleges; it numbered among its graduates Childers' kinsmen Thomas Erskine and Hugh himself, and his favourite poet, Tennyson. Moreover, it was full of 'aristocratic and upper class families on whom the destiny of Empire and country would depend'.[22] Here was the place for Erskine Childers.

The summer of 1889 was spent exploring some of Tennyson's old haunts, then on a trip to the wilds of Connemara. The latter produced Childers' first attempt at a sustained piece of writing, in the form of an account of his journey, a somewhat overwritten piece that nevertheless displays glimpses of his talent. Less fortunately, it was apparently a soaking on this adventure that brought on sciatica, which was to leave him with a permanent limp. Then in October it was Cambridge – for many young men, of whatever generation, a formative influence.

IV

Childers followed the then normal practice of taking rooms outside the College in his first year, at 5 Bridge Street, a few yards from Trinity's Front Gate. There he adapted quickly to the demands of undergraduate life, revelling in its responsibilities and its freedoms, its freshness, and the stimulus of other bright minds. In his first term he wrote to his sister, Dulcibella, revealing some of his enthusiasm for this new life:

> Oh by the way, I must emphatically *refuse* to be silhouetted in my cap and gown, as you cruelly suggest. It is the stamp of the innocent freshman, fresh from school, glorying in his membership of an ancient and august institution, with whose academical cloaks he is permitted to invest his person. That I am that innocent freshman, fresh from school and even to some extent participating in the above sentiments, I unhesitatingly admit: but that I should stamp the same in indelible characters upon a clumsy bit of card would be, I consider, a gratuitous insult to myself, and all connected with me – so there! (As you said to me.)[23]

The educational value of a university is as much informal as formal, and Childers made some good friends. The closest was Ivor Lloyd-Jones, the son of a Folkestone clergyman and another Haileyburian, who shared and fostered Childers' subsequent enthusiasm for the sea and – in Robert Barton's words – whose 'ebullient presence and ready address formed a counterpart to Perk's rather quiet, retiring manner'.[24] Walter Runciman was also a sailor (an enthusiasm born of his father's position as a prosperous shipowner), and a man with a major political career in front of him. Perhaps more intriguing was Childers' association with Edward Marsh. Later best known as Winston Churchill's long-suffering private secretary, Marsh also became a distinguished literary and artistic midwife. Rupert Brooke was his most famous protégé, but he was also the editor of *Georgian Poetry*, and an exceptionally discerning collector of modern art. The son of the Master of another Cambridge college, Downing, Marsh was a man of a sophistication of intellectual and aesthetic interest new to Childers. Maurice Baring, Lord Macaulay's great-nephews Charles, Robert and George Trevelyan, Walter Sickert's brother Oswald, and Bertrand Russell were members of his circle. 'We had been great friends at Trinity and later', Marsh wrote of Childers, 'and I knew him for one of the sweetest natures in the world.' Marsh has left us with this graphic and engaging picture of his Cambridge friends:

> What strikes me most when I look back on the life which I and my companions led at Cambridge is an extraordinary innocence and simplicity. I don't think the 'clear and serene air' in which I see it is an enchantment lent by distance – we really were a different kind from the distraught and turgid beings who people the current novels of adolescence . . . I don't think any of us were tormented and obsessed by sex as our successors appear to be – we had no known 'affairs', and I can remember only two of my known intimates falling in love. We were all tingling with intellectual curiosity, arguing on every subject in the firm belief that we should thus arrive at the truth; mostly hard workers for the sake of work, with little thought of our 'careers'; keen politicians, nearly all Liberals, aware of the 'storms that raged outside our happy ground' but not much irked by them; great readers in general literature, both English and foreign; respectfully and rather externally interested in the other arts, especially music, but hardly at all in any form of sport. We lived in with a high degree of plainness, entertaining one another mainly at breakfast, generally on eggs which we had personally 'buttered'; dining almost every evening 'in Hall' and meeting afterwards for the consumption, not of whisky and soda, but of cocoa, a drink for which I have since lost the taste. Taken together, it seems now to have been a very civilized form of life.[25]

Stimulated as he was by this sort of company, Childers also took the opportunity in his first year to travel abroad: a visit during the Easter vacation of 1890 with his sister Dulcibella to Italy. Apart from a trip to his grandfather in Nice when he was five, this was his first journey outside the British Isles. It was also his first direct exposure to the culture that had been the substance of his largely Classical education. E. M. Forster later captured in several of his novels the impact of the warm south on reserved and emotionally immature Englishmen, but Childers' impressions seem to have been predominantly aesthetic. Writing of the trip to his uncle Charles (as ever, very much *in loco parentis*), he remarked – perhaps a little tritely – that 'It cost between £20 and £29 and I can't help feeling it was worth ten times that! The pictures at Florence alone were an education in themselves, and Ancient Rome was so fascinating, and that queer silent sunny Venice, and the grand gothic cathedral at Milan, and the delightful sunsets from behind Tivoli, and from Galileo's tower above Florence, and Fiesole at Cantosa and the tower of the Doge's Palace at Venice, and a host of other places I shan't forget!'[26]

For his second year Childers moved into College, and immersed himself in its life. His sciatica precluded the running and rugby that he had enjoyed at Haileybury, but in the autumn of 1890 he took up rowing, winning a respectable position in the Trinity Second Boat. His recreations were also intellectual. He had been elected to Trinity's debating society, the Magpie and Stump,[27] in the November of his first year, and henceforth was a regular contributor to its meetings. His opinions were largely orthodox: he supported the motion that trade unions were detrimental to the country's interests, and held very much his uncle's views on the topical issue of Gladstone's second Irish Home Rule bill. 'Mr Childers pointed out some of the dangers of the proposed scheme,' we read. 'The case of Ireland was exceptional owing to its proximity, and the national aspirations were incompatible with our own safety.'[28] This is the first direct reference we have to his views on the issue to which he was later to devote his life, and it is interesting to see his relative indifference here to the nationalist cause. Despite the vehemence of his discussions with the Reverend Waller, like most people he seems to have taken his social and political opinions from his background relatively uncritically. As he later wrote, he 'grew up steeped in the most irreconcilable sort of Unionism'.[29] Only gradually was this to change.

There was also the Classical Tripos[30] to occupy him, for which he had the benefit of Marsh's tutor, Arthur Woolgar Verral. An early enthusiast for regarding the Classics as works of art rather than exercises in verse, Verral was nevertheless a dedicated linguist. 'He had the most scrupulous sense I have ever known of the value of exactness in language,' Marsh wrote. 'There was nothing academic in this; no one took more pleasure in novelty or audacity of expression if on close inspection it was justified and held water; but he would never tolerate an approximation to the meaning required.'[31] Although he appeared only in the second half of the second division of the Tripos in June 1891, such exactness – almost pedantry – was both his father's hereditary and Verral's more practical legacy to Childers. His placing must have been a disappointment for a college exhibitioner, however, and was perhaps instrumental in his decision to change to law for his remaining two years at Trinity. Law led to rather more obvious practical opportunities than Classics, and he may also have had in mind the career of his ancestor Thomas Erskine.

While mastering this new subject took up much of Childers' time, he was also developing in other directions. As early as his first year at Trinity he had become the college representative on the *Cambridge Review*. He was characteristically self-deprecating about this to his uncle Charles: 'I have blossomed into a college correspondent to the 'Review', an extremely unimportant office requiring no literary merits beyond a faculty for recording facts with brevity.'[32] In reality, both the *Review* and Childers' duties were rather more exacting. Founded in 1888 as a 'journal of University life and thought', it celebrated its fiftieth year with a roll-call of its 'galaxy of literary celebrities . . . to name but a few, Sir Edmund Gosse, A. C. Benson, G. K. Chesterton, F. Anstey, Rupert Brooke, Flecker, Sir Walter Raleigh, Quiller-Couch, E. V. Lucas, Erskine Childers and Archibald Marshall'[33] – a distinguished list. In the Michaelmas term of 1892, Childers became the *Review*'s editor, which plainly suggests journalistic ability, as well as a degree of respect from his peers beyond the gates of his own college. It is worth noting, however, that this esteem was not enough to get Childers very close to the Apostles, the undergraduate society of intellectual luminaries that later spawned the Bloomsbury group.

The second pointer for the future was the Magpie and Stump affair.

Childers had remained a regular participant in its debates, and in due course became successively its secretary and treasurer, positions from which the presidency generally followed. His debating style, however, though rational, earnest and logical, had about it a certain prolixity with which some of the society's members found fault. In the spring of 1892 they put forward an opposing candidate for the presidency, demanding that there should be a formal ballot. Posters around Trinity posed the question 'Which do you prefer? Mr Gordon's common sense or the intolerable gas of Mr Childers?'[34] The issue caught the imagination both of Cambridge and of the world beyond, London's *Pall Mall Gazette* regarding it as of greater interest than the concurrent local elections. The undergraduates, predictably disdaining worthiness in favour of panache, elected the eccentric Wykehamist George Hamilton Gordon, who celebrated with a fireworks display in Trinity's Great Court, the sort of incident typified by Evelyn Waugh as 'the sound of English county families baying for broken glass'.[35] In college history it went down as the Gordon Riots.

'Till the war came to confound all epochs,' wrote Marsh, 'my life divided itself in retrospect into three parts: before Cambridge; Cambridge; since Cambridge.'[36] Childers would not have so stressed Cambridge. He was at ease there, had apparently come to terms with himself and his parents' tragedy, had made some very pleasant friends – had developed his journalistic and debating skills, developed intellectually, perhaps emotionally. But it was not for him the Pauline experience it was for Marsh, who excelled at Trinity, and whose promise there marked him and his closest friends for prominence in later life. Although he came down in June of 1893 with a First in Law, Childers was neither of quite such intellectual calibre, nor quite of Marsh's inner circle. Indeed, the subsequent paths of the two men to an extent call to mind *The Riddle of the Sands*, in which the narrator Carruthers remarks of his companion Davies: 'We had both gone down in the same year . . . I had passed brilliantly into my profession, and on the few occasions I had met him since my triumphant début in society I had found nothing left in common between us. He seemed to know none of my friends, he dressed indifferently, and I thought him dull.'[37] Childers was perhaps here drawing a parallel between Marsh's spectacular subsequent progress at the Colonial Office under Joseph Chamberlain, and his own rather more stolid path. Childers was yet to burn with the hard, gem-like flame of Marsh.

As an undergraduate, only in his reflections on the death of Tennyson did the exceptional in Childers become apparent. 'His death seems to me to have just added the perfecting touch to his almost perfect life,' he wrote to his sisters. 'He just went out on "such a tide as moving seems asleep, too full for sound or foam, when that which drew from out the boundless deep, turns again home". You and I owe more to him than even we are faintly conscious of, I think. For my part there is hardly a good aspiration or a good notion in me which has not either been heightened or originated by him. Now he has died there seems no change – there are his words and his music still, only just with the added touch of perfection and consecration. Oh, I think such a life, such a life's work, and such a death are a treasure of unimaginable value to all English-speaking people.'[38] Here are several indications of the deeper Erskine Childers. Most obvious is his sensitive and passionate response to the poetry itself, to its music and its aesthetic qualities. There is also a moral response, a heightening of ethical sensibility and a desire, not that of many of his contemporaries for leisure and pleasure, but for virtue and for good. Then comes the note of Empire, admiration for a life of value, not to the Greeks, the French or the Germans, but to the 'English speaking people'. Finally, there is Childers' appreciation of the value, not merely of the life, but also of the death of Tennyson. Matched with a reserve masking considerable intellectual and emotional ardour, such qualities seem to define Childers at his coming-of-age.

Whether they were 'native impulses' from his ancestry or the 'stucco crusts' of environment, these qualities were to take him to some curious places.

4
A Double Life

1894–1897

'Few realized that the unobtrusive little man with the glasses and the sciatic limp was leading a double life. He let none of us know – until the information tumbled out one day, quite by chance – that his weekends were spent in the Thames estuary, sailing single-handed a scrubby little yacht.'

Basil Williams

I

His education in a formal sense complete, it was now time for Childers to set about making his way in the world. In the autumn of 1893 he followed Dick Whittington's steps to London, apparently with a view to making his living at the Bar. With his studies at Cambridge in mind and the inspiration of Thomas Erskine behind him, he had followed custom by joining one of the Inns of Court, the Inner Temple, in the year before his graduation.[1] He wrote on 22 October 1893 to Walter Runciman, 'I am starting for London tomorrow in a rather vague and lost frame of mind as I don't know whom to read with or where to live!',[2] but thereafter the trail grows cold. At the time the process of studying for the Bar was relatively informal, and with whom Childers read, and for how long, we do not know. He certainly found himself rooms in the Inner Temple. He re-emerges, early in 1894, not reading for the Bar but as an aspirant to a Clerkship in the House of Commons. In this may be seen the hand of his cousin, Hugh Childers.

Hugh Childers was by this time an established mentor. The recipient of the Queen's anxious enquiry over the matter of naval beards had been a leading Liberal for more than thirty years. He had taken an interest in the Childers children since their bereavement, and was particularly solicitous of the undergraduate Erskine following his uncle Charles's sudden death in 1890: as a friend of the Master of Trinity, Dr Montagu Butler, he had every opportunity to keep an eye on his kinsman. A man with a high sense of public duty, he could scarcely have been better placed to whet Erskine Childers' appetite for the art of the possible, to indicate where life and Childers' talents might best meet, and – the times being what they were – to influence its happening. Whether he actually discouraged Childers' legal studies, we do not know, but his suggestion of a Clerkship must certainly be regarded as astute. Unlike Churchill, famous already as being his father Lord Randolph's son, Childers was at this time almost unknown. His retiring manner argued against hope of success as an MP, but his father's legacy of a penchant for accuracy and detail, his own legal training and his facility with words made a Clerk's job – recording the business of the House of Commons and its various Committees – an entirely sensible choice: it would provide an excellent apprenticeship in political and parliamentary life for one of Childers' skills, and one which could be regarded either as a career in itself, or possibly as a stepping-stone to something more ambitious.

Thus, at some stage towards the end of 1893, the Bar was abandoned. The following January Childers enrolled at the crammers, W. B. Scoones, close to the Strand. With a clear objective in view, he now excelled himself by coming third in that year's civil service examinations. As who one knew was often as important as what one knew in obtaining such appointments as the Clerkship, the way must have seemed clear for a man of Childers' political connections. But the Civil Service Commission deemed him 'unfit', because of his sciatica. It was only on the insistence of the Clerk of the House himself, Sir Reginald Palgrave, that the appointment was made,[3] to begin in the new year.

Childers could now relax. Summer was here, and he induced a number of Trinity cronies to join him in Wales for a few days' break. Both Marsh and Bertrand Russell were of the party, Marsh writing somewhat sourly to Charles Trevelyan that 'Childers has turned us all into fishermen.'[4] Then, as would long remain his habit, Childers returned to Glendalough. His initial plan was to spend the rest of the summer there, going off from time to time for a little coastal sailing.

Romantic that he was, however, a fresh idea struck him. With five months to spare before he was obliged to take up his duties in Westminster, there was time for some quite extensive travel. He had written once to one of his sisters of his enthusiasm for Tennyson's *Ulysses*, declaring, 'And do read Ulysses. There are some splendid lines in it and every word is exactly the best and most beautiful one – "The long day wanes: the slow moon climbs the deep/Moans round with many voices. Come my friends/Tis not too late to seek a newer world." These lines always send a strange thrill through me and are half responsible for any longing I ever have to desert civilisation and "wander far away – on from island unto island to the gateways of the day" – and so on. If ever I disappear for a year or two, you will know what sent me.'[5] So it was that, early in October, he was writing excitedly to his friend Walter Runciman, 'Do you know any firm running *sailing* vessels to the West Indies?'[6]

For several weeks he busied himself with the idea, but then a domestic crisis at Glendalough meant that Childers had to stay and help his aunt manage the estate. He had to remain in Ireland for the autumn, escaping at Christmas only as far as Florence. He then began work as Junior Assistant Clerk at the House of Commons in January 1895, at a salary of £100 a year.

II

Every boy and every gal
That's born into the world alive
Is either a little Liberal
Or else a little Conservative

Iolanthe

It was as good a time as any to be introduced to the idiosyncrasies of Britain's Parliament. Nine months previously Gladstone's resignation, on the plea of ill-health, had drawn to a close a political career of unique distinction spanning more than sixty years. To the ageing Queen his departure was doubtless welcome; she had greeted his return to power in 1892 with the remark that 'The danger to the country, to Europe, to her vast Empire, which is involved in having all these great interests entrusted to the shaking hand of an old, wild and incomprehensible man of eighty-two and a half, is very great!'[7] Disraeli had died when Childers was still at prep school, but the passing of the old Liberal signalled the real end of the rivalry of the two dominant political personalities of the Victorian age. And the curtain had yet to rise on the battle royal of their successors, the continuers of the great political dualism of Liberals and Conservatives celebrated in *Iolanthe*, the two poles of mainstream English political thought in which Childers was to be involved.

Gladstone had been succeeded in March 1894 by his fellow Liberal, Lord Rosebery, on whose behalf Commons business was conducted by a deputy, Sir William Harcourt. Although not an unprecedented arrangement, it was scarcely conducive to efficient government, and the situation was further exacerbated by the disinclination of the pair to communicate except at the most formal level in Cabinet, and through the system of despatch boxes. Their joint administration lasted some sixteen months, and was characterized by little other than futility. Childers remarked in the spring of 1895 that 'this impotent and moribund government seems to take continual fresh fizzles of life and seems determined to stick in till it is forcibly kicked out.'[8]

The election of July 1895 ushered in a new world. The Liberals were dismissed by a considerable Conservative majority, and Lord Salisbury was returned to power to form his third Government. Though neither a Gladstone nor a Disraeli, the plump, bearded Salisbury was a man of tremendous gifts who encompassed the positions of both Prime Minister and Foreign Secretary, performing the two tasks largely independently of his colleagues' advice. As has been observed, 'only vaguely responsible to his colleagues in the Cabinet, he was for many years able to conduct the foreign policy of England by himself.'[9] This he famously, if not especially accurately, described as 'to drift lazily downstream, occasionally putting out a boathook to avoid a collision'.[10] At the same time, his Cabinet is generally regarded as having been 'one of the strongest that has ever held office in Great Britain'.[11] Most notable among its notables was Joseph Chamberlain. The son of a shopkeeper, he had made his fortune manufacturing screws in Birmingham before turning to politics. Scarcely a traditional member of the governing classes, he was a man marked equally by talent and ambition. Moreover, his choice of the Colonial Office – hitherto of 'very low status'[12] – was the clearest possible indication of the immediate political future, matched only by the nation's rejection of the party that had failed to recognize the swelling Imperialistic tide. Between them, Salisbury and Chamberlain were to dominate the next seven years, much as Gladstone and Disraeli had dominated the 1860s and 1870s. Childers was therefore introduced to the Commons during what was effectively an interregnum, during which he was able to find his feet before the next great age.

Fin de siècle London was almost as novel to Childers as was the House of Commons. His early memories of the city before his removal to Ireland were slight, and neither Haileybury nor Trinity had much encouraged jaunts to the capital. It was still, of course, the 'London of horse trams with halfpenny fares, and hansom cabs; of crystalline bells and splattering hoofs';[13] still, too, the world's largest city, hub of the Empire, and the repository of just about everything a man might need or desire. Much more dramatically even than it is today, it was a city of rich and poor. In the villages of Kensington and Chelsea the most genteel of lives might be lived within four miles of the East End – and of lives of an extremity of squalor that Seebohm Rowntree was soon to expose. The grand was very grand, but the poor remained Dickensian.

Childers had found rooms at 2 Mitre Court, in the Inner Temple. There he lived amid the privileged, in a cloistral calm reminiscent of Cambridge. His hours at the Commons were scarcely onerous, and outside them his family connections and those from Haileybury and Trinity opened a number of doors through which, rather diffidently, the young man passed. In *The Riddle of the Sands* Carruthers notes his own 'triumphant debut in society', but Childers was too shy to triumph. Although as a keen yachtsman he had joined the Cruising Club in 1895, for several years he does not even seem to have belonged to any one of those institutions to which a man of his background might have been expected to gravitate, the gentleman's Club. His was not yet Carruthers' regime of 'office, club and chambers';[14] neither was it the literary world of Wilde, Beerbohm and the *Yellow Book*, to which he might have aspired.

The House of Commons itself provided a social life, of course, and its ambience was to his taste. Although Hugh Childers had resigned as an MP in 1892 (and was to die in 1896), his name and acquaintance spelled friendship for the young man. Childers' colleagues, too, were congenial. The Clerk, Sir Reginald Palgrave, took a genuine interest in the young man he had been so determined to add to his department, and inevitably Childers was also befriended by the other young clerks, of whom there were a dozen at his own level. Later he wrote to one of them of the scene in the Clerk's Office: 'The office is just the same. Dicky is crouching over *The Times*, his spectacles scraping on the paper. Tupper is laying down the law on the right of succession to the [Clerk's] Table. Doyle is telling indecent stories and Columbe, Fell and Legge are capping them. Gibbon is solemn and subdued, Porter and Bramwell are in the country.'[15] This was to the fellow-clerk who became a life-long friend – Basil Williams, son of a Somerset barrister, educated at Marlborough and New College, Oxford, and three years Childers' senior. In due course Williams became a distinguished professional historian, and wrote one of the best and earliest short studies of his friend, in which he recalled Childers' early days at the Commons. He noted both Childers' reticence and his quality of extreme concentration: 'He seemed a particularly quiet, almost retiring colleague, who did the work allotted to him efficiently and without fuss, but for the rest made no great mark, and in his leisure moments had a peculiar power of abstracting himself from all extraneous interests.'[16]

This reserve, this marked reluctance to draw attention to himself, almost a colourlessness, made the eventual revelation of how Childers spent his spare time seem the more remarkable to Williams: 'We were astonished when we heard that our quiet friend was wont, in the long recesses from Parliamentary business allowed us in those comparatively placid times, to go away, often alone . . . in a little cockle-shell of a boat, navigating through the storms of the Channel or the North Sea, or threading his way through the complicated shoals of the German, Danish or Baltic coasts.'[17]

III

Childers may well have dabbled in boating on Lough Dan, near Glendalough, as a child. There is also a stray reference, from Ivor Lloyd-Jones, to the schoolboy 'sailing strange craft on the Lea'.[18] Lloyd-Jones was himself a sailor, and together he and Childers occasionally escaped from Cambridge to go yachting on the Norfolk Broads; at this time Childers and his brother Henry also kept a small craft for sailing on Lough Dan. There was little very serious in this, but once his Civil Service examinations were over in the summer of 1894, something altogether more ambitious was planned. He and Henry, who had recently left Sandhurst, decided to buy a sea-going boat. In an article for *The Times*, Childers later wrote of this puzzling onset of sea-fever. 'At twenty-one or twenty-two [the writer] and a brother, educated in different places and for different professions, with no special aptitude or propensity for the sea, but rather a well-grounded physical aversion to it, with no stimulus from friends, and in the face of solemn warnings of relations, felt themselves impelled simultaneously, in the manner of demented chickens, to take to the water.'[19] They did so in *Shulah*, a thirty-five-footer which had impressed them as a 'seaworthy sailing yacht'. However, as Childers continued in the article, 'Having very vague notions of the constituents of seaworthiness, we pitched on an ex-racing six-tonner whose absurdly disproportionate draught (for cruising, that is) of eight and a half feet, struck us as ensuring the requisite qualities.'[20]

During the summer of 1894, interrupted only by Erskine's trip to Wales, the brothers initiated themselves into the joys and tribulations of seamanship. They cruised from Kingstown – now Dun Laoghaire – north as far as the west coast of Scotland, and south to Land's End. In the course of these trips the limitations of the boat became obvious: her draft precluded entry into the shallow harbours of the British coasts. She was sold a few months after Childers had begun work in the Commons, and immediately replaced by the *Marguerite*. Jocularly nicknamed *Mad Agnes* after Childers' aunt Agnes Barton, this eighteen-foot half-decker quite fitted Williams' description of 'a scrubby little yacht'.[21] Certainly, too, Childers' ventures in her quite belied her size.

A cruise in the summer of 1895 took him from the yacht's base at Greenhithe, close to Deptford in the Thames estuary, round the Kent coast to Southampton, and then across the Channel to Boulogne. Anyone who has sailed a small boat in the Channel will know this for a feat, and it won him the Cruising Club's Admiral de Horsey cup for the best cruise of the year – a considerable achievement in only his first year of membership. The following three years, until he sold *Mad Agnes* in the summer of the Queen's Jubilee in 1897, saw Childers sailing all round this part of the coast, from Orfordness in the east to beyond the Solent in the south.

It seems to have been the physical and emotional challenge of sailing which appealed to Childers: a test for him to overcome. Much as he had risen above the emotional trauma of his parents' death and the loneliness of boarding-school, so too did he rise above the perils of the navigation of small sailing-boats in difficult tidal waters – perils that were all the more real before the advent of auxiliary engines, radio, efficient weather forecasting, or a proper marine rescue service. In a sensitive and lyrical piece which captures some of the curious pleasures of sailing in small boats, Childers himself hints at its appeal, writing of 'persons of regular habits and settled tastes, prudent, fastidious and punctual, who embark on voyages in small, half-decked sailing-craft, where they are starved and drenched by day and racked by night, where they undertake labour of the most novel and irritating kind and approach problems for which the accumulated experience of their lives is valueless'. And yet, he continued,

> . . . when the *sturm* and *drang* are past, and out of the shock of the seas and the smart of the spray they glide before the weakening evening breeze into some quiet haven or cove, to drop the anchor close to trees which never looked so green or cottages which never looked so snug and homely, their spirit rebounds with a leap, painful memories become sanctified, ennobled, glorious, the mystery of pain has been solved, the riddle of happiness guessed. Something has been conquered not only by power but by love; the world is grown to double its own dimensions, and is seen for the first time in harmony. New values have established themselves upon the wreckage of old standards of utility and qualification.[22]

The *Marguerite* was replaced by the yacht that was to provide Childers with his fame – *Vixen*, a converted ship's lifeboat of some thirty feet, described with very little poetic licence as *Dulcibella* in *The Riddle of the Sands*. In a letter to Walter Runciman, Childers called her simply 'a very ugly little 5-tonner with no headroom'.[23]

The first and most memorable of *Vixen*'s voyages was in the autumn of 1897. This was the experience from which *The Riddle of the Sands* germinated, and in the sea-log of which are to be found many echoes of the novel. Parliament having gone into recess, which then, in a very gentlemanly way, generally lasted until the following February, it was Childers' plan to cross the Channel to Boulogne. Then he would turn west and south to Bordeaux before taking the canals of rural France down to the Mediterranean. He completed the first leg to Boulogne single-handed, but the winds then turned contrary. He was joined by his brother Henry and Ivor Lloyd-Jones, and the threesome turned north. By early September they found themselves in Amsterdam, where weather too poor for a return across the North Sea drew their attention to the Dutch and German Frisian Islands, 'stretching away for a hundred sea-miles and separated from the mainland by from five to eight miles of sand, in great patches which are mostly dry at low water.'[24] Childers continued, 'Whether this region is known to many English yachtsmen I do not know; for our part, in default of better, we found it a delightful cruising ground, safe in any weather and a novel and amusing mode of getting to the Elbe and so to the Baltic . . .'.

It was thus that the end of September found them at Norderney, where 'a voice from the gloom made one or two perfunctory enquiries, and then all was silent'. Interspersed with that most favourite of Arthur Davies' occupations, kedging off, they then sailed east to Wangerooge, past the mouths of the Jade and the Weser, and up the Elbe to Cuxhaven. The newly opened Kaiser Wilhelm ship canal, some fifteen miles up-river, would take them to the Baltic. Small craft were towed through; *Vixen* found herself 'lashed alongside the *Johannes* schooner, bound for Kapplen . . . skipper Bartels, a right good sort, who helped us a lot . . . his boy steered for us both, and we had long yarns in our cabin'. By 9 October they were at Holtenau, the eastern end of the canal, and by the 17th in the Schlei Fiord celebrated in the novel. Then they headed for Dybbol, near Sonderberg, which had seen the last stand of the Danes against the German invasion of 1864. There Henry left the boat to return briefly to London (Lloyd-Jones having already gone back), and Childers returned to Flensburg in early November to pick him up. The elder Childers brought with him a fine load of stores, highly reminiscent of 'the collection of unwieldy and incongruous packages' that Carruthers took to Flensburg: 'loads of guns, cartridges etc., big new double oil stove, and our fine old Shulah compass'. On their return they encountered Bartels in Kiel once more, were back in Cuxhaven by the following day, and found themselves once again at Wangerooge on the 25th. Then the weather deteriorated, and on 29 November they were seeking shelter at Bensersiel. Here the log, at its most dramatic, has found its way almost point for point into the novel:

> Groped three-reefed to the Bensersiel channel and anchored outside for water. Wind grew to even worse gale, with heavy rain and hurricane look in the sky. A waterspout passed us at a distance of about 400 yards. We were in the centre of a cyclone, we supposed, about 11, for the wind suddenly veered to the northeast and blew a hurricane, making our anchorage and Bensersiel a lee shore. It was half-flood, and we decided to start, but how to get up anchor? Couldn't get in a link, as it was. In view of slipping it, we buoyed it ready: then got up sail, three-reefed, and tried to sail it out of the ground. Just giving it up when it came away and we got it up. Then bore away for Bensersiel. Got into the channel but found the booms almost covered by an abnormally high tide and very hard to see. Henry stood forward while I steered. Soon got into breakers and found it a devil of a situation. Fearful work with tiller under so much sail. One or two heavy gibes at turns of the channel. When close inshore, sea less bad – missed booms altogether and grounded, but blew off again. Whole population on the beach yelling. Tide so high all dunes were obscured, but H conned her skilfully on, and we were soon tearing in to the mouth of the 'harbour', about 15 feet wide, at about 7 knots. It was a tiny basin with not even room to round up. Tried to get sail down but peak jammed; let go anchor with a run, luffed, and just brought up in time with the bowsprit over the quayside, and received the bewildered congratulations of the people who seemed to think we had fallen from the sky.

The voyage was almost over. When the weather cleared they sailed south to Terschelling, where they arranged for *Vixen* to be laid up for the winter. On 15 December they caught the steamer back to Harwich.

* * *

It had been quite a trip. In three months Childers had visited four countries, weathered innumerable storms and squalls, and sailed more than two thousand miles. In a modern thirty-footer with the contemporary conveniences of yachting, it would be a feat of some endurance, seamanship and courage: in Childers' day it was, justly, described as an epic.[25]

This holiday pointed up the paradox in Childers' character implied by Williams: on the one hand, the 'person of regular habits and settled tastes', the punctilious servant of Empire and officer of the Crown, passing his days recording the deliberations of others; on the other, the ardent adventurer and man of action who seemed to need the outlet, the 'strenuous physical expression',[26] provided by the challenge and the risks of the sea. Echoes of this tension and disjunction are to be found in the remarks of Carruthers about Davies: 'An armchair critic is one thing, but a sun-burnt, brine-burnt zealot smarting under a personal discontent, athirst for a means, however tortuous, of contributing his effort to the great cause, the maritime supremacy of Britain, that was quite another thing . . . To hear him talk was to feel a current of clarifying air blustering into a close club-room, where men bandy ineffectual platitudes, and mumble old shibboleths, and go away and do nothing.'[27] Childers' own passion was rising. A passion quite for what had yet to emerge, but passion it was.

IV

'I don't quite understand your not liking Frenchmen,' wrote Edward Marsh to Bertrand Russell in 1894. 'Is it simply because they are unchaste? It is very disgusting – all the ones here fornicate pretty regularly from sixteen years old, and talk about it in a way that would sicken me in England – but it's merely a matter of education.'[28] If education was indeed the issue, Childers' own might be progressing apace both at sea and in the Commons, but seems to have been merely marking time elsewhere. As Marsh himself – admittedly not exactly an enthusiast for the opposite sex – noted, undergraduate Cambridge in the 1890s was not a place into which women much intruded. Yet in London this was scarcely the case. Russell himself lost little time in marrying, and Childers, as a more than presentable 'man about town', must have done his fair share of the obligatory taking of ladies down to dinner. He was clearly attracted by women: on his trip to the West Indies in 1898 he certainly noticed one of his fellow travellers, 'Miss McCarthy, golden haired, eighteen or thereabouts, and a very good sort with no rot about her.'[29] Yet there are few suggestions of any grand attachments for Childers in his first years in London, although he seems to have been on affectionate terms with one of the daughters of Henry Yates Thompson,[30] a prominent literary figure, sometime secretary to the Viceroy of Ireland, and friend of the Bartons.

Childers may perhaps have been constrained by his domestic circumstances. By 1897 he could afford to put into practice a long-desired plan to provide his sisters with something approaching their own home, and Sybil moved into a flat he had taken in Glebe Place, just off the King's Road. Then, as now, this was an exclusive backwater. In 1901, joined by Constance and Dulcibella, they moved a few hundred yards away, to Carlyle Mansions in Cheyne Walk, another 'good' address. This happy arrangement, by which Childers could feel that he was fulfilling his responsibilities to his orphaned sisters, nevertheless had some obvious limitations: one of his reservations at the time of his engagement to Molly in 1903 concerned the problem of what would become of the home he had made for his sisters.

His responsibilities for his sisters apart, his earliest and closest relationships – with his parents – had been too soon and painfully truncated: he would be neither the first nor the last to feel a consequent reluctance to risk the hurt implicit in other close alliances.

There was, however, one subject which undoubtedly lay close to Childers' heart: that of his country and her Empire.

5
Imperial Guard

1896–1900

'Don't you think it would be splendid to do something for one's country? Normally, alas, I'm an idle man on the whole, and I feel this is a chance of useful action.'

Erskine Childers, 1900

I

Leaving aside the rather special case of Ireland, Britain had had an Empire worthy of the name since the late seventeenth century. Only in the eighteenth century did 'Empire' become a matter meriting much concern, however, in connection first with India, then with the independence – or otherwise – of the colonies on the eastern seaboard of America. By Childers' day Britain had passed the stage where she could either feed herself, or thrive commercially on the basis of home markets alone, and colonies, as sources of raw materials and markets for manufactured goods, were seen by many as crucial to her economic supremacy. This was equally the case with the newly unified states of Italy and Germany. In a sense, therefore, dividing up those parts of the world not already 'allocated' to the major European powers came to be seen as a matter of necessity rather than choice. In practice, this meant Africa: the struggle for that continent was on. Between 1870 and 1914, almost the entire continent was divided between the major European powers. Men such as Cecil Rhodes made of the business a very pleasant virtue: 'We happen to be the best people in the world, with the highest ideals of decency and justice and liberty and peace, and the more of the world we inhabit, the better for humanity.'[1] In this way did Imperialism become, not merely an agreeable commercial arrangement, but a veritable creed. The erosion of traditional Christianity had perhaps created a spiritual vacuum that this nationalistic crusade for the betterment of humanity swelled to fill. Of his adventures in South Africa, working under Lord Milner, John Buchan wrote:

> I was more than a convert, I was a fanatic. I dreamed of a worldwide brotherhood with the background of common race and creed, consecrated to the service of peace; Britain enriching the rest out of her culture and traditions, and the spirit of the Dominions like a strong wind freshening the stuffiness of the old land . . . The white man's burden is now an almost meaningless phrase: then it involved a new philosophy of politics, and an ethical standard, serious and surely not ignoble.[2]

Childers, who had been distraught at his loss of a conventional Christian faith, for a time embraced the new creed with the same enthusiasm as Buchan. In 1903 he was to remark approvingly that 'one can set no limits to the possibilities of an alliance of English-speaking races';[3] similarly, of his *alter ego* Davies he wrote, 'The key to his character . . . was devotion to the sea, wedded to a fire of pent-up patriotism struggling incessantly for an outlet . . .'[4]

Agreeable though it could be for its practitioners, this colonizing process was hardly characterized by passive acquiescence, either among the rival colonial powers or on the part of indigenous inhabitants. Most serious of the various squabbles that arose was the simmering issue of the Boers, in which Germany was involved – or had involved herself.

The South Africa of a century ago was a small and rather introspective Boer colony. Dutch farmers who had settled in the south-eastern quarter of South Africa at the end of the seventeenth century, the Boers were of interest to the British for the most legitimate of Imperial reasons. During the Napoleonic wars it had been necessary to annexe Cape Town to protect what was, before the opening of the Suez Canal, the only sea route between Britain and the Far East. An uneasy relationship was established between the English and Dutch. The former were keen to protect trade and ultimately – certainly this was the aim of Cecil Rhodes – to create a great British 'corridor' between Cairo and the Cape; the latter were determined to maintain their independence and traditional way of life, which included the keeping of slaves. The Boer, after all, 'considered himself also a member of a master-race, the rock and fortress of a European civilisation in the midst of the inferior millions of native tribes'.[5] There were skirmishes from time to time between these scions of civilization, most notably at Majuba Hill in 1879, when the British were defeated and the Transvaal declared its independence from the Crown. Even then, all might have stumbled on without more serious conflict, had it not been for the discovery of gold in the new republic, in 1886. This attracted a new breed of adventurers to the Transvaal, most of whom were British, and who came to be known by the Dutch as *Uitlanders* or outlanders. Between these two groups, conflict soon arose. The causes were various, but culminated in the fact that while they were very heavily taxed, the Uitlanders were permitted no measure of political power. In December 1895 Rhodes, premier of Cape Colony and forever jealous of the Transvaal's independence, instigated an ill-judged raid, supposedly with the aim of righting the Uitlanders' wrongs, led by Dr Starr Jameson. It was a disaster. The Uitlanders failed to rise in response, and the raiders – no more than 400 strong – were stopped in their tracks, captured, and put on trial. It was at this point that Germany manifested an interest.

Towards the end of the nineteenth century Germany was still a relatively new nation-state. As recently as the 1860s she had been no more than a loosely confederated group of princedoms, some no larger than Surrey. Under Otto von Bismarck, the greatest continental statesman of the age, she had been unified into a coherent, politically stable, economically prosperous and industrially ambitious nation. Her coming-of-age she had announced by her defeat of the French and seizure of the industrial heartland of Alsace-Lorraine in 1870, the year of Childers' birth. Now she, too, was ambitious for an Empire, declaring her desire for 'a place in the sun' alongside Britain. The Jameson raid provided an ideal pretext for extending Germany's existing interests in German South West Africa. A racial affinity between the Dutch and the Germans was proclaimed, and in January 1896 the Kaiser sent a telegram to the Transvaal's president, Paul Kruger, which was capable of an interpretation implying Germany's willingness to act with the Boers against Britain: 'I sincerely congratulate you that, without appealing for the help of friendly powers, you with your people, by your own energy against the armed hordes which as disturbers of the peace broke into your country, have succeeded in re-establishing peace and maintaining the independence of your country from attacks from without.'[6] This was seen as provocative, at a time when such sabre-rattling between countries was not uncommon, and when a small-scale war between professional armies was seen as a perfectly acceptable way of settling international differences. British public reaction to what came to be known as 'the Kruger telegram' was extreme.

Parliament was in recess at the time, and one of its clerks was on holiday on the French Riviera, doubtless reflecting on his first year in Westminster. Childers wrote, very much in the language of the day, to his Cambridge friend Walter Runciman:

> I am so excited about the African business that I can hardly think about anything else. What a damned insolent puppy that Emperor is, I would like nothing better than for him to land his dirty marines in Delagoa Bay [on the eastern seaboard of Africa], but the whole of Europe seems against us, not to mention America. Lloyd-Jones is here and we spend the day in telegram hunting and Emperor-cursing and expressing a sublime confidence in the tenacity of the Anglo-Saxon Race.[7]

At it happened, this particular affair blew over. Joseph Chamberlain sent Sir Alfred Milner as High Commissioner to South Africa with a view to reconciling the demands of the Uitlanders with Kruger's stance, and Childers returned to his Commons duties without having his confidence in the Anglo-Saxon race put to the test. Kruger, however, was deeply suspicious of the British, and intransigent in the matter of the Uitlanders' civil rights – at least, in denying them. For three years the situation smouldered on; Milner finally wrote in despair to Chamberlain, 'There is no way out except reform in the Transvaal or war'.[8] He was proved right, hence Churchill's later observation, 'I date the beginning of these violent times from the Jameson Raid.'[9]

II

In the meantime, Childers was as usual devoting most of his considerable spare time to sailing. In the spring following the Jameson raid, *Mad Agnes* took him and a crew that included a new friend, William Le Fanu, on an Easter cruise of the east coast. Le Fanu, distantly related to the writer Sheridan Le Fanu, was a member of a distinguished Anglo-Irish family, his father being the Commissioner of Public Works in Ireland. Le Fanu had been educated at Haileybury, but was some nine years older than Childers; they met in London, through 'the Irish connection'. He had trained as a solicitor, and was tall, and a fine oar. The two were soon on close terms, Le Fanu constituting an ideal crew. That year, as they pottered around the Solent, Childers got to know the nooks and crannies of that richly varied cruising ground. The following Whitsun saw the two men back on the east coast in weather sometimes entirely characteristic of the time of year – it was very early in the season for yachting in a half-decked boat. The trip, though, proved useful, for the flats of the Essex coast were identified by Childers in *The Riddle of the Sands* as one of the two proposed German invasion sites.

Then came *the* national event of 1897, the Queen's Diamond Jubilee. This was an occasion which could scarcely pass by a man of Childers' mental stamp.

It was inevitable that a celebration of some sort would mark this great jubilee. It was Chamberlain's idea, in his capacity as Colonial Secretary, to focus on colonial premiers rather than crowned heads, thus distinguishing the occasion from the Golden Jubilee of 1887. Equally, it would reflect the Imperial temper of the times. What could be better? To the Queen, the matter of the precedence of the various princes and premiers presented problems: as she remarked in her journal of 4 June, 'We always kept forgetting someone, which was maddening.'[10] Still, the plan as a whole was agreeable enough. The official celebration on the day itself was to comprise a great procession through central London of the military representatives of the multifarious peoples of the Empire. The then stupendous sum of a quarter of a million pounds was spent on street decorations, out of public funds, and 2,500 beacons were lit all over the country. This was on the Tuesday, 21 June 1897. The following Saturday at Spithead would see a Review of the Fleet.

Given his patriotism at the time, this occasion was as important for Childers as for any of the Queen's subjects. In Glebe Place he was, in a sense, in its midst, since most of the colonial contingents attending the Jubilee were encamped barely half a mile away, in the grounds of the Royal Hospital, Chelsea. The House was sitting during the period of the Jubilee, so he may have seen the great procession; he was certainly present, with Le Fanu, at the Spithead Review. With 164 ships of the Royal Navy, in addition to those of ten other nations, it was the largest peace-time demonstration of naval power ever witnessed – and witnessed it was, by some 35,000 officers and men, in addition to the tens of thousands of civilians on the shore. The *New York Times* was inspired to write of 'the Greater Britain which seems so plainly destined to dominate this planet',[11] and most other observers took a similar line. Yet even on such an occasion, a minority of doubters thought the great Review an insubstantial pageant. Catching the mood of the more prescient, Kipling made a plea against Imperial grandiloquence:

The tumult and the shouting dies;
The Captains and the Kings depart:
Still stands Thine ancient sacrifice,
An humble and a contrite heart.
Lord God of Hosts, be with us yet,
Lest we forget – lest we forget![12]

A month later Parliament went into recess, and Childers set off on his voyage to the Frisians, and beyond to the Baltic. On his return to London in December, he set his affairs in order before once again travelling to spend Christmas in St Moritz. He was back at work in the House of Commons until April, then took the steamer across the North Sea to rescue *Vixen* from her winter berth at Terschelling, sailing briefly to the east-coast flats before returning her to the Hamble early in May. The latter part of spring, and the summer, were again spent nosing in and out of the various little havens around the Solent. By Childers' standards, the season was to be short: on 12 August, the day the House rose, *Vixen* was laid up, and after his usual visit to

Glendalough, in late October he set off for the West Indies, as a passenger on a tramp steamer, the SS *West Indian*. Arranged by Walter Runciman, this was the trip he had intended to take four years previously, in the autumn of 1894.

A hundred years ago the Caribbean was rarely visited by the English – unless they had specific colonial duties there, the islands being largely under British rule. It was a region exotic and remote and, for Childers, infinitely romantic. His responses to the trip were at first suitably Imperial. 'There's the captain,' Childers recounted to his sisters, 'a wiry little Welshman, flaming red, full of queer yarns and taking a great interest in foreign politics. Hearing little, as he's generally at sea, he gets me to coach him in all the contemporary questions, so I am giving him sound imperial policy on the Cretan, Egyptian, Armenian and other questions . . . We go at it hammer and tongs . . .'[13] Similarly, he found the islands, in that year of 1898, pure Kipling. He quoted to his sisters:

> To the cool of our deep verandahs,
> To the blaze of our jewelled main,
> To the night, to the palms in moonlight,
> And the firefly in the cane.

That is the West Indies: 'On from island into island to the gateways of the day.'[14]

Yet there was more to the experience than this. Hitherto, Childers' writing had been attractive enough to be very occasionally published, but was little marked by any particular talent. Now, in his twenty-ninth year, a tone of voice mature, confident and much more obviously his own began to emerge in his letters home. An excellent example is his description of the ship's third officer on the voyage out, 'an old, dour, silent, grizzled man of sixty-two, looking like some gnarled tree trunk on a blasted heath. He never speaks or unbends, except to the cabin kittens when he thinks he is unobserved; he then expands in elephantine tenderness. A strange, silent riddle of a man.'[15] This is pure Childers: the acute observation of character, the expressive simile, the delicacy, and the happiness of 'elephantine'.

There were also, in the West Indies, opportunities for the sort of blue-water sailing that was entirely novel to a man weaned on the cold, rough, yeasty waters of the Channel and the North Sea. It had been Childers' ambition to sail – in his own words – 'one of the little negro-manned sailing vessels which ply a humble and precarious trade between the islands.' This he did, to Grenada, on a craft called *Faith*. In a later newspaper article he remembered that happy time: first, securing his berth from the captain:

> I led up, with a hint of practical nature, to the question of accommodation. 'You shall have the dog-house, Sir,' he said, evidently meaning to confer a high distinction, though the offer made me thoughtful.

Then the voyage itself:

> In a universal chatter and laughter, we had our various meals by the light of the moon, while *Faith* yawed unsteadily through half the points of the compass. Someone was giving casual attention to the helm; someone else hovering wistfully about the side-lights, which seemed to be the victims of an intermittent disorder; but the general impression to my eye was that of a party of children out for a frolic, without any question of a serious commercial enterprise.[16]

IV

If there was something in this, for Childers, of a dream come true, less agreeable events were simultaneously occurring on the far side of the globe. In November of 1898, a Boer jury acquitted one of their own policemen of shooting an Uitlander dead. As a symptom of their diminishing confidence in Milner and Chamberlain, the Uitlanders addressed a petition of protest directly to the Queen. This could hardly be ignored, and a conference was arranged between Milner and Kruger to attempt to resolve the crisis.

Childers, having returned to England in December, was an engrossed observer of events which proved to mark a great turning-point in the development of Britain's relations with her colonies. For him, it was an issue with both patriotic and professional aspects, and in consequence he felt he could not risk his customary lengthy cruise that summer of 1899: he took *Vixen* no further than the Isle of Wight. In June the conference ended in failure, and it was the Boers who eventually issued the ultimatum that made war inevitable, when at the end of September the Orange Free State joined with the Transvaal in determining to fight for complete independence from the Crown. Nevertheless, the likelihood of the Commons Clerk becoming involved seemed remote. As the two Boer republics of the Transvaal and the Orange Free State had a population of barely 100,000, it was plain that the British Army would not be long gainsaid. Moreover Childers, with a military training limited to the school cadet force, his spectacles, and his sciatic limp, was hardly military material. Writing to his sister Dulcibella from France in October 1899, where he was touring the Dordogne with William Le Fanu, he remarked, 'We are anxious about the Transvaal but find the press give a good deal of news here – of course venomously hostile. I am collecting cartoons on the subject and have one or two very choice ones.'[17]

The Boers, however, were not to be easily cowed. Avoiding direct confrontation with a numerically superior force, their small, highly mobile and independent units went in for guerrilla tactics. Expectations presaging those of 1914 – that the war would be over by Christmas – began to subside. Then came Black Week, in December 1899, when disaster befell each of the three British columns moving north-east from the Cape to quell the Boers. Defeats at Magersfontein, Stormberg and the Tugela River left three thousand British dead. From the most prestigious of the volunteer militia forces, the Honourable Artillery Company, came a call for reinforcements. Basil Williams, who had been present at the Commons investigation into the Jameson Raid where he was much struck by the character and evidence of Rhodes, was among the first to answer it. To Childers, spending Christmas at Glendalough, he wrote, 'You should come over at once and volunteer. I've already taken steps to do so.'[18]

Shades of Davies! To a patriotic man of Childers' romantic temperament, it was irresistible. He at once packed his traps and left for London. 'The fact is,' he wrote to his sister Dulcibella early in January, 'I've been longing to go out for some time. Don't you think it would be splendid to do something for one's country? Normally, alas, I'm an idle man on the whole, I fear, and I feel this is a chance of useful action.'[19] A few days later he added: 'Heaven knows I shall be sorry enough to leave you all, but something impels me here and I feel it's right. Yet it's no good dwelling on the serious side. It's after all a splendid adventure!'[20]

With great persistence, he had secured a position as driver in the same battery as Williams, in charge of the two horses which pulled a 12-pounder wheeled Vickers Maxim gun, formally attached to the emergency reserve unit of the Honourable Artillery Company known as the City of London Imperial Volunteers. His duties were menial, and his influence over the course of events was likely to be nugatory, but it was certainly something of a change from what Childers later characterized to Williams as the 'cigarette-smoking, gossiping, bottom-warming, Bradshaw-studying life at Westminster'.[21]

After a month's barrack training in St John's Wood, the CIV embarked on the transport SS *Montfort* in the midst of a snowstorm in the early hours of 27 February 1900. They disembarked at Cape Town more than three weeks later and spent a few days at Green Point Camp. Then they edged north: first to Stellenbosch; subsequently by train to Piquetberg Road, some eighty miles from Cape Town; then, on 17 May, to Bloemfontein.

Childers' concern both on the voyage out and in their travels north was that they might be too late to see any real action. The new commander in the field was Lord Roberts, an Anglo-Irishman like Childers, and Britain's best-loved general. Roberts had driven north in February with great success to relieve Magersfontein, while General French had lifted the siege of Kimberley and Sir Redvers Buller that of Ladysmith. It was no rout of the Boers, but retreat they did. Pretoria was soon in Roberts' sights. Then, as fever broke out among his troops, the pace slackened. The Boers, everywhere, resumed their sporadic harrying. A few miles north of Bloemfontein, on 26 June 1900, Childers' battery at last saw action.

> Walk – march – trot rang out to the battery, and we trotted ahead down the hill, plunged down a villainous *spruit*, and came up on to the level, under a pretty heavy fire from the *kopje* on our left [he wrote]. For my part, I was absorbed for these moments in a threatened mishap to my harness, and the dread of disgrace at such an epoch. My off horse had lost flesh in the last few days, and the girth, though buckled up in the last hole, was slightly too loose. We had to gallop up a steep bit of

> ascent out of the drift, and to my horror, the pack saddle on him began to slip and turn, so I had to go into action holding on his saddle with my right hand, in a fever of anxiety, and at first oblivious of anything else. Then I noticed the whing of bullets, and the dust spots knocked up, and felt the same sort of feeling one has waiting to start a race, only with added chill and thrill.

Later he added: 'There was a load off our minds this night, for the HAC had at last been in action and under fire. All went well and steadily.'[22] Just a day after celebrating his thirtieth birthday, Childers had been 'blooded'.

Roberts now forced his army the last miles to Pretoria, driving the Boers before him. Childers' battery followed, seeing further action against the scattered Boers on several occasions before themselves reaching Pretoria, on 14 August. The following day they were reviewed by Roberts: 'He was standing with a large staff at the foot of the steps. The order "eyes right" gave us a good view of him, and very small, fit and alert he looked.' Quoting Kipling, Childers continued:

> Oh, 'e's little, but 'e's wise,
> 'E's a terror for 'is size.[23]

Childers' battery was now attached to General Paget's brigade, which had the job of scouring the district around the railway line that ran north to Petersberg. Almost at once he was afflicted with an infected foot, and by 30 August had been invalided out to the Imperial Yeomanry Hospital at Pretoria. There, quite by chance, he encountered his brother Henry. The latter had been in Canada at the outbreak of the war; he had volunteered for a mounted infantry unit, and himself been slightly wounded. 'It was a strange place to meet in after 17 months, he coming from British Columbia, I from London,' wrote Childers. 'A fancy strikes me of the way in which the whole Empire has rallied for a common end on African soil.'[24]

Childers hankered to rejoin the battery, but his foot was slow to heal, and by September it was clear that the major actions of the war were over, and only sporadic resistance seemed likely to remain. Lord Roberts was returning to England, and the CIV were among the first of the volunteer units to be dismissed. By November, courtesy of the SS *Aurania*, Childers was home.

V

The experience of the Boer War was as profound for Childers as was Cambridge for Edward Marsh. 'Every man', said Johnson, 'thinks meanly of himself for not having been a soldier, or not having been at sea.'[25] Childers, of course, could already very much pride himself on his seamanship; now he could take pleasure in his soldiering, too, and in having overcome quite a challenge in order to do so. As Williams noted in his memoir, 'At first he was not considered a very promising soldier, for he not only had to wear glasses – in those days an almost unheard-of singularity in one of the rank and file – but he also had a limp in one leg.' And yet, as Williams observed, 'over those months Childers earned the liking and respect of officers and men, not only for his thoroughness and unassuming courage as an artillery driver, but still more for his unselfishness in all the little difficulties of campaigning life, his modesty, and his transparent fitness of character. He was a man with whom the roughest would never think of taking a liberty.'[26]

Liberty was of course the matter at issue, and given Childers' later fondness for republics – or for one republic, anyway – his attitude regarding South Africa is intriguing. Although his respect for the Boers is clear, both as an army and as individuals,[27] more characteristic is not so much his assumption of the justice of the British cause, as his absolute celebration of that justice. In many respects the Boer entanglement proved a catalyst for republican thinking in Ireland, and an independent Irish brigade fought alongside the Boers against the British. Yet the majority of Irishmen remained loyal to the Crown, and Childers encountered some of them. As he remarked, 'It was pleasant to hear the rich Cork brogue in the air. It seems impossible to believe that these are the men whom Irish patriots incite to mutiny. They are loyal, keen, and simple soldiers, as proud of the flag as any Britisher.'[28] Yet despite his belief in the justice of the British cause, Childers was too intelligent, too close an observer, and too much a delver into his own conscience not to ponder the British involvement in South Africa very carefully – an involvement much criticized in both the European and the American press. Moreover, as a close companion throughout these months he had the thoughtful Basil Williams, who later wrote: 'Here, when we were tired of playing piquet with a precious but greasy pack of cards, we would talk of all things under the sun until we rolled over to sleep . . . Both of us, who came out as hide-bound Tories, began to tend towards more liberal ideas, partly from the jolly democratic company we were in, but chiefly, I think, from our endless discussion on politics and life generally.'[29]

There was also the matter of Britain's military competence. The Boer War marked the end of the 'Pax Britannica', a thoroughly agreeable period for the British which had lasted – with the solitary exception of the Crimea – since the ending of the Napoleonic wars at Waterloo in 1815. The Kruger telegram hinted at the possibility of another major European war, and events in South Africa then suggested quite how poorly Britain was prepared for such an eventuality, and how friendless her policy of 'splendid isolation' had left her. If this was apparent in the 'bottom-warming, Bradshaw-studying life at Westminster' – and it was – it was even more so on the *kopjes* of Bloemfontein. Soon, like Thomas Erskine before him, Childers would take up his pen as an active and percipient critic of his country's military arrangements.

Though he was to become critical of the military mind in due course, for now he was, above all, exhilarated to have done something for his country – and perhaps in the doing he had resolved some of the latent tensions in his character. There was to be a campaign medal, the Freedom of the City of London, the great celebration of City of London Imperial Volunteers Day in the City itself – but first of all, on their return to Southampton and then to the capital, the Company were received as conquering heroes. Childers later recalled,

> . . . that wonderful journey to London with its growing tumult of feelings, as station after station, with their ribboned and shouting throngs passed by . . . The rest seems a dream; a dream of miles of upturned faces, of dancing colours, of roaring voices, of a sudden dim hush in the great Cathedral . . . and finally of the entry once more through the old grey gateway of the Armoury House. I expect the feelings of all of us were much the same; some honest pride in having earned such a welcome; a sort of stunned bewilderment at its touching

> and passionate intensity; a deep wave of affection for our countrymen . . .[30]

In Childers' eyes the Boer War was his first real 'chance of useful action' – a yearning for which was to become a critical component of his personality – and it was one he seized.

6
The Riddle of the Sands

1900–1903

'Davies in *The Riddle of the Sands* was every bit Childers.'
Ivor Lloyd-Jones

I

Gratified and surprised though Childers was by the Company's reception, he had another reason for pleasure that day. Quite unintentionally, he had become an author.

Childers' habit of regaling his friends and relatives, when separated from them for any period, with letters recounting his doings, was of course a commonplace in that age; 'a line' Lord Curzon once dropped his wife from New York ran to a hundred pages. Childers was a fine correspondent, with a style by now easy and unselfconscious, full of sharp, finely observed detail, and a very winning line in humour. Of an adventure which was the greatest in his life to date, he would as naturally wish to write as his correspondents would wish to hear details from him, and he wrote sufficiently regularly to provide in many respects a very full picture of his seven months on the veldt. Written especially for his sisters, these letters gave them treasured glimpses of their brother's skirmishes at the other end of the world. Letters were often passed around a wide circle of family and friends, and so it was that these found their way into the hands of the Yates Thompsons, to whose daughter Childers had once been mildly attached. Here they provided not simply a personal record, but a fascinating narrative of the war as seen from the perspective of this engaging gentleman-ranker.

The country was agog at the daily developments in the war; would the public at large not be enthralled by Childers' story? Mrs Thompson in particular thought so, and persuaded her brother-in-law to think so too. He was Reginald Smith, of the publishers Smith, Elder and Company, a prestigious firm who published Charlotte Brontë, Meredith, Trollope, Browning, and Childers' own great favourite, Thackeray. An Etonian and another graduate of Trinity, Smith's 'salient characteristic was consideration for the sensitive race of authors'.[1] Indeed, he was so courteous as to travel to Southampton to be on the pier to meet the *Aurania* the day she docked. There and then he agreed with Childers final details regarding the publication of the letters – already in hand. Just weeks later *In the Ranks of the CIV* appeared, dedicated to 'My Friend and Comrade, Gunner Basil Williams'. The book may still be read with pleasure today, but has long been out of print; as it was the immediate precursor of *The Riddle of the Sands*, it merits brief comment.

By the end of 1900, the publication of dispatches from South Africa was scarcely a novelty. Among others, Arthur Conan Doyle had written *The South African War*, and Winston Churchill had augmented a growing reputation for enterprise and dash with *London to Ladysmith* and *Ian Hamilton's March*. Churchill's two volumes of collected journalism constitute an interesting comparison with Childers' work. The former are very much *de haut en bas*, encompassing a broad strategic sweep and a fine understanding of the larger movements of the war; in the latter, by contrast, the view is immeasurably more restricted, being that from the bottom of the military pile. This had its own fascination, for before 1900 the story from the ranks had rarely been told. 'The fact is – and I fancy this applies to all sorts and conditions of private soldiers – in our life in the field, fighting plays a relatively small part,' wrote Childers. 'I doubt if people at home realise how much in the background are its dangers and difficulties. The really absorbing questions are those of material welfare – sordid, physical, unromantic details, which touch you at every turn. Shall we camp in dry blankets? Biscuit ration raised from three to three and a half! Dare I take my boots off tonight? Is it going to rain?'[2] This sense of the day-to-day life of the rank and file, new to the public and fresh, very well complemented the sort of diet that newspaper coverage – Churchill's included – had already given them.

Facts and details of this nature are something which *In the Ranks* shares with *The Riddle of the Sands*. Both books also convey the author's sense of humour. 'A camp rumour is a wonderful thing,' Childers observes. 'Generally speaking, there are two varieties, cook-shop rumours and officers' servants rumours. Both are always false, but there is slightly more respectable mendacity about the latter than the former. The cooks are always supposed to know if we are changing camp by getting orders about rations in advance. Having this slight advantage, they go out of their way to make rumours on every sort of subject. How many scores of times they have sent us to the front I shouldn't like to say.'[3] Childers' personality, too, shines through. As *In the Ranks* progresses we come to know, to appreciate, and finally to love our workmanlike, self-deprecating and thoughtful guide – first to the regime of camp life, then to the relative rigours of the campaign, finally to the dangers of being under fire. Ivor Lloyd-Jones later remarked upon Childers' 'Utter selflessness, honesty, courage and simplicity . . . I can think of no virtue he lacked – but those I have mentioned were the outstanding ones.'[4] To those traits as displayed in the South African book might particularly be added modesty, and charm.

In the Ranks is a very different book from *The Riddle of the Sands*, and not such a good one. One of the many charms of the novel is the close interplay of character between Davies and Carruthers; and while Childers would probably have been unable to compass such a counterpoint had it not been for his almost constant companionship with Williams during their seven months on the veldt, the absence of anything similar in *In the Ranks* is perhaps inevitable, since Childers' intention was simply to keep his sisters informed. Then, *In the Ranks* is of course a series of letters, based on actual experiences written of as and when they occurred – albeit edited later; accordingly, although it has a certain narrative force, it lacks the drive and carefully paced climax of its fictional successor. In every sense it is an apprentice work, preparing its author for the novel that was to come.

In the Ranks was well received on publication, had generally good reviews, and was in a third printing by Christmas of that year. Its success also led to Childers' friendship with the Commanding Officer of the Honourable Artillery Company, the Earl of Denbigh and Desmond, who was to induce him to travel to Boston.

If the early months of 1901 brought the excitements of authorship, they were also unsettling ones for Childers. In January the Queen died, bringing to its end an age, in Britain, of unparalleled peace, prosperity and (in many respects) progress. Her death was widely – and rightly, as events were to prove – seen as heralding a less certain age. Childers himself, while he deprecated the extent of the eulogies, yet wrote to Flora Priestley that he had 'a superstitious feeling that her death closes our greatest epoch, as her crowning certainly began it'.[5] The Queen herself had been wont to declare, 'What will become of my poor country when I die? If Bertie succeeds he would spend his life in one whirl of amusements'[6] – a well-founded concern. And the war dragged on. Although there had been so much euphoria associated with the HAC's return, the Boers under Botha, De Wet, de la Rey, Smith and Kritzinger masterminded a brilliant rearguard guerrilla action, and it was May of 1902 before peace was finally achieved.

Childers had anticipated this course of events, but it gave him no pleasure to see it. He deplored the way the task in which he had been involved was left half done, and was torn between his professional and domestic responsibilities in London, and a desire to go back to help complete it. Writing to Williams in January 1901, he remarked that 'Other things being equal I would drop [Westminster] if I saw a chance of more active work, but other things are not equal. My clear duty keeps me in England and I can't forgo the assured income for a doubtful future.' Equally, as a recent participant rather than a mere distant observer of the war, he found the over-simplifications of public and press comment hard to take. To Williams he continued, with a self-righteousness that was new: 'Ever since I came back I have been irritated and disgusted by the tone of the press and other ignorant persons towards the Boers. It was worth going out there if only to learn to respect them. Otherwise the excesses of the anti-Boers would have made me pro-Boer.'[7] He no doubt sympathized with Churchill, whose adventures in South Africa had also engendered in him a respect for the Boers, and who observed in his maiden speech in the House of

Commons that spring, 'If I were a Boer I hope I should be fighting in the field.'[8] It was not a popular remark.

Basil Williams, too, was unsettled. He soon resigned from his clerkship to work in the Transvaal under Lord Milner's auspices, as one of his 'kindergarten' of bright young minds, mainly from Oxford. Behind him, in his half-completed history of the HAC's South African involvement, he left an opportunity for his friend. The sponsorship of Lord Denbigh as Commanding Officer led to Childers being drafted in to finish the task. At the same time, from as early as January of 1901, two months after his return from South Africa, Childers had been worrying away at the idea of a novel set in the Frisian islands. Although this called for a different approach from the letters that comprised *In the Ranks*, the tossing-off of a novel was something of a commonplace among young men of the time: in 1900 Churchill had published *Savrola*, an entirely readable thriller. In due course these two literary tasks began to encroach seriously on Childers' spare time, but for a while sailing continued to provide some of the adventure his nature craved.

Vixen, for all her merits in the shallow waters of the Frisian islands, was a cramped and uncomfortable craft, and her owner now hankered after something larger. The old life-boat had long been quartered at Alexander Moody's boatyard on the Hamble, and here in April 1901 Childers part-exchanged her for *Sunbeam*, an elderly fifteen-ton yawl bought in syndicate with William Le Fanu and a Cruising Club friend, Alfred Dennis,[9] all three of whom were now living in Carlyle Mansions. Soon Childers was at her helm, with all sorts of friends on board; Basil Williams has given us an engaging picture of him in charge of the boat.

> Aboard *Sunbeam* there were no fits of brown study, no undue modesty in the skipper. He was an undoubted despot and we land-lubbers had to do what we were told to and look sharp about it without any back-talk, whether it was hauling at a rope, or taking a hand at the helm, or doing something mysterious with a marlin spike and the lee-scuppers . . . Of course he was entirely responsible for the navigation – though his powers were not put to any severe test on this occasion; but one saw enough to feel that one would be perfectly ready to trust oneself to him in any gale or sudden squall off the most treacherous of coasts.[10]

Sunbeam was used for little more than jaunts around the Solent until 1903 when, *The Riddle of the Sands* completed, she took her owners to the Baltic. If it was less of an epic than the voyage of 1897, this 1,870-mile round trip was still an achievement. With 'a small cabin boy who had never even *seen* the sea before', Childers followed the now familiar route to Terschelling, Cuxhaven and Brunsbüttel, through to the archipelago between Denmark and Sweden. There, in the height of summer, they met the most dismal weather. Childers' account in the Cruising Club *Journal* gives some of its flavour:

> We anchored together with all the other vessels in a spot which promised good holding ground, well round under the shoulder of the cliff, and under shelter of it; a heavy ground swell running in, and we rolled horribly. At 9 p.m. the wind veered still further round to NW and blew a heavy gale. As we were, however, the land was still just – and only just – a protection, and we rode it out there all night, the anchor holding well, though the sea was considerable. Some of the other vessels, including the German yacht, dragged and got sail up and shifted still further round. We kept anchor watches, and the night was a rather anxious one, but all turned out well. None of us will forget the scene that night: the little *Sunbeam* plunging her bows into the short white seas and the great pale cliff rising above.[11]

II

The House of Commons, meanwhile, continued to provide Childers with both his bread and butter and his political education.

The 'khaki election', which had taken place while he was homeward-bound in the *Aurania*, was intended to exploit the emotions of a military victory: in fact, it had left Lord Salisbury with a majority no greater than before. Absolute victory in the war had in any case yet to be achieved; and the ensuing eighteen months were dominated by squabbles over the matter between the government (particularly Joseph Chamberlain) and the Liberal Opposition (especially Lloyd George). A Welsh nationalist from a poor background who had entered the House in 1890, Lloyd George was one of the figures who exemplified the dramatic changes taking place in the country. He was a man for whom women displayed a weakness that was rather galling to other men, but his wit and oratory were nevertheless such as to command a measure of Childers' respect. Certainly he felt there was some basis in Lloyd George's relentless criticism of the government's management of the tail-end of the war. However, when he was introduced to the pro-Boer Irish Nationalist John Dillon, once a lieutenant of Parnell, Childers made it quite clear in which camp he still stood. Writing to Williams in March 1902, he remarked:

> Dillon is very rabid just now. I was calling on the Matthews the other day and found there him and his wife (she was a Miss Matthew). Lady Matthew was very genial and introduced me to them as 'the Mr Childers who defended De Wet'. This annoyed me frightfully as it was as good as stamping me as a fellow pro-Boer of Dillon's. So I said: 'Yes, and I'm delighted to see Bruce Hamilton's men have captured all the stores today.' There was an awful, icy pause, and then Kathleen Matthew dragged me away to a remote window and gave me tea.[12]

Twenty years later, Childers and Lloyd George – and Churchill – were to meet face to face across the table at which the treaty would be negotiated that finally divided England and Ireland, putting an end to a period of seven hundred years of British history.

For Childers, though, the days of extremism lay still far in the future. The Irish parliamentary party had split following Parnell's disgrace and death in 1891, and only now, more than ten years later, was it beginning to refocus around the more temperate figure of John Redmond. In these days of Imperialist fervour over the South African war, Home Rule was in any case low on the nation's agenda, although of sufficient moment to divide the Liberal Opposition. Childers' own comments to Williams at this time flesh out his continuing Unionist position:

> He [Campbell-Bannerman] and Asquith are trying to form a vigorous party, but they will be more impotent than ever, I expect. I don't admire CB generally, but I think he shows pluck in sticking to Home Rule now – and Rosebery cowardice in chucking it. The principle it depends on is not really affected by Irish disloyalty during the war, which is Rosebery's pretext. The theory is that to satisfy their grievances will make them loyal. I'm not a Home Ruler, but I recognise that this is the principle which animates a true Home Ruler.[13]

Increasingly, however, the year 1902 was consumed by writing. Once the Parliamentary recess had begun in August, Childers went sailing for a fortnight in the *Sunbeam*, one of his companions being the clerical friend of his adolescence, Edward Waller from Glendalough. Then it was a case of ploughing on with the novel. 'My sisters are in Ireland,' he wrote to Williams, 'and I am camping in the flat trying to finish my book. I have rather overworked at it, I'm afraid, and don't feel very fit. Reginald Smith has promised to read it when it's done but I don't feel very hopeful about it.'[14] Completing the work to his own satisfaction, he escaped at the end of the year to St Moritz, where he spent a pleasant month with his sisters. On his return he found his doubts had been fully justified: the book, Childers wrote to Williams, 'displeased [Smith] in many respects'.[15] Smith's demands for revisions trespassed on Childers' work both in the Commons and on the HAC history. Indeed, so pressed was Childers for time that he almost failed to meet Smith's deadline. There was then the disagreement over whether Childers should be cited as 'author' or as 'editor', and the writing and inclusion of the final postscript in response to the government's defence initiatives of that spring. The book was at last published, on 27 May 1903, to a reception already described.

III

The contemporary success of *The Riddle of the Sands* was partly attributable to the extent to which it embodied and dramatized increasingly widespread fears concerning the ambitions of Germany. Beginning with the Kruger telegram, these fears were then reinforced by the building of the Kiel ship canal linking the Baltic to the North Sea, and by the passing of the various German Navy Laws.

Bismarck, creator of the unified Germany, had in 1890 been obliged by Kaiser Wilhelm to resign; the architect of all this naval activity was Admiral Tirpitz. Twenty years before, at the time of the Franco-Prussian war, the German Navy had been summed up in the happy phrase, 'a collection of experiments in shipbuilding'[16] – hardly acceptable to a state which aspired to challenge the commercial supremacy of Great Britain: a fleet as powerful and as prestigious as Britain's was the aim of both the Kaiser and Tirpitz, even though it was rather less justifiable on grounds of a need to protect colonies and food supplies. The succession of German Navy Laws, from the first in 1898, made increasing provision for a large and modern navy; their culmination was the naval 'race' between the two countries which was in itself the opening act of the Great War. As Davies puts it so splendidly in the novel,

> Here's this huge empire, stretching half over central Europe – an empire growing like wildfire, I believe, in people, and wealth, and everything. They've licked the French, and the Austrians, and are the greatest military power in Europe. I wish I knew more about all that, but what I'm concerned with is their sea-power. It's a new thing with them, but it's going strong, and that Emperor of theirs is running it for all it's worth. He's a splendid chap, and anyone can see he's right. They've got no colonies to speak of, and *must* have them, like us. They can't get them and keep them, and they can't protect their huge commerce without naval strength. The command of the seas is *the* thing nowadays, isn't it?[17]

Childers had accurately described the book to Williams as a 'story with a purpose', and the British reading public recognized and appreciated its intention of highlighting the reality of the fact that England's traditional enemy, France, had been replaced by an ever more ambitious Germany, and the limitations of national preparedness for a European war. The book was thus exceptional in the way it caught and exploited the mood of the times, yet it was scarcely the only one to have done so: as far back as 1870, *The Battle of Dorking* had rehearsed a German invasion, and from the turn of the century onwards such books were published quite literally by the dozen, among them *The Coming Waterloo*, *A New Trafalgar*, *Pro Patria*, *The Invaders*, *Black Fortnight*, and *Seaward for the Foe*.[18] That these are now forgotten, while *The Riddle of the Sands* is still widely read and enjoyed, indicates that Childers produced something which transcended his original intentions.

It was perhaps not surprising that a man schooled in the Classics should have given his story the simplicity and unity of purpose the Greeks so admired. The Quest – as Davies and Carruthers come to call it – for Dollmann's motivation in attempting to wreck Davies is pursued unerringly, and without digression. From the arrival of the letter from Davies which lures Carruthers to Flensburg, through the meeting with Bartels, the journey to the islands, the encounter with von Brüning, the trip to Memmert and the inspection of the conspirators, right down to Carruthers' feint to Holland and doubling back to the islands and the final climax on Norderney, our attention is relentlessly held. This narrative force provides the backbone to the book, with its triumphant culmination in the two men's achievement of their 'double aim':[19] the traitor is vanquished and England saved, the girl is won.

Satisfying though this is, an air of contrivance and implausibility might be felt were it not for the book's vraisemblance, what the author himself called 'what is meant to be convincing fact'.[20] Most novels, of course, aim at a sufficient plausibility of character, action and setting to enable the reader to suspend disbelief in what at one level he *knows* to be fiction; but the way in which this is done and the extent to which it succeeds varies a great deal. Childers' approach is one of dedicated realism, in which a concrete, detailed and graphic description of situation and character tends to make us less observers of the scene than participants in it. Here is Carruthers, experiencing his first real storm, in a doubtfully safe anchorage:

> [Davies] busied himself with his logbook, swaying easily to the motion of the boat; and I for my part tried to write up my diary, but I could not fix my attention. Every loose article in the boat became audibly restless. Cans clinked, cupboards rattled, lockers uttered hollow groans. Small things sidled out of dark hiding-places, and danced grotesque drunken figures on the floor, like goblins in a haunted glade. The mast whined dolorously at every heel, and the centre-board hiccoughed and choked. Overhead another horde of demons seemed to have been let loose. The deck and mast were conductors which magnified every sound and made the tap-tap of every rope's end resemble the blows of a hammer, and the slapping of the halyards against the mast the rattle of a Maxim gun. The whole tumult beat time to a rhythmical chorus which became maddening.[21]

It is this quality of particularity that lends such vividness to the book and allows us, if not to suspend disbelief, then to find entirely credible what on cold reflection is perhaps only barely so. In this context Daniel Defoe and Robert Louis Stevenson are sometimes mentioned as forerunners of Childers, but more interesting, perhaps, is Childers' own influence on later writers. Certainly it is difficult to imagine John Buchan, Graham Greene or John le Carré writing quite as they have, without an infusion of Childers. All create vivid fictional worlds quite as full of graphic detail as *The Riddle of the Sands* – though not always with Childers' lightness of touch. As noted earlier, Childers drew on the log for his own voyage to the Baltic in 1897 when writing the novel, and characters as well as incidents have been lifted directly from the one to the other. This is not to belittle the imaginative art of the novel: the strength of the story really depends not on those incidents drawn directly from life, but on the coherent amalgam of events and of people, both experienced and imagined. For von Brüning, for instance, there is no obvious model, and a lesser writer might have been tempted to draw a caricature; yet this would have vitiated Childers' over-riding purpose, and his naval commander is a plausible figure, a formidable threat. Urbane and intelligent, appreciative of these idiosyncratic Englishmen yet at the same time carefully investigating their activities, he duly wins their respect: '"He's a thundering good chap, anyhow", said Davies; and I heartily agreed.'[22]

The Riddle of the Sands is also an enduringly witty book. Humour had long been the stock-in-trade of Childers' correspondence, though in his youth the effect was sometimes strained. By the time *In the Ranks of the CIV* was published, however, he was master of an easy, often self-deprecating humour and wit. Memorable in the later novel are 'the rough woollen garments' purchased in Kiel for the Islands, 'all of a colour chosen to harmonize with paraffin stains and anchor mud' . . . 'Then there were the naval books. Davies scanned them with a look I knew well. "There are too many of them," he said in the tone of a cook fixing the fate of superfluous kittens. "Let's throw them overboard."' . . . 'As an ornament the [Rippingille] stove was monstrous and the taint of oil was a disgusting drawback; but after all, the great thing – as Davies said – is to be comfortable, and after that to be clean.' Apart from these incidental touches, there is something more structural in the counterpoise running throughout the book between Carruthers and Davies, which often generates humour. The shabby, workaday woollen garments which so suited Davies would scarcely have been natural to the elegant Carruthers, who by Kiel 'had irretrievably damaged two faultless pairs of white flannels'; the German in which Carruthers was so at home is also the language in which Davies 'compassed a wonderful . . . phrase to the effect that "it might come in useful"'; the first meeting at Flensburg contrasts the ludicrously accoutred and luggaged guest with his embarrassingly practical host.

Character is of course the essence of what Childers in his 'editor's introduction' called the 'warm human envelope'[23] of the novel: John Buchan observed that the characters are 'the most truly realised of any adventure story I have met'[24] (it is also true to say that they are as convincing as those in many novels with literary pretensions well beyond those of Childers'). There is Davies – Davies, of a peculiar diffidence and absent-mindedness matched only by his enthusiasm for the sea and dedication to the craft of navigation and art of seamanship; Davies, with his execrable German, his unfailing sensitivity and kindliness, his penchant for jettisoning both the useful and the useless; Davies, so full of useful maxims; Davies, who in annoyance declared, 'I wish to heaven we had never come here. It comes of landing *ever*.'[25] We know Davies in his light and in his shade – inside out. Carruthers is cleverly drawn as his foil – superficially everything Davies is not, he sets off and contrasts with his companion. He is a professional and social success, as against Davies' failure; he is articulate, self-assured and debonair: an imposing façade . . . with, perhaps, little behind. The growth and deepening of Carruthers, as he learns to value the solid over the superficial, the shabby *Dulcibella* over Dollmann's glittering yacht *Medusa*, is one of the less sung pleasures of the book; it is these experiences which Childers, in his capacity as 'editor', declares 'had left a deep mark'[26] on Carruthers' character and habits.

With the Dollmanns, particularly the daughter, Clara, Childers is less sure. As has been remarked, he seems to have conceived the book without this element, and to have included the romantic interest in deference to his sister. Despite so being 'spatchcocked' into the novel as originally conceived, Fräulein Dollmann works well structurally, providing an additional challenge for the Quest, and a sufficiently entertaining sub-plot. As a character she is less satisfactory, for although her attraction for Davies is adequately conveyed, the reader is not quite made to feel it. At this time Childers was, of course, more familiar with women as sisters than as lovers. His sister Dulcibella wrote to him on his engagement: 'Do you remember how piteous were my appeals that you should write a "*love*-story" – and you declared you knew nothing about it and were incapable and now – oh how sweet Molly must be!'[27] Herr Dollmann is similarly only partly realized: not for some years was Childers to encounter any *real* villains. At his worst, Dollmann resembles the more melodramatic element in the works of Childers' acquaintance Arthur Conan Doyle: ' "Not so loud, you fiend of mischief!" He turned his back, and made an irresolute pace or two towards the door, his hands kneading the folds of his dressing-gown as they had kneaded the curtain at Memmert.'[28]

It is of course entirely possible to overrate *The Riddle of the Sands*. Joseph Conrad, to whom Buchan gallantly compared Childers, had published *Heart of Darkness* in 1899, followed in 1904 by *Nostromo*. Henry James and Thomas Hardy were only just past the peak of their powers; H. G. Wells was in his prime; E. M. Forster, James Joyce and D. H. Lawrence were about to burst on the literary scene; and other considerable writers were at work. The age was, in short, the heyday of the English novel. As a generalization, it might be said that, morally, the best works of the period are more challenging than Childers', while aesthetically they are in some respects more imaginative. Yet *The Riddle of the Sands* has remained, over the years, a celebration of a certain sort of Englishman and Englishness, a celebration of the end of a time and place clear-cut, unambiguous and as wholesome as W. G. Grace . . . on which the shades were in fact fast falling. It is a golden portrait of a high-minded, heroic, masculine and yet curiously sensitive England which – if it ever existed – vanished with the war that in a sense the novel sought to avert. As Churchill said of *My Early Life*, the book is 'a picture of a vanished age'.[29]

Quite apart from the book's literary merits, the relationship between its characters and their creator is intriguing. There are probably few first novels from which an element of autobiography is absent, and in many it is the driving force. The 'obscure Burmese administrator'[30] of the novel's opening paragraph might almost be Robert Caesar Childers; the diffident and absent-minded Davies might be his son; while the Carruthers who 'knows the right people, belongs to the right clubs, has a safe, possibly brilliant future in the Foreign Office'[31] might be that same son, but on another day and with a little added panache.

As has often been remarked, there is undoubtedly a great deal of Childers in Davies; as Ivor Lloyd-Jones remarked simply, 'Davies in *The Riddle of the Sands* was every bit Childers'.[32] The superficial resemblances are obvious – as are the differences: Childers was an academic and professional success whose literary fluency is hardly echoed in Davies' stilted log-book entries and childish spelling, and whose library extended well beyond Mahan's *Influence of Sea-Power* (in two pieces). This lends weight to Andrew Boyle's view[33] that Davies and Carruthers loosely represent two sides of Childers' own character, and indeed it might seem that in the novel Childers was exploring aspects of his own personality, more or less consciously, in a sort of Platonic dialogue. Certainly he examines the Shakespearian theme of the varying and opposing merits of thought and action, to say nothing of the tensions between them. In this sense Childers is the man of thought, Carruthers, who aspires to emulate the man of action, Davies.

This is not of course to say that there were no models for Carruthers, who is clearly less Childers than is Davies. Ivor Lloyd-Jones and Childers' brother Henry have often been proposed as obvious candidates.[34] Equally, Childers had been intimately associated with Basil Williams in the year preceding the book's composition, so surely some hint of Williams has found its way into Carruthers? And much the same might be said of William Le Fanu. Similarly, it was Bertrand Russell who, like Carruthers, spent a period in Germany after graduation, while Edward Marsh was the possessor of his fastidiousness and dandyism, 'groomed to a nicety and invariably composed in manners'.[35] Finally, there is a serendipitous footnote to be recorded. Childers joined the Savile Club in 1903; in May of the following year, so did a man named Carruthers.[36]

Yet in the last analysis it is the character of Davies that is most revealing in terms of self-portraiture. There are the descriptions of the well-springs of Davies' character, particularly that love of the sea that also so animated his creator, and the 'fire of pent-up patriotism' like that which had taken Childers to the veldt. Of equal significance are the delicacy of Davies' conscience as regards any use of Fräulein Dollmann as a source of information about her father, and the extremes of reserve that mark his relationships with women: '"I find it very difficult to tell people things," said Davies, "things like this." I waited. "I did like her – very much." Our eyes met for a second, in which all was said that need be said as between two of our phlegmatic race.'[37] Above all, there is the matter of Davies' 'chance': '"I can't settle down," he said. "All I've been able to is potter about in small boats; but it's all been *wasted* till this chance came. I'm afraid you won't be able to understand how I feel about it; but at last, for once in a way, I see a chance of being useful."' Carruthers continues: 'Once set on the road he grasped his purpose with childlike tenacity. It was his "chance".'[38] This is the Childers who had seized what he called 'a chance of useful action' in Africa – the same Childers who, as he grew older, would seek other and further such chances and, with greater rather than less urgency, a cause to which he might dedicate his life. We may also here read into Davies – and Childers? – a sense of personal inadequacy, and a desire to expunge this by rising to – perhaps creating – great challenges.

In the novel, all this leads to success; in the harsher school of life, the outcome would perhaps be less certain. Like Davies, Childers was a man who discovered a great challenge to which to rise; sadly, he was not to meet with the same success. Indeed, as Roy Foster has noted in his essay on Childers, 'it is interesting that Dollmann is presented as the epitome of corruption because he adopted another country, implacably opposed to the mother country: a creature of "magnificent perfidy" according to the narrator. It is oddly prophetic of how Childers himself would be described.'[39]

7
Molly

November 1903

'I cannot find words to tell you what Erskine means to me.'
Molly Osgood, 1903

I

The success of his novel led to a further literary commission, when Leo Amery approached Childers to write the fifth volume of *The Times History of the South African War*. Amery, the general editor of the series, had himself already completed the first two volumes. A contemporary of Churchill at Harrow and a neighbour of Childers in Chelsea, he was fast establishing himself as one of the leading journalists of his generation. A diminutive figure of startling energy, he was nicknamed 'the pocket dynamo'.[1] Later he turned, with much success, to politics. Amery had already persuaded Basil Williams to tackle the fourth volume of the *History*, and was evidently impressed by the grasp of strategy displayed in *The Riddle of the Sands*. The financial terms Amery offered seemed attractive, but Childers had misgivings about the amount of his spare time the task would involve; eventually, he accepted.

One of Childers' conditions was that he should have time to finish the Honourable Artillery Company memoir before beginning the new commission: Lord Denbigh was keen to see the job done. Childers had maintained his connection with the HAC since his return from South Africa, drilling regularly at the St John's Wood barracks and occasionally joining their camps; and thus he first heard of the plan that the Company should return the visit made in 1896 by the Boston branch of the HAC. At the end of September, on the liner SS *Mayflower*, Childers set off to the New World.

The visit of the HAC was the highlight of Boston's social calendar that autumn. The rights and wrongs of Britain's military involvement in South Africa had, of course, been much discussed in the city of the Boston Tea Party, where so many people were of Irish descent and thus especially sensitive to British Imperialism. Some Bostonians had even done a little background reading in preparation for the visit: Molly Osgood had found and much enjoyed a volume called *In the Ranks of the CIV*. The great day – it was 2 October – came. The *Mayflower* docked, the guns of Fort Warren boomed their salute, and the great parade began. It passed up Beacon Hill, where the whole Osgood family had assembled to watch. The younger daughter was at the window, and later told a friend how 'her eye was drawn to the figure of her husband. She seemed to have felt at once they were destined for one another. She met him at dinner that evening and he, too, knew at once they would never be parted.'[2]

The Osgoods were an old and distinguished Boston family. A Captain John Osgood had been one of the early East Coast pilgrims, having sailed in 1638 on the original *Mayflower* to settle in Andover, Massachusetts. There the family had prospered. A descendant was involved in the Boston Tea Party and the subsequent War of Independence, and there was a distant connection with the sixth President, John Quincy Adams. Dr Hamilton Osgood was himself a distinguished physician, with a particular interest in the study of the mind that was soon to make the name of his friend and contemporary Sigmund Freud.

Of Dr Osgood's two daughters, the youngest lacked good fortune. Molly's early skating accident had left her crippled and seldom free from pain, and she was never able to walk without the aid of sticks. Like her sister Gretchen, however, she was a fine musician and singer, also something of a beauty. Furthermore, her physical incapacity had provided her with every opportunity to develop her mind. Writing in old age, she happily recalled her Boston youth.

> I have especial love for that library, for when I was fourteen years old and just beginning to walk on crutches, they used to let me spend days

reading there though so young, and I learned to climb ladders up to the high shelves and to read there for hours. I was an omnivorous reader. The Old Corner Book Shop was another beneficial source. I could not go to school and this was all of it sheer joy and a long voyage of natural discovery for me – such wonderful books I read.[3]

Cultured though the Osgoods' home was – in Childers' words, 'crammed full of beautiful things in exquisite taste'[4] – it was as far from Glendalough politically as it was in miles. Gretchen's husband Fiske Warren was an active anti-imperialist, rich enough to give generously to the cause. The Osgood family history added a certain allure to republicanism, and Dr Osgood habitually encouraged workers for that great nationalist cause of the time, Ireland. Most prominent among these was John Boyle O'Reilly, editor of *The Pilot*, the voice of the American Irish, who was also the author of *Moondyne*, an autobiographical novel telling of his time in Australia, serving a term of penal servitude for provoking mutiny in the 10th Hussars. He was a member of the revolutionary Fenian movement that had grown out of the tragedy of the famine and, with his black beard and merry eye, to Molly he epitomized all the romance of republicanism. Of him she wrote, 'I myself was very young but I knew him through my father who told me of his life, his heroism and devotion to all those who needed help. He was a man of high honour and a passionate Irishman.'[5]

So Molly's was an odd childhood, intellectually free yet physically constrained, and its peculiarity was compounded by her own decision, at the age of fifteen, to be 'finished' at a school abroad. She was very fond of her family, but had begun to feel the need – despite, or even perhaps because of, her disability – to establish her independence.[6] So this remarkable girl induced her parents to send her alone, across the Atlantic, to a school, Dieudonné, on the outskirts of Paris, run by a woman with some of the force of will of Molly herself, the Marquesa de San Carlos. Under the Marquesa's guidance, Molly flourished. She perfected her languages, her social graces, and learnt to play the guitar in the passionate Spanish style; she became the object of the affections of a distinguished elderly Frenchman and star of the Comédie-Française, Constant Coquelin, who created the name-part in Edmond Rostand's *Cyrano de Bergerac*;[7] and she sent home warm, chatty, highly affectionate letters to her parents and her sister, which form an interesting contrast to her future husband's.

> Your dear letter made me glad, and I wanted so much to have you for a few minutes to hug, or to tell you how much I love you. You would be happy if you could see me here. The chateau itself is simple and uninteresting as I expected, but the surroundings well make up for the deficiencies. It is so absolute country here, and every day I have two hours out of doors, [in] which I either take long walks in the beautiful old ivy-grown woods of the chateau, or I drive through long stretches of open country and cultivated fields, with the peasants at work in their blue blouses . . . The girls are all very nice I am glad to say. There are two or three I like very much. Then the Marquesa and all her daughters are perfect ladies, and cultured, and I am already very fond of them.

Here is a warmth and emotional spontaneity that Childers was not able to express. Yet there was also in Molly something of the vivid awareness of beauty, the sensitivity, and the spirituality of the man she was to marry.

> It was an absolutely still night, not warm but not too cold, the air was clear as crystal, and we had a full moon. We walked the broad step of wooded land belonging to the Marquesa. The moonlight made everything clear even in the thick woods, all the leaves having quite gone. Every tree-trunk shone like silver and each cast a shadow on the glistening fallen leaves. We came to a gate which led into a good stretch of open fields . . . there we stood and looked at the rolling country. The moonlight was intensely white, and one could see for miles and miles . . . Suddenly in the North it began to grow pink in streaks. It was the Aurora Borealis, which became rosier and rosier until it was now over almost all the sky, stretching in long curved ribbons like rainbows. During that time all longing to see you vanished. I felt you both so tremendously close that I could almost see you . . . it was like a vision.[8]

At the end of her spell at Dieudonné, Molly had a difficult operation which would enable her to bear children. Such was her courage in the face of this that her father rewarded her with a trip around the world. Then she returned to Boston.

Dr Osgood's brother-in-law Sumner Pearmain was a stockbroker, banker and anglophile. He was particularly interested in literature, and numbered H. G. Wells among his English friends. Childers sent his letter of introduction to the Pearmains on his arrival in Boston, and was promptly invited to dinner. Mrs Pearmain decided that he should take their niece Gretchen Warren in to dinner; then difficulties arose. Childers, who had somehow acquired a black eye and mislaid his luggage containing his dress clothes, wrote to Mrs Pearmain, begging to be excused. The Pearmains waved aside Childers' embarrassments, only to discover that Mrs Fiske Warren had fallen ill. Her sister Molly was persuaded to take her place and so, on 3 October 1904, Childers sat beside her at dinner. Despite the black eye, it was love at first sight.

The courtship was decorous but rapid. Superficially the attraction between the intelligent, bookish and high-minded pair, with a difficult childhood in common, was unsurprising. It was also a mutually appreciative meeting between the old and new worlds. On his first visit to the States, in 1895, Churchill had written to his brother, 'Picture to yourself the American people as a great lusty youth who treads on all your sensibilities, perpetrates every horror of ill-manners, whom neither age nor just tradition inspire with reverence – but who moves about his affairs with a good-hearted freshness which may well be the envy of older nations of the world.'[9] Childers, too, was struck by this freshness, and found particularly appealing the very natural and open affection which Molly showed her parents, and which she enjoyed in return. Indeed, the hitherto essentially reserved Englishman found all this warmth infectious. Writing to his aunt Agnes at Glendalough of his engagement he could declare,

> I am amazed and overcome sometimes with my own good fortune. I don't know why such a thing should happen to me. I am utterly unworthy of it, utterly. She is one of the noblest women living, I believe . . . Now here is the paradox. She of whom they all derive strength and wisdom was in childhood helpless on a bed of suffering. The result is a wonderful character, true and sweet and strong beyond belief. Every day I have fresh evidence of her magical influence on all people she has met and always helped. As for me she is swiftly making me . . . I know that I have wasted my chances terribly, not taken enough and not given one hundredth part enough. The result is a miserably tainted and imperfect thing: but I have found her and have hidden nothing from her . . . somehow I feel myself that my whole scope is unleashed through

> her and I have not only done better things myself but can do more to help others, exercise a wider sympathy.[10]

This was heady stuff, denoting depths of emotion long denied, long suppressed. Childers' passions, perhaps all the more powerful because of their earlier sublimation, had found a very happy human focus, one which would form the cornerstone of the remainder of his life.

Yet the unhappy hint of self-abasement evident in Arthur Davies also had its counterpart in Erskine Childers. In letters written some fifteen years after the event, Molly alludes to an occasion shortly after their engagement when Childers seems to have qualified his proposal, having taken it into his head that, much as he adored her, the higher path was to reject the joy she offered. The question in 1919 was whether the couple should go to live in Ireland, to help tackle the worsening crisis there; Molly suspected her husband wished to follow this course, not necessarily because it was the right one, but simply because it was the most difficult. 'This very thing nearly made our marriage impossible,' she commented. 'You thought the harder way the right way and that you must deny yourself me.'[11] Childers, emotionally deprived in his childhood, had perhaps taught himself to make a virtue of this deprivation, of his independence of mind and heart. As a consequence, it is possible that emotional involvement and commitment seemed a vice, or at the least a weakness. This trait seems in some ways to have led to his final tragedy.

Childers and Molly were married in Boston's Trinity Church on 6 January 1904. Dulcibella had travelled from London to be Molly's chief bridesmaid, Robert Barton from Glendalough to be his cousin's best man. The wedding, celebrated by Bishop Lawrence of Massachusetts, generated considerable press coverage, as a society occasion of some note. The *Boston Herald* billed it as 'an international romance', describing the bride as a 'petite blonde, with Titian hair and a face of surpassing sweetness', and the bridegroom, elsewhere, as 'an Englishman of prominence, an author of note'; 'Most elaborate were the church decorations,'[12] countered the *Globe*.

After a few days in New York, the couple boarded the liner *St Louis*, to honeymoon in Europe. 'My darling mother' – as Childers, tellingly, now addressed his mother-in-law – 'Your children are sitting side by side surrounded by heaps of letters, telegrams, cheque books etc., for the ship is approaching Plymouth and we are preparing our rather bulky mail. We are *utterly happy*. It grows and deepens every day in that for me I find such depth and wealth in Molly as I can not sufficiently fathom or grasp. Your very loving son, Erskine.'[13] Their honeymoon took them to Florence, one of the places Childers had enjoyed as a young undergraduate. In February he wrote again to his sisters, at the conclusion of the trip. 'We are here back again in Paris with our honeymoon behind us and a strenuous life before.'[14]

Thus began the marriage which was perhaps Childers' greatest single 'chance'.

PART TWO

The Blessed Angel

'Blessed angel, I feel lonely for you – my love and prop, my wisdom and second self.'

Erskine Childers, 1908

8

A Terrifying Happiness

1904–1908

> 'It terrifies me almost to think how much I love you because of the fear of what would happen if I lost you. I don't know where I end and you begin.'
>
> Erskine Childers, 1906

I

Life for Childers only began, he was fond of declaring, after he met and married Molly. Yet in its externals his life in the year following his honeymoon remained largely unchanged. His sisters had offered to vacate the Carlyle Mansions chambers, but this was something the Childerses could of course not accept; instead, they found a new apartment of similar size just a few hundred yards down the Thames, in the pleasant nook of Embankment Gardens, backing onto the grounds of the Royal Hospital. It was soon painted, papered and furnished to suit them both, and remained their home for the next fifteen years. When Parliament was sitting Childers still usually walked rather more than a mile to the House of Commons, where his work, if not his seniority, was much the same as it had been in 1895. His circle of friends, although steadily increasing, was for the time being at least still largely drawn from among the bright, well-educated, forward-looking but scarcely iconoclastic group he had found congenial at Cambridge. And again as at Trinity, he tended to know and be known by those who were becoming the leaders of Edwardian England – people like Churchill, Marsh, Bertrand Russell and the three Trevelyans – while not quite being one of them himself.

Externals might remain much the same, but for the inner man, life had been transformed. An intrinsically reserved man, Childers nevertheless both thought and felt deeply, and was capable of profound friendship with the relatively few people he knew very well and trusted, such as Ivor Lloyd-Jones from his youth, and William Le Fanu and Basil Williams from his early maturity. But in his wife he had found an intellectual equal with whom he could also fall in love, and to whom he could expose some of the considerable vulnerabilities resulting from his childhood and his temperament. It was to his wife that he was able to confess the first agonies of religious doubt he had suffered at the time of his mother's death – doubts that returned when he was brooding over the very question of his proposal to Molly, and which she later described as 'a stage for him of agonizing regret and intense longing to know. His doubt was to him intellectually like the lack of food to a starving creature.'[1] It seems unlikely that such confessions were ever made to Williams or Le Fanu. For this introspective man to have as a constant companion an equal to whom he could reveal his greatest aspirations and deepest fears was an unmitigated joy.

One result of having Molly as both wife and confidante was that the pace of Childers' political development now gradually quickened. Of her role in this, Molly observed, long after her husband's death: 'I'm thinking over the growth and evolution of Erskine's political philosophy. One might be inclined to think certain experiences as occasions for big alterations in his mental outlook. Yet it was an almost continuous process – change taking place as a result of his scrutiny of life and his constant research. But it can be said that our companionship had an accelerating influence. For the first time he was expressing his thoughts without reserve . . .'[2] Sixty years on, her obituarist wrote of Molly's later life in Ireland: 'Many political writers of the time agreed that the real power behind the de Valera revolutionary movement was Erskine Childers, and that the power behind Erskine Childers was his wife.'[3]

Basil Williams took a similar view, remarking in his memoir: 'Of this marriage I will say no more than this, that whatever anyone else may have thought of Erskine and Molly Childers, one thing nobody could doubt, that they felt and thought for the rest of their lives almost as one being.'[4] Williams' ambivalence about the marriage of his old friend is plain, while some of Childers' family were inclined to regard his young wife as headstrong, the man himself as beguiled. The Reverend Charles Childers had died in 1896, but his widow in due course took it upon herself to comment in a letter to Childers that his 'faith had been undermined by love, rather than deepened';[5] he was stung to reply:

> It's a very long and difficult subject to go into and I doubt if there's much use in saying very much about it, because in matters of religion differences in temperament make it almost impossible for people of different faiths to understand one another's point of view. But this much I can say. My belief, in the orthodox sense, in Christian tenets . . . was shaken and finally overthrown long before I met Molly; and off and on, from school onwards, I suffered the keenest intellectual misery from the change – for this reason: that while I was dissatisfied with the old faith, I had not the backbone and character to carve myself a new one, which should really represent me, my inmost spiritual nature. Well, since I met Molly I have been happy. Contact with the sweetest and strongest nature I have ever known has given me what I needed – I say this in humility – character, faith, religion. I have a spiritual life such as I never knew before; and I love good in its widest sense, as, to my shame, I never loved it before I knew her.[6]

In *Howards End*, published some six years after the Childerses' marriage, E. M. Forster writes of the 'glass shade . . . that cuts off married couples from the world.'[7] Ultimately, the precise nature and balance of this particular relationship is of course unknowable; yet there is no doubt that what could well be seen as a marriage of true minds had a profound effect on Childers' development. Whether it was quite the force that some supposed, the reader alone must judge.

For Molly, the early months in London must have been bewildering. As the couple's friend Sir Frederick Pollock lightly remarked, this had been 'a modern marriage of capture – her husband went to Boston with the Hon. Artillery Company and brought her home'.[8] The previous autumn Molly had been settled in Boston, living at home, one of a close-knit family. Suddenly she was wife rather than daughter, hostess rather than guest; and an observer of – soon a participant in – the social and intellectual world of the highly privileged of Edwardian

London. Boston was and remains a sophisticated and civilized city, proud of its history, home too of an intellectual and social élite: it was, after all, the city where the Lowells talked to the Cabots, and the Cabots talked only to God. Nevertheless, it was not the hub of the British Empire at its zenith. As Churchill later put it,

> In those days English society still existed in its old form. It was a brilliant and powerful body with standards of conduct and methods of enforcing them now altogether forgotten. In a very large degree everyone knew everyone else and who they were. The few hundred great families who had governed England for so many generations and had seen her rise to the pinnacle of her glory, were inter-related to an enormous extent by marriage. Everywhere one met friends and kinsfolk. The leading figures of society were in many cases the leading statesmen in Parliament, and also the leading sportsmen on the turf. Lord Salisbury was accustomed scrupulously to avoid calling a Cabinet when there was racing at Newmarket, and the House of Commons made a practice of adjourning for the Derby.[9]

In fairness and in passing, it should perhaps be noted that this last reflects Salisbury the pragmatist, rather than Salisbury an enthusiast for the turf: the Prime Minister once remarked tartly to his wife that 'Our political arrangements are necessarily hung up until some particular quadruped has run for something.'[10]

Her marriage gave Molly the entrée to a society which comprised an interesting mixture of intellectuals, artists and senior civil servants. Writing to his father-in-law not long after returning from honeymoon, Childers related that they were 'going out a good deal and there is very little time . . . for the quiet life. But we have had some interesting parties: with the Sargents: John Sargent and Henry James were there . . . and Sir George Clarke . . . the ex-governor of Australia and a present member of the triumvirate who are re-organizing the National Defence System and giving us a new army and war office.'[11] Yet it was inevitable that Molly should not at once feel herself at ease – and that some of these people should prove more to her taste than others. At first, the Childerses saw a good deal of Erskine's Cambridge friend Edward Marsh. In 1904 he was still at the Colonial Office, but soon to be noticed by the fast-rising Churchill and established as his personal private secretary by the end of the following year. 'And yet not personal in the ordinary sense,' Molly later observed, 'just faithful, and absolutely exact and painstaking, never making mistakes, never thrusting himself forward. Like his flat. He was a planned person – charming, very nice, interesting, read fine books, perhaps he collected poets.' Continuing, she compared Marsh unfavourably with the Meynells – he the editor of a literary magazine, she a prominent poet: 'In that house was salvation and understanding and passionate love for real talent in others . . . how one cares for people like that!'[12]

The political ambience, too, could sometimes jar. At twenty-six Molly was not, of course, a political sophisticate, yet her husband's job and her own background, intelligence and temperament ensured that she took an interest, and formed opinions. It was perhaps not to be wondered that a denizen of the New World should find the Conservative Balfour administration that succeeded that of the ailing Salisbury unsympathetic, the old guard of the English ruling class stuffy and hidebound. Equally, however, Molly was sufficiently of her own class and time to want little truck with the nascent Labour movement which was beginning to be of political significance in both England and Ireland. Her husband's friends at this time were becoming increasingly liberal, in the several senses of the word: his old Cambridge friend Walter Runciman was now a Liberal MP, as was their acquaintance Churchill – indeed, in 1900 they had contested the same seat, Runciman emerging the victor. With the Liberals' more broad-minded views – on Empire, on the burgeoning movement for women's suffrage, and in favour of modest social reform – Molly, unsurprisingly, felt more at home.

But of course the mainspring of Molly's life was her husband. Although the two really scarcely knew one another when they were married, the first eighteen months after their return to London revealed how well matched they were, and how deeply in love. It was a devotion utterly reciprocal. Childers wrote to his wife that 'It almost terrifies me to think how much I love you because of the fear of what would happen if I lost you',[13] and Molly replied, 'I meant just to say that with the inspiration you give me I feel no task however herculean would be too great, for through you I draw upon universal strength, and can draw help without end.'[14] The marriage appears to have been as close physically as it was emotionally, and both were ready for children as soon as they might appear. To their joy, in the spring of 1905 Molly found that she was pregnant, and in December of that year Erskine Hamilton Childers was born.

'We have a wonderful life together', wrote Childers. 'And the child has crowned it all.'[15]

II

It was natural that, like any happy newly-married man, Childers should want his wife to know his pleasures, his friends, his pursuits, his touchstones. One of his first cares was to introduce her to those relatives at Glendalough who had been unable to make the journey to Boston for their wedding, and in particular to his beloved aunt, Agnes Barton. In April 1904 Molly first made the acquaintance of the land which, fifteen years later, was to become her home. 'When I first came to Glan we arrived late at night,' she later wrote. 'The next morning before breakfast we went out together and I stood beside him looking at the trees and the lovely growing things. "Tell me just what you feel about it," Erskine asked. "I feel it is the first time in my life I have stood upon home ground." "That is just what I was praying you would feel." '[16] To his mother-in-law Childers enthused, 'Molly is enchanted by the place and enchanted with Aunt Agnes and is of course – need I say it – endearing herself to everyone.'[17] Soon the Osgoods themselves would cross the Atlantic, visiting Glendalough and then settling in a house in Oxford.

Childers was also touched by the enthusiasm with which his wife came to share his passion for the sea – and with admiration, in view of Molly's disability. No sooner had the sailing season of 1904 begun than he was gently introducing her to the pleasures of the sea, aboard the *Sunbeam*, which Childers still owned in syndicate. At first it was a question merely of acclimatizing her to sailing in the Solent. So well did Molly take to the rituals and challenges of the water, however, that she was soon urging her husband to venture further afield – to Cornwall, or even France. In May 1904 Childers wrote proudly to Mrs Osgood from Plymouth: 'I wish you could have seen Molly yesterday. It was a test day – strong wind, lumpy sea, heavy rain all day and a long sail with a head wind most of the way from Dartmouth here. She sat in her oil-skins and sea-boots and sou'wester by the mizzen all day long, looking such an able little sailor-girl and such a sweet and fascinating one too, so cheerful and happy despite the cheerless conditions.'[18]

With characteristic generosity, the Osgoods decided to give the couple a yacht of their own, as a wedding present. Designed and built by the Scottish-Norwegian Colin Archer, who had made his name with Nansen's *Fram*, she was to be an elegant forty-four-foot ketch. She was named *Asgard*, which means 'home of the Gods' in Norse, and is also an ancient version of the Osgood family name. Her design was agreed between Childers and Archer by the end of 1904, the boat was delivered from Larvik the following August, and the bill was settled by way of a Baring Brothers' bankers' draft. With the season already late and Molly pregnant, sailing in the new yacht that year was restricted to the south coast, although the whole of September was devoted to a cruise that took them as far as the Helford River in Cornwall (later the inspiration for Daphne du Maurier's *Frenchman's Creek*). Since Molly's enjoyment of the sea so happily matched her husband's, something more ambitious was planned for after the baby's birth – no less than a return to the Baltic. 'I am so excited to think I am going to see *The Riddle of the Sands*' country',[19] wrote Molly to her father – although in fact *Asgard*'s substantial draught would preclude too close an inspection of the Frisian islands themselves.

Asgard slipped anchor from Burlesdon on the Solent in August 1906, following much the same course as *Vixen* in 1897 and *Sunbeam* in 1903, to Texel, Terschelling and Kiel. Then, after the usual tow through the canal, they found themselves in Childers' 'beloved and lovely Baltic, with its clear tideless waters, delicious scenery, a vast variety of snug harbours, and friendly, hospitable folk.'[20] Soon they were in Flensburg, then they sailed as far north as Åhus. By mid September the weather had turned; Molly wrote to her parents of a splendid passage up towards Copenhagen:

> You must picture us to yourselves at this time with a close beat of thirty miles before us, the sun shining, the sea rising like lightning, and the *Asgard* simply laughing with the rollick of it. Smothered in spray, clinging to our positions, and simply loving it. The crew worked hard

> at the sheets, and I at the wheel . . . the sea was high and hollow, very short, which continually stopped *Asgard*'s course. She could dance over two, but the third often caught her. Nevertheless they all said they had never seen a boat so buoyant and quick . . . It was very hard tacking. Once in a while she wouldn't do it, if two or three seas struck her bows. Erskine lowered topsail and took two more reefs in mainsail – making three for the first time. It was a question as to whether to lower mainsail, but we had to try to get somewhere before dark and pick up these very important buoys off sands, etc. He decided rightly; the *Asgard* was splendid under that rig, and simply made us love her ten times more.[21]

It was a glorious voyage, covering more than 1,100 miles, ending only when they laid the boat up for the winter at Svendborg. It set the seal on Molly's love for the sea; if possible, it had even augmented her love for her husband. Later she wrote, 'When we lay in our cabin we would listen to the water rustling under her forefoot – what a sound! Or if at anchor: do you hear that lap-lapping? What is adrift? And then he would slip up . . . and I would hear his soft foot-falls . . . on the deck. He taught me to listen and feel for the faintest shudder – one can describe it in no other way – part sound and part sensation of the dragging anchor.'[22] She became, in Childers' own words, 'a trained seaman', who could 'navigate, keep watch, and steer';[23] one, moreover, with particularly acute eyesight – a gift which often proved invaluable. And many years later she wrote lyrically, in an introduction to yet another edition of *The Riddle of the Sands*, of 'those who put forth in great or small sailing ships in search of adventure'.[24]

III

The fulfilment of Childers' personal life in the first two years of his marriage doubtless precluded great professional strides. The birth of his son at the end of 1905 coincided with his completion of ten years' service in the Commons, where he was plainly quite comfortably situated. The work suited him as well as it ever had, without making undue demands on his time and energy; it kept him in touch with the political heart of the Empire, particularly with the military developments in which he had been interested since the Boer War; and it provided the substance if not the whole of his income: he continued to write occasionally for the newspapers on military matters and on sailing, and he had a significant private income. It was not, however, work in which he sufficiently excelled for him to aspire to the highly responsible and respected position of Clerk of the House, as perhaps envisaged by Hugh Childers. Neither was it cast in the heroic mould so attractive to Childers' *alter ego* Davies – and nor was it the future envisaged for him by his wife. From the beginning of 1906, Molly began to urge her husband to take a more active role in the political life of the country.

This was something from which his clerkship precluded him, since those responsible for the recording of parliamentary business were – not unreasonably – constrained from active support of any political party. For the constitutionalist Childers then was, becoming active politically meant becoming an MP. In light of his experience of South Africa, it is not surprising that his affinities now lay increasingly with the Liberals, who were overwhelmingly returned to power at the end of 1905. This victory must have whetted his enthusiasm for politics, as must the elevation early in 1906 of Runciman and Churchill from the back benches to under-secretaryships in Sir Henry Campbell-Bannerman's new administration. For the moment, however, opportunities were limited. With no general election in immediate prospect, it would be a question of being adopted as a candidate in a by-election. In any case, such time as Childers could spare from his young family and the House was largely taken up with writing.

The history of the Honourable Artillery Company in South Africa had finally appeared in the autumn of 1903, to a satisfactory reception. *The Athenaeum* noted that its 'joint editors' (Williams and Childers) 'were skilled writers and most competent editors for a record of the service of the HAC'. The *Financial Standard* felt that 'this excellent compilation of facts' reflected 'the greatest possible credit on the editors'. The *Leeds Mercury* noted lyrically that 'nothing could be more calculated to inspire that proper pride of patriotism which must always be the true incentive of good soldiering.'[25] This was all well and good, but against the success of *The Riddle of the Sands* it counted little. Not surprisingly, there was considerable enthusiasm for a successor to the novel. As early as the summer of 1903, Childers' artistic mentor Flora

Priestley was urging him to prepare himself for the life of a man of letters by seeking inspiration in Greece, the traditional cradle of English literary careers. Childers' reply provides an important insight into his mentality: 'I cannot meet your mood in the matter of Greek things,' he wrote. 'I am not an artist . . . and you are . . . No, I don't believe I shall ever go to Greece for fear of false, no not exactly false emotions, but of ways of thought which it is no use my following, but which would in themselves be a . . . temptation to follow.' He continued, 'I believe I want action more than anything. It has always been the best for me.'[26]

Action he certainly wanted, and although it was acute of him to recognize this powerful need in himself, it is reasonable for us to regret that he pursued no further the imaginative path indicated by *The Riddle of the Sands* and, to a lesser extent, *In the Ranks of the CIV*. These are rich, human books with a strong moral perspective. As Basil Williams put it: 'To many of us it has always appeared a deplorable loss to English literature that Childers . . . abandoned the rich vein of human feeling which he revealed in his first two books, and devoted himself thereafter to books with a purely propagandist or political aim.'[27]

At first he turned to the volume in *The Times History of the South African War* series Leo Amery had suggested he write in 1903. This Childers finally set about after completing the HAC history. Writing to his sister-in-law in the summer of 1904 he remarked, 'I am very busy, having taken up the history work definitely – *Molly* dictated the terms – a year to do it and £400, which was more than they offered. At the moment I am a little appalled by the magnitude of the work . . .'[28] The extensive research the book demanded, including personal correspondence with both Kitchener and Milner, in fact occupied Childers for more than three years, until its publication in 1907.

Childers was also following up his old fascination with the German North Sea coast. As Maldwin Drummond revealed in his study of the military background to *The Riddle of the Sands*, early in 1906 Childers was busying himself preparing a paper entitled *Remarks on the German North Sea Coast in its Relation to War Between Great Britain and Germany – with a Note on the Dutch Coast.*[29] This was partly stimulated by his return to the Baltic with Molly in *Asgard*, but also by growing public concern that with Germany, and not with France, lay any future threat of European war. France had in fact become an informal ally following the settlement of various differences in the Entente of 1904; she was also on amicable terms with Russia. When in 1907 Britain herself came to terms with Russia, the Triple Entente was born. Conversely, the gap between Britain and Germany seemed ever to widen, and the Triple Entente became more and more delicately balanced against the Triple Alliance of Italy, the old Austro-Hungarian empire, and Germany herself. Hence the inspiration for Childers' agreeable plan to reverse the principle of his novel with an English invasion of the Frisians. What could be better? There are three specific suggestions: a blockade of the coast; a blockade of the Kiel canal; and the seizure, first of the islands, then of the mainland beyond them. (The note on the Dutch coast highlighted its vulnerability to German attack.)

This paper was dispatched to his friend Sir George Clarke, then serving on the Committee of Imperial Defence. The official response was discouraging, the reply remarking that 'an invasion in the direction you mention appears to present very great difficulties, the distance at which the covering fleet must lie, the exposed position, the distance over which the invading force would have to be "boat transported", and the distance when landed of any very important objective renders that portion of the coast as of comparatively doubtful advantage, should invasion be contemplated.' Nevertheless, the reply did stress the value of 'any fresh information gained by yachtsmen and others'[30] of the coast; and the idea was indeed later taken up by Churchill, when he reached the Admiralty. From all this, intriguing consequences were to arise.

In the meantime, Childers plodded on with the South African book, frequently working even at his desk in the House. When it was eventually published, it seemed his labours had been worthwhile: reviews were generally favourable. 'A very difficult task admirably performed'[31] commented the *Daily Chronicle*, and the consensus of opinion of the extensive notices was that the writer had excelled in bringing together into a coherent narrative the disparate actions that constituted the phase of the war that was his subject. Inevitably, however, the book lacks the 'warm human envelope' that made Childers' strategic thinking in *The Riddle of the Sands* so very readable; it would only be of interest to a specialist today.

The book does nevertheless provide an interesting comparison with *In the Ranks of the CIV*, indicating as it does the extent to which Childers' thinking on the war and its political rationale had developed over the space of five years or so. The *History* does of course cover the final phase of the war, well after Childers' departure from the veldt in the autumn of 1901; and the genesis of the two books was very different – the one a contemporary and personal record from the ranks, the other written from the much more considered and distant perspective of the historian. That said, it may be remembered that the early book is very largely uncritical, either of British motivations and intentions towards the Boers, or of the conduct of the war; the latter is clearly critical of both. 'The British aim', Childers declares in the *History*, 'was not merely conquest but the absorption of a free white race, a race no longer retaining the weaknesses of colonial pioneers, but firmly rooted in the soil. It was an aim unparalleled in the history of our nation . . . save the great struggle with her own colonies in North America.' Similarly, Childers lambasts the conservatism of the army, in failing sufficiently quickly to abandon the cavalry sword in favour of the rifle used so adeptly by the Boers. 'The regular cavalry formed the permanent foundation,' he writes. 'But the profound conservatism which . . . characterised this arm, debarred it from setting such an example of vigorous originality as was urgently needed for the conduct of the campaign.' Again he found a helpful comparison in America: 'The best lessons for the cavalry were to be learnt, not from the continental wars of the 'seventies but from the American Civil War of the 'sixties, when men of our own race, unhampered by prejudice or tradition, attacked and solved cavalry problems on fresh and original grounds.' That 'continuous process of change' that Molly had identified was certainly under way: Childers' views were now becoming distinctly liberal, not to say radical.

Childers reserved his most trenchant criticism for the final chapter of the volume, which covered the protracted negotiations for peace in the spring of 1902. The main issue was the terms of the surrender. 'Broadly speaking,' Childers wrote, 'the difference was that Milner, from the political point of view, favoured unconditional surrender;

Kitchener, primarily from the military but incidentally from the political point of view, was content to obtain a surrender on terms.' The author himself was now very much of the Kitchener camp, perceiving absolutely no virtue in the humiliation of a people whose character, rights, and military capabilities he had come to respect; perceiving, moreover, no virtue for the Empire in being seen, both in its Dominions and elsewhere, to so behave. It was Childers' misfortune that Amery, the editor of the series, was very much of Milner's persuasion. The chapter as finally printed was so toned down that Childers disclaimed it: 'Mr Amery, in his capacity as general editor, has largely remodelled my draft of this chapter and, as it now stands, he is solely responsible for it.'[32]

That an author and editor should disagree on such a matter was hardly unusual, but for Childers both the political perspective and the intransigence were new. In a particularly critical review, the *Daily Telegraph* complained that the book was 'far less a judicial summary drawn from a comparison of evidence from many quarters, than the dogmatic assertion of positions which present themselves as certain to a man who has gone through a very limited experience of his own.'[33] Likewise, even Williams later conceded Childers' occasional self-righteousness, noting that he 'never hesitated a moment when he saw his way clear to a course as the right one to follow, nor, when he saw fit to alter old opinions and so cut himself adrift thereby from old friends and associations, would he compromise with his determination to carry out his convictions.'[34] There is something to admire in such behaviour; whether it is invariably wise is perhaps less certain.

IV

After three years' work on the South African book, some rest and recreation in the summer of 1907 seemed in order. At the end of the Baltic cruise in 1906, when the *Asgard* was laid up at Svendborg, something on these lines seems to have been planned. To her father, then increasingly ill with angina, Molly wrote at that time: 'If we took [*Asgard*] back to England we should not be able to get farther afield than this, whereas leaving her here, we can go to the Gulf of Finland next summer, and the year after either sail home or, if there is a constitutional government in Russia by then, sail in Russian waters.'[35] *Asgard*'s log books for this period are missing, however, and no other indications of her travels exist. Yet the yacht was evidently retrieved from the Baltic at some point, and it remains the belief of the Childerses' younger son, Robert Alden Childers, that his parents explored the Gulf of Finland in the summer of 1907.[36]

At this time Childers also began to be involved with an interesting group known as the Sunday Tramps. It had been founded in 1879 by Childers' friend Sir Frederick Pollock and that Eminent Victorian, Sir Leslie Stephen. Pollock was a distinguished academic lawyer, sometime Corpus Professor of Jurisprudence at Oxford; and his *Introduction to the History of the Science of Politics* was a favourite text of Childers'. Stephen was the first editor of the *Dictionary of National Biography*, one of the leaders of the Victorian intellectual hierarchy, and father of the novelist Virginia Woolf. Pollock and Stephen were both keen walkers – Stephen, indeed, was a noted mountaineer – who, based as they were in London, found their opportunities for exercise somewhat circumscribed. The idea was to make use of the excellent suburban railway service by taking a train to a spot about twenty miles out of town, walking for a similar distance, and then training back from wherever they reached. Considering the mental calibre of its founders, it is scarcely surprising that the ethos of the society should have been as much intellectual as athletic. Its 'ballade' celebrated both qualities:

> If in short you feel somewhat inclined
> For fresh air and a six hours' grind
> And good metaphysical talk –
> With a party of writers in mind
> You should go for a Sabbath day's grind.[37]

Innocent – not to say arcadian – in its aims, the club's membership might have been used as a roll-call of the English savants of the day. Early members included a future Lord Chancellor (Lord Haldane), Roger Fry, John Buchan, Ralph Vaughan Williams, Goldsworthy Lowes Dickinson, Desmond MacCarthy, the three Trevelyan brothers, and Geoffrey and Maynard Keynes. Basil Williams joined the group in 1907 on his return from South Africa to pursue an academic career, and perhaps introduced Childers. Soon the latter was striding through the Home Counties in the company of these intellectual heavyweights – generally but not invariably completing the course: one day he was among those who 'weakly remained at Merstham'.[38] Childers himself remarked, 'I like the Tramps'; and, with a hint of his usual insistence on moral and intellectual development, 'I think they have done me some good.'[39]

Yet the real leitmotif of these first four years of marriage was less intellectual than emotional. When parted for even the briefest of periods it was the couple's habit to correspond, and it became Childers' custom to write to Molly every year on her birthday, 14 December, wherever he might be. As a series, these letters form an extraordinary testimony to their love, varied in expression if uniform in their lyricism and, through all the pressure of later events, utterly constant in devotion. 'My sweetest angel,' Childers wrote on 14 December 1907, 'Sitting opposite to you and our darling little baby I am overcome with tenderness and love and a sort of wonderful exaltation. I see your beautiful and noble face and I see his little baby features unformed but also beautiful and noble and I see his bright curls pressed against your breast and the whole miracle of it comes home to me with double strength. It is just a symbol of my salvation and my life and all my future . . . I love you and adore you for ever.'[40] A note scrawled from the House of Commons committee office in 1908 to ask, prosaically, for the 'MS of my war-chapter', concludes, 'Blessed angel, I feel lonely for you – my love and prop, my wisdom and second self.'[41] These expressions were utterly unforced and natural, and entirely reciprocated. Childers had found his mate, and his relationship with Molly bears comparison with others fabled or factual, of their own or any other time.

It was characteristic of Childers' fortune throughout his life that even this halcyon period should have been marred by sorrow. Dr Osgood fell victim to his angina towards the end of 1907, leaving his wife to a long widowhood. Then Molly's second pregnancy, in 1908, proved difficult and painful, and the deformed son born that July very shortly died. The baby was christened Henry, after Childers' brother. The event, which would have saddened any parents, was particularly harrowing to those of such sensitivity. Its effect on Childers himself was to revive all his agonies and uncertainties, never very far from the surface, about the ultimate nature and purpose of human life. According to Molly, it proved decisive to his religious thinking. 'When he came to me after spending the night with our dead baby boy's little body beside him and told me he was sure we were immortal, he accepted it as a man does light from the sun . . . everything follows from that consciousness of eternal life . . . of an eternal plan in which mankind had an eternal share and duty.'[42] This small death introduced a harsh note of the ephemeral into a relationship that was, after all, only in earthly terms a paradise.

9

'This great turning-point in our lives'

1908–1912

'His creed, ingrained from his early youth, was in his own conscience.'
Molly Childers

I

Absolutely secure in his domestic base, it was from this time that Childers – then thirty-eight – turned his energies and interests increasingly towards public questions and public life. With the Liberals in power under Campbell-Bannerman, there was a distinct change, now welcome to Childers, from the jingoism of Salisbury and Chamberlain. Campbell-Bannerman himself took particular credit for the solution of the problems in South Africa – so dear to Childers' heart, so firmly associated with him in the public's mind.

Following the end of the Boer War there was clearly neither a necessity for nor merit in Britain remaining for ever in South Africa as an occupying force, while some measure of self-government for the descendants of the original white settlers seemed desirable. Campbell-Bannerman's career, like Childers' own, had encompassed a passage from right to left, and – urged on by Winston Churchill in his first major task as a Cabinet minister – he took the view that complete colonial self-government should be granted, in the first instance to the Transvaal. On the heels of a long and costly war fought over this very matter, the generosity and prescience of this proposal was both remarkable and controversial. The notion was very much to Childers' taste, but Balfour, now leader of the Opposition, declared it 'the most reckless experiment ever tried in the development of a great colonial policy'.[1] Indeed, the only Conservative to vote for the proposal was F. E. Smith – who, fifteen years later, was to play an important part with Childers, Churchill and Lloyd George in the Irish settlement. The result of Campbell-Bannerman's policy was to place in power in the Transvaal the former military leaders, General Botha and General Smuts, who 'led their people in a determination to do as Campbell-Bannerman had done by them, and use their liberty in the same spirit of reconciliation in which it had been granted.'[2] Campbell-Bannerman died in 1908, but his work had been done. In due course the four separate South African parliaments, of the Transvaal, Orange Free State, Natal and Cape Colony, voluntarily constituted themselves a self-governing dominion, as the Union of South Africa. A happy accommodation was thereby reached between Britain and a colony with the strongest of national aspirations. Needless to say, the whole matter was regarded with a great deal of interest in various other Imperial trouble spots, notably Egypt, India, and Ireland.

Home Rule for Ireland had now been part of Liberal ideology for more than a generation, much as an unequivocal Union between Britain and Ireland was a Conservative tenet. With a Liberal in Downing Street, devolution accordingly once again became an issue, particularly as the Irish Nationalists in Westminster under John Redmond were adopting an altogether more conciliatory line than they had under the strident Parnell – possibly a reflection of the fact that for once they did not hold the balance of power. Campbell-Bannerman's success in resolving the problem of South Africa lent the question of Home Rule a fresh impetus which continued under his successor Herbert Asquith. Asquith was a Yorkshireman with little of the directness associated with the county, a Balliol man, barrister and intellectual. Of a carelessness in dress unusual at the time, he was also the 'first Prime Minister since the younger Pitt who is said to have been manifestly the worse for drink on the Treasury Bench'.[3] Under him the Liberal cry became 'to make Redmond the Irish Botha'[4] – that is, leader of a semi-autonomous state on friendly terms with the Crown.

The paradox was that in some respects Ireland stood less in need of such an arrangement than at any time since the famine. It had for many years been Tory tactics to pursue a policy of amelioration towards

Ireland that was dubbed 'killing Home Rule by kindness'. By 1908 a neutral observer might have argued that many of the causes for Irish discontent had been quite fully addressed. Tory measures had culminated in 1903 in an act that was to have the effect of settling once and for all the long-running sore of the Irish land question. Financial incentives encouraged landlords to sell to their tenants, and they did so in sufficient numbers that by 1914 the matter could be considered closed. Similarly, the return of the Liberals to power saw significant improvements in housing and schools, the university system placed in Catholic hands, and the introduction of old age pensions. In short, the effect was one of 'social revolution'.[5] To many Liberals this seemed entirely satisfactory, and because of the majority they enjoyed between 1906 and 1910, Redmond's Nationalists were able to pressure them into nothing more dramatic in the way of Home Rule than the Irish Council – a very dilute form of devolution. Nevertheless, as Churchill remarked in a letter to the King defending the Transvaal settlement, 'Any intelligent community will much rather govern itself ill, than be well-governed by some other community'.[6] Additionally, the Irish cultural renaissance kept the question high on the agenda in Ireland itself.

This renaissance took the form of a promotion of the cultural identity of Ireland, quite independent of its association with Britain and the Empire. It was variously manifested, but chiefly found expression through the Gaelic Athletic Association, the Gaelic League and a literary revival. Briefly, the Athletic Association deplored the playing of English sports, such as cricket and rugby, which was particularly prevalent in towns where military units were stationed, and instead encouraged traditional Irish games like hurling, Gaelic football and hammer throwing. To complement this, Douglas Hyde[7] and Professor Eoin MacNeill,[8] leaders among those who recognized the power of a native language, through the League effectively revived the use of the Gaelic tongue; both men were later to play a large part in Irish affairs, the latter in association with Childers. Similarly, while the eighteenth and nineteenth centuries saw the flowering of a fine literary tradition in Ireland, beginning with Swift, Goldsmith and Burke and ending with Wilde and Shaw, its essence was neither one of Irish subject matter nor of the native tongue. These qualities were subsequently taken up in the early years of the twentieth century and given prominence by Lady Gregory, J. M. Synge and, above all, the poet and playwright William Butler Yeats, long associated with the Abbey Theatre. There was perhaps not much in any of these movements, taken in isolation; taken together, there was a good deal. And soon the renaissance acquired a political focus, in an organization known as Sinn Féin; founded in 1905 by Arthur Griffith, its name is normally glossed as 'we ourselves'. Its agenda was independence, but independence, as Griffith saw things, ultimately under the auspices of the Crown, and to be achieved by non-violent means.

Ireland was on the move, and its movement was noticed. As the Chief Secretary at the Castle, Augustine Birrell, remarked,

> The intelligence of England, never over-represented in Parliament, at last took cognizance of the change, and the Sister Island began no longer to be regarded as the dreary, dingy, disreputable politico-religious problem but a land with a literary and political tradition of her own, a 'point of view' of her own, and a genius of expression not confined to stale jokes and specimens of so-called Irish humour invented to gratify the crude tastes of the English traveller.[9]

For Childers himself, the issue of Ireland was certainly beginning to loom larger, but in 1908 scarcely the obsession it was to become. He had lived continuously in Ireland for only four years, from the age of six until he was ten; generally he had holidayed at Glendalough when he was at school and at Cambridge. Following his uncle Charles's death in 1890, he had helped his aunt Agnes and the new young master of the house, Robert Barton, with estate and family matters. From 1895 he was working in London and spending much of his spare time sailing; accordingly, his visits decreased, and after his marriage in 1904 he probably went to Glendalough no more than half a dozen times a year. This would not of course preclude an emotional attachment to his mother's country; quite the contrary – he loved 'Glan', and he had long loved the country. Yet at that time he was relatively ignorant of any Irish life or history beyond that offered by the particular and limited perspective of the long and winding drive leading out of Glendalough. Indeed, it seems to have been partly with a view to remedying this ignorance that in the late summer of 1908 he 'undertook a jolly motor tour with my cousin, Barton, through a good slice of central and western Ireland.' Writing to Basil Williams, he continued: '[it was] mainly to inspect co-operative societies in which he is much interested, and to which Sir Horace Plunkett[10] and a good deal many other well known people look for the salvation of Ireland. I have come back finally and immutably a convert to Home Rule, as is my cousin, though we both grew up steeped in the most irreconcilable sort of Unionism.'[11]

The co-operative societies, which owed much to Plunkett's initiative and enthusiasm, were schemes to improve the tenant farmers' production and distribution while keeping the profits of the improvements in the tenants' hands. Help of this sort was clearly necessary, since peasant life in Ireland in the early part of the twentieth century involved levels of poverty that today we would associate with the third world: very much Churchill's 'life passed in a one-roomed hut on a diet of potatoes'.[12] In an era only beginning to approach the concept of state intervention in such matters, any idea which would enable Ireland's poor to help themselves seemed a reasonable step to the good Liberal Childers then was; at the same time, it would have seemed to him that the broader responsibility for their own welfare embodied in the Home Rule movement would force the point home. As he was himself such a believer in individual independence, it is surprising only that he did not become a supporter of Home Rule rather earlier; it was another small step in Childers' continuing political development and a significant one in terms of the development of his political and personal ideals. Increasingly he came to believe that both individuals and nations should create their own salvation and work out their own destinies. As his wife later wrote, 'his creed, ingrained from his early youth, was in his own conscience.'[13]

II

Convert though he declared himself, it was to be some time – six years – before Childers did anything positive about this new belief, before he cloaked thought in the 'action' that, he had memorably written to Flora Priestley, was 'best for me'. Having dealt with South Africa in

The Times History, by the end of 1908 he was turning once again to the German question.

As Davies so sagely remarked in *The Riddle of the Sands*, 'The command of the seas is *the* thing nowadays.'[14] So it certainly proved, as the great naval race, stemming from the German Navy Laws, grew to occupy a significant place in the public mind. It was a race, not simply in terms of the number and quality of ships each nation possessed but, more importantly, in the competition for commercial and political supremacy which it symbolised. The rivalry was focused on a class of ships known as the dreadnoughts; these were in their day the equivalent of a nuclear deterrent, faster and better armed than either their predecessors or their German counterparts. Their commissioning represented an overturning of the view that 'France was the possible enemy, the passage to India the chief trade-route in need of protection, and the North Sea of small naval importance'[15] – the view that had prevailed in Navy circles until at least 1903, and which *The Riddle of the Sands* helped to erode. The first vessel in her class, *Dreadnought* herself, was launched in May 1906, and the intention was that four should henceforth be laid down each year. British Naval supremacy, British supremacy generally, might thereby be guaranteed. This plan of Balfour's Conservative administration was, however, significantly curtailed after the election of 1907 when the Liberals came to power, with their greater commitment to major innovations in social welfare. Thus the spectre of the inadequacy of Britain's preparations for a European war that had so animated *The Riddle of the Sands* – and had animated the paper prepared for Sir George Clarke – was once again raised.

Childers' response again took literary form, with two volumes of what Williams later dubbed 'propaganda', in preparation between 1908 and 1910, and published respectively in 1910 and 1911. They were *War and the Arme Blanche*, and *The German Influence on British Cavalry*. 'Arme blanche' was the contemporary military term for the cavalry sabre, a weapon which the campaigns of the Boer War had suggested to many besides Childers should have been relegated to the museum by the advent of the rifle . . . but which the British Army persisted in using. As Winston Churchill later observed, there was more to this matter than mere weaponry:

> Instead of a small number of well-trained professionals championing their country's cause with ancient weapons and a beautiful intricacy of archaic manoeuvre, sustained at every moment by the applause of the nation, we now have entire populations, including even women and children, pitted against one another in brutish mutual extermination, and only a set of blear-eyed clerks left to add up the butcher's bill . . . war, which used to be cruel and magnificent, has now become cruel and squalid.[16]

Much though Churchill might deplore this development, he was determined, both before and after the Great War, to ensure that due military preparations should be made for probable future circumstances. This was also Childers' stance, his two books comprising a highly intelligent repudiation of the cavalry philosophy, with a wealth of historical detail and contemporary analogy. As Childers put it in the second volume, his objective was 'to sweep away root and branch the tactical system founded on lance and sword, and create a new system based on rifle.'[17] His studies in the matter took him to the army's training grounds, and even to the citadel of the man in whose train he had followed in South Africa: Lord Roberts himself. A postcard to Molly in September of 1909 from Swindon reads simply 'Following a cavalry brigade. Very dull. Love, E.C.'[18] A few days later he wrote, 'I have seen two fights but can't find the cavalry anywhere. The battlefield is so huge. Wired Roberts to Wantage and met him there by chance soon after. I think he had forgotten all about me and bolted to his lunch.'[19] Forgotten or otherwise, Childers nevertheless persuaded the old soldier to endorse his studies, by way of an introduction to *War and the Arme Blanche*. 'With every word of this I agree,' Roberts wrote, 'and it must be remembered that my judgement is based upon personal and first-hand knowledge. Why did our cavalry fail? Because they did not know, because they had never been required to know, how to use the principal and most useful weapon with which they were armed.'[20]

Despite the pincer movement on the part of an old professional and a man who might still conceivably be described as a young turk, these strictures when published were far from welcomed. 'Military opinion in this country has been considerably agitated by a remarkable book recently published, *War and the Arme Blanche*,' declared one reviewer.

'The book is an uncompromising attack on what its author regards as old-fashioned notions about the functions of cavalry in war, and a lively discussion has been carried on in service quarters.'[21] In view of the general conservatism of institutions and the particular conservatism of military people, this reaction was perhaps not surprising. Nevertheless, in theory Childers might reasonably be regarded as protesting too strongly; in practice, he certainly was.

The book was very widely reviewed and generally seen by the reviewers as providing a fascinating and trenchant contribution to a matter certainly of military interest; *The Scotsman* declared it 'one of the most remarkable contributions to our military literature to have seen the light in recent years.'[22] Yet it was not free of the dogmatism some had detected in his book on the South African war: as *The Outlook* noted, Childers' 'confidence in his own reading of the lessons of war causes him to look with contempt on those who have studied the question quite as earnestly, but who have reached different conclusions . . . It is to be feared that a style of this nature does little or nothing to stimulate sympathetic appreciation of the author's thesis.'[23] In the book's Conclusion Childers concedes that he has 'written strongly, because I feel strongly about a point which every Englishman, soldier or civilian, has a right to feel strongly.'[24] In a way this was fair enough, but Childers signally failed to question whether writing strongly was the best means of achieving his end. In his use of his old dictum, 'Trust thyself. Every heart vibrates to that iron spring' to head his climactic chapter on Reform, it may appear that he allowed self-expression to predominate over his need to communicate with and persuade others.

The book – both books, for the second was no more than an addendum to the first – also of course raise a question as to the form in which Childers had chosen to express his views. *The Riddle of the Sands* was not just a novel, but a fiction composed with the specific purpose of heightening public awareness of the German threat. It is impossible to measure objectively the extent to which it actually did so, but in view of its contemporary popularity and the press coverage it generated – and the interest of the Admiralty – it might reasonably be considered to have been successful. *Arme Blanche* and *The German Influence on British Cavalry*, on the other hand, were technical studies aimed at a narrower audience; in eschewing the fictional in these efforts at persuasiveness, Childers cannot be said to have captured the imagination of the general public in the same way. And while the subject of weaponry was probably less suited than German invasion to dramatization, it is also arguable that it was less suited to Childers' talents. As Williams later wrote of these volumes, 'It was undoubtedly work worth doing, this exposition of old shibboleths and this attempt, partially successful, to introduce more enlightened methods in the training of the British Army; but one always felt it was a waste of his genius to be involved in such comparatively ephemeral controversy, when he might have been writing works of fancy and of charm which would live to delight mankind when these old controversies were forgotten.'[25] It is impossible not to sympathize with this point of view, yet at the same time to feel that delighting mankind was no longer (perhaps never had been) an objective Childers found sufficiently worthwhile. His was a driven personality; now – under his wife's tutelage – he was ever more determined that his life's work should be something of emphatic moral value. For a man of his background and education, in the age in which he lived, it was natural that this work should involve his country; and up to this point, in various manifestations – parliamentary clerk, soldier, military controversialist – it had done just that. The problem beginning to raise its head, whether Childers was conscious of it or not, was a feeling of ambiguity as to whether 'his country' was his father's – England; or his mother's – Ireland.

III

Valuable though Childers continued to see his literary work as being, the world of politics increasingly intruded on his life during 1910.

The policy followed first by Campbell-Bannerman and then by Asquith, of compromising the pursuit of absolute naval supremacy in favour of Government spending on social reforms such as pensions, was called into question in the winter of 1908/9. It was then discovered that Admiral Tirpitz, encouraged by what he took to be Britain's ambivalence concerning her naval supremacy, had redoubled Germany's efforts to challenge the dreadnought programme. Such was his success that it looked as though something approaching parity might be achieved within three or four years. This greatly alarmed the public and the Admiralty alike, underscored as it was by the clear message implicit in Blériot's cross-Channel flight of 1909. Conservatives throughout the country took up the demand for eight new ships to be laid down, summarized in the music-hall refrain: 'We want eight and we won't wait.' The Liberals eventually had to accede to the demand. As Churchill – now Home Secretary – ironically remarked, 'The admiralty wanted six, the treasury four, so we compromised on eight.'[26] (Four were to be laid down immediately, four later.) Desirable – essential – as these warships doubtless were, like the pensions, they had somehow to be paid for; the unprecedented sum of upwards of £15 million must be raised. To do so the Chancellor, in the person of that rising star, David Lloyd George, contrived the Budget of 1909, by which the larger proportion of the money required was to be raised in taxes such as increases in income tax and an extension of death duties, which would particularly hit the peers and the interests they represented.

This was a clever ruse. Since coming to power the Liberals had foreseen that the inbuilt Conservative majority in the House of Lords would lead sooner or later to their use of the veto to block legislation; they would have welcomed an excuse to seek a mandate from the voters for a limitation of the veto, and had already tried to provoke the Lords on previous occasions. Traditionally – a tradition stretching back over more than 250 years – the Lords did not reject or even amend finance bills (such as the Budget); for them to do so now would be a break with constitutional precedent which would enable the Liberals to call for reform. The Budget, passed by the Commons on 4 November, was sent up to the Lords, where their Lordships took particular exception to a tax which would have involved a land valuation scheme. Deeming this little less than state trespass, on the technicality that such a measure was illegal in a Finance Bill, they duly rejected it on 30 November, enabling Lloyd George to portray them as 'palpable constitution-breakers and rich men trying to avoid taxation.'[27] Asquith then moved and carried a resolution, 'That the action of the House of Lords in refusing to pass into law the financial provisions made by this House for the service of the year is a breach of the constitution and an usurpation of the rights of the Commons.'[28] The inevitable consequence was a general election, held in January 1910. Asquith and the Liberals were returned to power, but with a greatly reduced majority. The Irish now very much held the balance of power, and the price of their support was Asquith's promise to push ahead with reform of the Lords' powers of veto so that legislation on Home Rule could be initiated. (It should perhaps be remembered that the Conservatives, at this time, were more commonly known as the Unionist Party.)

With work on his two cavalry books largely completed, and the question of Home Rule rising to prominence again, Childers too turned his mind in that direction. Initially, he intended to write another book. Although a great deal of ink had been expended on the matter, both in the past and more recently, by way of newspaper articles, pamphlets and the like, there had been no thorough contemporary study of the Home Rule question by anyone of the status Childers by then enjoyed as a writer and – increasingly – a controversialist. His idea was to provide a historical review of the issue combined with practical proposals for a solution appropriate to the circumstances: to, as he put it, 'advocate a definite scheme of self-government for Ireland.'[29]

Even as he set to work on the book, however, he began to wonder whether the pen alone was sufficient. For more than four years now he had been urged by his wife to take up active politics, and was coming increasingly to feel the need himself. Writing to William Le Fanu at the end of 1909, he remarked, 'You are . . . without any burning political ideals and inclined to think that it matters very little, as I have often heard you say, who is in and who is out.' Then, in a passage that expands his remarks of some eight years previously regarding the importance to his temperament of 'action', he continues: 'I wish for my peace of mind I could be the same: but it is an odd thing that the older I grow the keener I get about things and the more acutely I feel the discomfort of caring, without the necessary safety valve that is simultaneously a sedative and a stimulant – action.' That year of 1910 Childers would celebrate his fortieth birthday. Contemporaries such as Churchill and Runciman, who had unswervingly followed political careers, were now Cabinet Ministers. With his Irish background and his increasing sympathy for Home Rule, was his pen really a sufficient weapon? If Home Rule was anyone's cause, it was Childers'. With the Boer War he had seized his chance of action, as he had with his proposal to Molly. Surely parliamentary candidature, a chance of playing a part in the action rather than merely observing or commenting upon it, was the next step? 'I don't agree with your diagnosis of the Commons,' Childers continued to Le Fanu. 'It presents the greatest career of all and excites the greatest ambitions.'[30]

Nevertheless, it is clear that Childers agonized over this decision, as he agonized over much else. At an age when most men are settled in their careers, he was proposing a dramatic change in his. In candidature there was no guarantee of success and, if he was elected, no guarantee of permanency as an MP: as the Senior Clerk he now was, he was assured of absolute security, £800 per annum, and a pension. For a man with responsible views towards a growing family – Molly was again pregnant – it was by no means an easy choice, and one which was much debated by the Childerses in the tense months following the election of January 1910 and the subsequent struggle to control the power of the House of Lords.

Visiting Glendalough once again in the summer recess, largely to work on his Home Rule book, focused Childers' mind. Certain as he became during that visit, both of the justice and of the inevitability of Home Rule, he became clearer, too, as to the part he himself should be playing. By the autumn it was settled, and Childers resigned from his clerkship in October 1910, fifteen years after first entering the Commons.

IV

The political backdrop to this decision was one of mounting drama. In February 1910 Asquith introduced a Parliament Bill which provided for abolition of the Lords' veto on all bills designated Finance Bills by the Speaker, and that other bills should become law with or without the consent of the Lords if passed by three successive sessions of the Commons. His introduction was accompanied by an announcement that if the Lords failed to pass the Bill, he would advise the Crown to take the necessary steps – that is to say, the creation of as many as 500

Liberal peers, to swamp the Conservative majority there. A bitter battle was joined, in the midst of which, suddenly and quite unexpectedly, on 6 May 1910, Edward VII died. 'His final collapse was a matter of hours, and the nation, which only one bulletin had prepared for it, was utterly stunned.'[31]

Childers, as befitted a man close to the pulse of government, took a more restrained view of the King's death, remarking to Sumner Pearmain that 'a sort of orgy of false sentiment has been washed up here . . . the press knows literally nothing, and lords [*sic*] him to the skies as a wise and benevolent statesman who has controlled the destinies of Europe and what not!' Nevertheless, he was more than ready to acknowledge the crisis that the new King, George V, had to face. He continued: 'There is a bitter party struggle between Liberal and Tories, Commons and Lords. There is only one constitutional means ultimately of enabling a representative house to enforce its will, and that is by the creation of a number of peers sufficient to secure a majority in the Lords, otherwise there might be an eternal deadlock and paralysis of government.'[32] Out of courtesy to the new King, so as not to embroil him in controversy at the moment of his accession, a Constitutional Conference to resolve the crisis began to meet from the middle of June 1910, comprising four representatives from each of the two major parties. When its failure was announced five months later, it emerged that the main stumbling-block to agreement was 'not so much any general constitutional theory, as the particular desire of the Conservatives to block Irish Home Rule.'[33] The impasse between upper and lower House, between Conservatives and Liberals, remained unbroken. Parliament was dissolved in December 1910, and it was accordingly at an election in which Home Rule was once again a live issue that Childers sought to stand. Writing to Molly, Childers declared, 'I am preparing myself steadily and coolly for the future. I am longing *somehow* to do something for the cause.'[34]

Philosophic conversation being somewhat easier of achievement than practical results, these longings were to be frustrated for several years yet. Influential friends were of course valuable, and Walter Runciman was at once prevailed upon to prod the Whips' Office into finding a suitable seat for which Childers might be proposed as the Liberal candidate. Soon he was on his way to Suffolk headquarters, where he was wanted to stand at Sudbury – or so he had been assured. When the contrary proved the case, a telegram from Runciman dispatched him to Shrewsbury – with similar results. 'This is another Sudbury fiasco,' he wrote to Molly, 'only much less excusable because the local people wrote to headquarters *asking* for a candidate on Saturday. Now it seems they don't want to fight. Nothing personal to me! I know they liked me . . . I shall decide in the morning what to do – too tired now.'[35]

It was a dispiriting introduction to practical politics, but Childers did not repine. With the election now only days away, his own candidature had to be abandoned. Instead, he would travel to Rugby to help Basil Williams fight a rural constituency in Warwickshire, Williams having 'no permanent gentlemen to do the things I can do'.[36] It is a commonplace that first-time candidates very rarely win seats, so this was in any case probably Childers' best way of gaining some useful experience of the hustings. And this experience turned out to be a considerable revelation to someone who so far had in many respects led a very sheltered life. As he wrote to Molly on 13 December, he was to meet

> Liberals of all classes and see the way they look at things instead of the somewhat doctrinaire atmosphere in which we upper classes discuss our politics in London. What an eye-opener it would be for Aunt Aggie and people like that, whose nature it is to regard all Radicals either as dishonest or crack-brained, to see some of the meetings I have seen, the sound sober sense that is talked in earnest, shrewd, *good* faces of hard-working men and women, the sense of the ideal they have as well as the practical, and to know moreover what a real hard *sacrifice* it is to many of them in country districts to profess liberalism.[37]

For this alone, Childers' first foray into politics had been worthwhile.

Yet the election left the Liberals with their earlier small majority reduced by two; and Basil Williams failed against what Childers described as a 'deadweight of slow silent Toryism in that division which it will take years to move'.[38] The constitutional debate dragged on until August of the following year, when the Lords finally passed the Parliament Bill introduced by Asquith in January 1910, having failed to amend it to exclude Home Rule from legislation which could become law without their consent. The provisions of the Bill were to have a most mischievous effect.

Despite Childers' failure to stand as a candidate, the end of 1910 and the beginning of 1911 were exciting times for him. In May 1910 the *United Services Magazine* had made the following report: 'Those who have read Mr Childers' brilliant book *The Riddle of the Sands* will not be surprised to learn that one of his predictions has been fulfilled. Germany has strongly fortified the Island of Borkum, ostensibly to guard against invasion, but in reality for offence purposes . . . This new development upsets the balance of power in the North Sea, and our own government must meet it by a corresponding increase in our naval strength.'[39] Now, prompted either by this fortification or by Childers' proposals of 1906 which engendered the Admiralty request for information about the area, two British naval officers had spent the summer of 1910 doing some quiet investigations in the region; in August they were caught, on Borkum itself, and their trial that December in Leipzig was widely publicized. Captain Trench was reticent as to their activities, but when his companion's counsel produced a copy of *The Riddle of the Sands*, Lieutenant Brandon disclosed he was a close student of the book, having read it three times. To the English public this both confirmed what the two men had been up to, and heightened the perception of Childers as an expert in such matters – which was useful in providing him with the pretext for a newspaper article, as well as stimulating sales of the novel. Less usefully, it endowed him with a reputation as a man knowledgeable about spying and subterfuge that he by no means entirely deserved.

With another son, christened Robert Alden Childers, born in January 1911, this was also a time of characteristic domestic felicity. Writing to Molly on her birthday as usual, Childers declared, 'My heart is so full on this birthday that I can hardly find words to express all I feel. First I thank God on my knees that I, happiest of all men on this earth, have had one more year of love and companionship of the noblest woman ever made . . .' Then he turned to the steep hill that now lay ahead.

> We stand now on the threshold of a new life. We have decided together and I feel as if in a mysterious way it was the common act of two souls made into one . . . But without you, how could it have come to pass? Without your exquisite faith in me and your trust that I, by your side, am able to live and work for an ideal, and am strong enough to make worthy sacrifices, which all of us, you and I and our darling children must bear the brunt of, such as it is I say it again, that I *know* we are right . . . our instinct pointed the way and we followed it, not blindfolded, but certainly, steadily and trustfully.[40]

In a letter of about the same time to his mother-in-law, he described it as 'this great turning-point of [our] lives.'[41]

V

His hopes for a parliamentary seat temporarily dashed, in the new year of 1911 Childers returned to his study of the Irish question, to be called *The Framework of Home Rule*. His publisher having persuaded him that the subject's topicality dictated publication before the end of the year, Childers had a tight deadline to meet. Free of his Commons duties, however, he could at least work on the book without being distracted by the Parliamentary calendar, and the book progressed apace. It was apparent that a fairly lengthy visit to Ireland would be necessary to enable him to do full justice to his subject, and this Childers undertook in the spring of 1911. He spent some six weeks travelling all over the country, sounding out the very considerable variety of opinion of all sorts and conditions of Irishmen.

Despite the undeniable improvements to many aspects of life in Ireland, the country by then was a pot beginning to warm nicely. In the south the streams of nationalism and republicanism manifested in bodies like the Gaelic League and Sinn Féin were stimulated by John Redmond's leadership of the Irish MPs at Westminster, and by the current Liberal enthusiasm to make him the 'Irish Botha': all well and good, had it not been for the traditional Unionist opposition to such ideas in Ulster. The issue was partly religious, of course; Protestants predominated in Ulster, and its people held by the old slogan, 'Home Rule is Rome Rule'.[42] In reality, this masked rather more material issues. The industrial revolution that had been the mainspring of England's nineteenth-century prosperity had largely passed Ireland by. She was a terribly poor country by comparison with her great neighbour, lacking in particular the natural resources of iron and coal, and burdened by an ever-increasing population. Belfast was in many ways the exception to this rule, where a commercial centre of considerable substance had been built up, based first on the linen industry, then on shipbuilding (indeed, a great ship was even then on the stocks in the Belfast shipyards: the *Titanic*). Naturally enough, Belfast was jealous of its connection with England, by far the most important of its trading partners, and saw any form of devolution as a threat to its prosperity; for the citizens of Belfast, the idea of any subjection of their great capitalist centre to the vagaries of the smaller southern city of Dublin was anathema. Following the fall of Parnell, the possibility had seemed remote; with the rise of Redmond, it seemed altogether less so.

In one of the many paradoxes of Irish history, Redmond's chief opponent, the leader of the Unionist movement, although a Protestant, was himself a Dubliner. Sir Edward Carson was an outstanding barrister who had made his name as Queensberry's counsel in the Wilde libel case. Of Italian extraction, massive in form and charismatic in presence, he became leader of the Unionists in February 1910, and took the chair of the Ulster Unionist Council shortly before Childers' visit in early in 1911. Before the end of the year the 'Ulster programme' would be in train – 'not merely to defy Dublin's Home Rule, but to prepare an alternative'.[43] Famously, it was to be ready 'the morning Home Rule passes, to become responsible for the government of the Protestant Province of Ulster'. In short, the plan was to actively resist any weakening of the link with Britain. A movement so contrary to the democratic constitution and traditions of Britain was odd enough in itself; it was odder still that it should be led by such an eminent lawyer: it was as though a Master of the Rolls was inciting armed resistance between Wales and England.

With his 'longing *somehow* to do something for the cause', Childers plunged somewhat unguardedly into this political labyrinth. He was not entirely without sensible advice and counsel. In Dublin he sought out his friend Sir Horace Plunkett, in whose company in 1908 he had made the tour of Ireland that had convinced him of the necessity of

Home Rule. Plunkett, like Childers, was a member of the old Ascendancy who nevertheless saw that there remained much to be put right in Ireland. His particular achievement lay in the considerable improvements of the lot of agricultural tenants, achieved through the Irish Agricultural Organization Society. He was keen to help the younger enthusiast, and Childers wrote to Molly that Plunkett thought it 'absolutely necessary for me to go North before writing my book, though he is also very anxious for me to stay here and see more . . . Barbour [an Ulster mill owner and prominent nationalist] comes on Friday and . . . wants to put me up and bring me in touch with the young crowd of Ulster Unionists.'[44] Accepting Barbour's invitation, Childers spent some days in County Antrim, plumbing opinion and seeking ideas. In a letter to Molly he remarked that 'They are all against Home Rule but moderate and would make it a success if it was inevitable, and they are the kind of men who *would* make a success of it in combination with men like Bob [Robert Barton] from the South.'[45] A few days later he appears rather less sanguine: 'Busy day yesterday – fire-eaters, moderates, home-rulers, indifferents – very interesting . . . I *don't* think Ulster will fight, mainly bluff.'[46] Returning to Dublin he encountered Sir Horace Plunkett's secretary, the poet and painter George Russell, or A.E., as he styled himself.[47] Childers was impressed: 'I had a fascinating talk with A.E. He is a marvellous man.'[48] He had gathered the facts; he now had merely to write the book. Returning to London, Childers 'scarcely lifted his eyes from his latest work until he had finished the last paragraph'.[49]

Published just in time for Christmas 1911, it was as thorough and elegant an advocacy of Home Rule as one might hope to find. It comprised, as he had planned, an historical review, a careful study of the comparable cases of some of the Dominions, and a reasoned and detailed specification for what amounted to autonomy for the whole of Ireland – Ulster included – under the Crown. In many quarters the book, appropriately, was as brilliantly received as his fictional masterpiece. *The Irish Times* thought it 'by far the most important contribution to the study of the Irish political problem to emerge since Home Rule re-emerged into the region of practical politics';[50] the *Daily News* called it 'the ablest and most clear-sighted book that has ever come from an English writer on the subject of Home Rule';[51] *The*

Glasgow Herald declared it 'probably the most fascinating book which has ever been written on this subject'.[52] Many praised the logic of the case, and the passionate sincerity with which it was presented; others were struck by the erudition of the colonial parallels, and the 'veritable brilliance of the author's handling of the need for Ireland's fiscal autonomy'.[53] Others praised the style.

But again there were several significant critical responses. It was perhaps predictable that the *Belfast Newsletter* should note Childers' apparent ignorance of the importance of the influence of the Catholic Church in the south, declaring that 'he seems almost unaware that its pretensions and its influence in Ireland enter in the smallest degree in the problem he seeks to solve'.[54] More seriously, the *Manchester Guardian* took issue with Childers' colonial comparisons, arguing that the differences between Ireland's situation and those of the more distant Dominions were far more important than the similarities and concluding, crucially, that his argument by analogy, although 'magnificent', was not 'politics, if by politics we are to understand the pursuit of the possible'.[55] The *Oxford and Cambridge Review* addressed the similarly serious point of Childers' tendency to gloss over the Ulster problem. 'He persists throughout the book in treating Ireland as a nation with one distinct individuality, of which Ulster forms merely a dissentient minority, to be soothed, argued with and, if still recalcitrant, overridden'. It also noted his increasingly dogmatic style, the 'invincible faith in his own doctrines'.[56] Perhaps most tellingly, *The Outlook* argued that while the book hung together 'as logically as an essay in higher mathematics', it was divorced from the realities of politics and the psychology of the Irish people. 'Does Mr Childers mean that if we fix Irish life into this admirable design, Irish character must conform to it?' No, *The Outlook* argues: 'Good statecraft under democracy is not a tyranny of ideals.'[57]

Idealistic the book certainly was, yet it was also highly expressive of Childers' own ideals. As we have seen, self-reliance, personal integrity and the 'creed of one's own conscience' had long been his touchstones; now, increasingly, they became part of his prescription for Ireland. His Imperialist phase well past, he was coming to feel ever more strongly that self-help and political self-determination were the best panaceas for the political problems of the country. Indeed, in this sense the book's title was deceptive, for in reality his argument was as much for independence as it was for Home Rule under the auspices of England. As he puts it in *The Framework*, 'What, in the Colonies, Ireland and everywhere else, is the deep spiritual impulse for Home Rule? A craving for self-expression, self-reliance . . . Home Rule is synonymous with the growth of independence and character. That is why Ireland instinctively and passionately wants it, that is why Great Britain, for her own sake, and Ireland's, should give it.' Finally, presaging events to come, Childers congratulates Sinn Féin for its contribution to this process, its purpose in his eyes being 'to inspire Irishmen to rely on themselves for their own salvation, economic and spiritual'.[58]

Yet was it enough just to produce another book? Childers was certainly feeling doubtful when he wrote to his sister Constance at the time of its publication: 'The book is just out and I hope will get to you soon. I feel it is a terribly forlorn hope, like the arme blanche books! An unpopular cause – I seem to be thoroughly identified now with such.'[59] In the autumn before publication he had already established, with Basil Williams, something arguably more practical: the Home Rule League. This group of influential British Liberal intellectuals, gathered together to lobby for devolution, soon spawned a series of lectures and pamphlets, to which Childers himself contributed a paper entitled *Home Rule: Its Form and Purpose*. As it was obvious that both English and Irish opinion had to be influenced, Childers returned to Dublin in the spring of 1912 to deliver this essay as a lecture. 'On the whole, I think it went off well,' he then wrote to Molly. 'The general argument met with approval and applause, except the latter part about the contribution to the future of the empire, which was *coldly* received.'[60] Such practical activities were doubtless a step in the right direction, and more was to come.

That May, Childers was unanimously adopted as one of the two prospective Liberal candidates for Devonport, the naval dockyard in the suburbs of Plymouth; it looked as though, at long last, Childers really would be able to do something thoroughly practical 'for the cause'.

10
The Liberal Candidate
1912–1914

> 'I am in the midst of a kind of vision, wondering how one can do most to help one's fellow man.'
>
> Erskine Childers, 1913

I

At Devonport Childers threw himself with energy into winning over the local electorate. Lodging at the Durnford Hotel in Plymouth, he was soon writing enthusiastic letters home to Molly, who was occupied with their new son. 'Just had an open air meeting, a fairly good one, I think, on insurance only . . . A pleasant interlude last night – a trip up river with the young Liberals. Inevitable speech at end of bridge of steamer. I got fascinated with an Irish family – Carroll – whose baby (about the size of Bobbie), called "John Redmond", saluted at the name and made what was meant to be a speech on Home Rule.'[1]

It was a misfortune that this momentum was so soon dispelled. Late in April 1912 the third Irish Home Rule Bill had been introduced by Asquith to the House of Commons, as bad a piece of news for Belfast as the sinking of the *Titanic* on the 15th of that month. Under the provisions of the Parliament Bill passed the previous year, the Lords could delay the passage of the bill into law by two years at most – until the summer of 1914. If the measure itself was one on which Ireland was much divided, the delay envisaged in its implementation seemed merely to make its opponents more intransigent; it also gave time for means outside the constitution of preventing its imposition to be devised and organized. In the autumn of 1911 Carson had declared his intention that the Ulster Unionists should be ready to assume responsibility for Ulster 'the morning home rule passes'; in January 1912, having obtained the appropriate permission from local magistrates, he began drilling a 'volunteer' force, the purpose of which was clearly to provide military support for such an assumption of power. Amateur military bodies such as this were an echo of various historic risings in the country, and were to become a painful feature of future events. Then, in July 1912 (some months after Childers' encounter with 'John Redmond' Carroll), the new leader of the Conservatives, Andrew Bonar Law, declared, 'I can imagine no length of resistance to which Ulster will go, which I shall not be ready to support, and in which they will not be supported by the overwhelming majority of the British people.'[2] This was an extraordinary statement: the leader of one of the two main political parties of the country that had defined modern democracy, openly supporting violent opposition to due constitutional processes. 'It is difficult to imagine a Disraeli or a Peel, a Salisbury or a Balfour so abdicating control. To pledge a great English party to follow a small Irish faction whenever it might lead would hardly have appealed to any of them.'[3]

It had been hinted that Asquith might call an election on the Home Rule issue, and it was in these circumstances that Childers had allowed his name to be put forward for the Devonport seat. In the course of the summer of 1912, attempts at compromise were made by those such as Churchill who realized that Ulster could not be coerced into accepting Home Rule. A back-bench Liberal proposed an amendment to exclude the northern counties of Antrim, Armagh, Down and Londonderry – the heart of Ulster. This, the first formal proposal to destroy the integrity of a community that many saw as a nation in its own right, was summarily rejected by Asquith. Yet at the same time he himself showed no signs of a constructive will to break the impasse, by an election or by any other means. During the summer of 1912 this remained a tenable stance, but as the year withered and died it became less so. 'The habit, which grows on most prime ministers, of postponing decisions and trusting that time will untie the knots, obtained an altogether excessive hold on him. A phrase which he several times uttered early in 1911 – "wait and see" – was afterwards not unfairly made his nickname. Thus it was that down to 1914 he still had no clear policy, but remained poised on equivocations, waiting for something to turn up.'[4]

Needless to say, and notwithstanding his diplomatic remarks, postponement and prevarication were hardly to Childers' taste. He distracted himself by arranging to meet the two naval spies Brandon and Trench, just released from prison in Germany, and then paid his customary summer visit to Glendalough. There, in discussion with Robert Barton – himself now a fervent Home Ruler – he seems first to have explored other and perhaps more practical ways of forwarding the cause. If his political career was hanging fire in England, perhaps it might find some impetus in Ireland? For the moment, Childers did no more than take soundings, returning to London, then, periodically, to Devonport in the autumn and winter of 1912. 'Last night was a *frost* and we were disgusted,' he wrote to Molly in January 1913. 'No preparations, very small attendance – stony cold school-room hung with big, obvious texts. I spoke about Ulster . . . Also, I think, was rather eloquent about Home Rule as a whole, but that wasn't reported at all. Such is fortune!'[5]

Nevertheless, that same month the Home Rule Bill cleared its first hurdle, being passed by the Commons, and to celebrate the event a dinner was given to Asquith by some of the Irish Nationalist MPs. The guests included several from outside Parliament who had contributed to the cause, among whom Childers was the most prominent. 'When called upon for a speech,' recorded Basil Williams, 'he attributed, as was his wont, all the credit to others.'[6] The episode was heartening, but for Childers such private plaudits, while gratifying, were no longer really sufficient. It was now more than two years since he had resigned his clerkship in the House of Commons, and while public commitment to the cause he had made his own was widespread, there was also a good deal of public resistance, especially in Ulster. In terms of his own career, no one had yet had the opportunity to vote for or against him in an election of any sort – not since the Magpie and Stump days. As Asquith's policy appeared increasingly to be one of procrastination, there seemed little immediate chance for any sort of resolution.

'I am in the midst of a kind of vision,' Childers wrote one day to Molly on the train to Plymouth, 'wondering how one can do most to help one's fellow man in the exacting business of politics, wondering how we can use ourselves to best advantage – one's brain and other faculties in the midst of issues so vast and obscure, and seeing how one can get into the soul and essence of the Devonport problem. It's all so obscure.'[7] It was perhaps not surprising that Childers, with his high-flown sentiments, was gradually finding himself at odds with his more pragmatic fellow-Liberals at Devonport. He resented the tradition that candidates should make charitable contributions to local causes, especially – and perhaps not unreasonably – if such 'contributions' manifested themselves in liquid form. This rigour makes Childers an interesting contrast to Churchill, now First Lord of the Admiralty, who once confessed to his mother that 'I do not care so much for the principles I advocate as for the impression which my words produce and the reputation they give me. This sounds very terrible. But you must remember we do not live in the age of Great Causes!'[8] Even at this early stage, Childers was far from possessing this particular brand of pragmatism, and as the spring of 1913 blossomed into summer, his thoughts began to turn again to the notion of Ireland rather than England as providing him with the opportunity – the chance – he craved.

First, though, in June of that year, the Childerses once again returned to German waters, and to the Baltic beyond.

II

It was one of Asquith's misfortunes that he had to deal with no fewer than four major imbroglios, each of which from time to time, and sometimes at the same time, amounted to crises. Scarcely keynotes of the golden pre-war age we like to imagine, two of these problems – the rise in militant form of the labour and the suffragette movements – are of minimal concern here; not so those of Ireland and Germany, the latter now barely a year away from its culmination.

Despite the naval race that had continued unabated between Germany and Britain, exemplified by the 'We want eight' dreadnought refrain of 1909, diplomatic relationships between the two countries had remained satisfactory until 1911. That May, the Kaiser had visited

London for the unveiling of the Queen Victoria Memorial; then, at the end of June, Germany precipitated a European crisis by sending the gunboat *Panther* to the Moroccan port of Agadir. A Franco-German agreement of 1909 had endorsed Morocco's independence, guaranteeing German commercial rights and access while France (desiring a protectorate) had assumed the primary political role – to the extent of sending a force, in April 1911, to protect the European residents against a tribal uprising around the capital, Fez. Yet the French action might be altogether more aggressively construed and, so construing, Germany reciprocated by seizing Agadir. In London this was seen as an aggressive act against a country – France – with whom England had increasingly friendly relations. More importantly, it provided Germany with a convenient base for operations in the Mediterranean, and Germany's continued presence might threaten Britain's sea-lanes to West Africa and the Cape. Formal objections followed, and Britain sent a warship to lie alongside *Panther*. This resulted in silence from Berlin for seventeen days, between 3 July and 21 July – and in dramatically rising tension. Then Lloyd George, in a speech at the Mansion House, threatened war. 'I would make great sacrifices to preserve peace,' he stated. 'But if a situation were to be forced upon us in which peace could only be preserved by the surrender of the great and beneficent position Britain has won by centuries of heroism and achievement . . . then I say emphatically that peace at that price would be a humiliation intolerable for a great country like ours to endure.'[9] This turned the tide, and although in September war still seemed so close that the Cabinet ordered the patrolling of the South-Eastern Railway against a possible invasion, by November the *Panther* had been withdrawn.

In reality, however, this incident was prelude rather than swan-song. One inevitable consequence was to push Britain and France further into one another's arms, particularly with regard to the disposition of their navies. It had of course been one of Childers' aims, with *The Riddle of the Sands*, to promote the establishment of a North Sea fleet, and the Anglo-French Entente of 1904 had enabled this process to begin; the crisis of Agadir ensured its completion. In the autumn of 1912 British ships finally assumed responsibility for the North Sea, the Channel and the Atlantic; the French for the Mediterranean. Then, that October, war erupted (yet again) in the Balkans. In a sense, this was but a 'little local difficulty'. Essentially, though stripped of its labyrinthine details, it represented an indirect conflict between the two great powers of continental Europe – Russia, attempting to expand south, and Germany, busy with the Berlin-to-Baghdad railway. Neither the conflict itself nor any outcome favouring either major party was desirable from the British point of view, as the world's greatest trading nation favoured peace over war, and deprecated any alteration in the balance of power in Europe. The usual conciliatory conferences were arranged in London (London did a fine trade in the conference business over these years), but the treaty signed at the end of May failed to provide a resolution, and war broke out again with a Bulgarian offensive against Serbia and Greece at the end of June.

These events, which were the prologue to those of the following August, 1914, also coincided with the Childerses' Baltic trip.

Setting sail from the Hamble on 26 June 1913, they took as crew Gordon Shephard; two Americans, Barthold Schlesinger and Samuel Pierce; and a paid hand. The Childerses had first met Shephard in the summer of 1909. Another Anglo-Irishman, the son of Sir Horace and Lady Shephard, he had been named after that great imperialist, Gordon of Khartoum. He was an officer in the regular Army, described by a close friend as 'the most unmilitary soldier I have ever known . . . singularly clear-sighted, logically minded, and tenacious of an idea.'[10] Like Childers he belonged to the Ascendancy and was much concerned with the welfare of Ireland; he was also, when they met, already a committed Home Ruler. 'I dined yesterday with a great yachtsman,' his diary records of that first meeting. 'He is a clerk to the House of Lords [*sic*] but nevertheless a good Radical.'[11] An adventurer in the same mould as Childers, Shephard had been arrested while yachting in the Frisian islands, suspected of spying. He was also one of the first army pilots, and later became, at thirty-two, one of the youngest Brigadiers in the Royal Flying Corps. Patriotic, talented and daring, he had something about him of both Davies and Carruthers; he became very close to the Childerses, and after his death in 1918 Childers wrote a letter to *Yachting Monthly* which says as much about himself as it does about Shephard:

> I would like to say that he was not one who courted risk, but who, desiring to extend the limit of small yacht cruises and having decided to undertake some distant voyage, would carry through what he had undertaken. In his flying work the same quality was displayed. If a necessary undertaking presented difficulties, those difficulties were not allowed to stand in his way. Once having made up his mind to do a thing, he did it. Those who watched him at work will tell you of his singular wit and skill in minimizing danger and his delight in exercising these powers. But to imply that he sought risk for risk's sake and out of a dare-devil spirit is to ignore his purpose and fine intelligence, and the fact that in all he did every detail was planned out before hand and difficulties were weighted and allowed for. He was a type of Frobisher who, desiring to extend his knowledge, accomplished great things in spite of many dangers.[12]

The Americans were of less heroic stature; Childers later wrote to Flora Priestley of 'Schlesinger, an American friend and a sort of odd man casually picked up by S on his way from America – an altogether speculative proposition, who turned out not exactly a success and not exactly a failure – a sort of negative who came and went and left no trace. He was terribly nervous at first and used to wake me up and implore me to order sail to be shortened!'[13]

Their route took them as usual across the North Sea to the Kiel Canal, then through German waters to Stralsund, a beautiful medieval city in eastern Germany. Reflecting the change in the diplomatic climate between England and Germany, their reception was austere. 'When yachting in the summer of 1913 we noticed a marked change in the people in the German fiords we explored,' Molly later wrote. 'In former years small, friendly crowds assembled when we moored alongside quays and gave the strangers a warm welcome, others giving help of various kinds . . . But in 1913 we were received with scowls; no help was offered, the crowds were not friendly. Erskine decided to leave German waters.'[14] Maldwin Drummond also discovered that Childers' reputation in Germany meant that he was under official observation during this voyage.[15]

Asgard headed north-east to Visby, the ancient Scandinavian centre of Baltic trade, on to Helsinki on the southern tip of Finland, then across the mouth of the Gulf of Bothnia to Stockholm. Here, having 'made good from Hamble 1505½ miles in 27 days',[16] Shephard and the two Americans departed. The Childerses lingered for a couple of days before sailing south to Kalmar on the eastern coast of Sweden to pick up a new crew, one of whom was the teacher and writer Alfred Ollivant, who later evocatively described the passage:

> The winds were contrary. We beat all down the Baltic, and south of Oslo, ran into a gale. Some tackle broke away at the masthead and had to be lashed down – Childers, already grey, lame and the eldest of us by some years, went aloft to do it. A little figure in a fisherman's jersey, with hunched shoulders and straining arms, the wind tearing through his thick hair, his face desperately set, he tugged, heaved, fought with hands, feet and teeth, to master the baffling elements and achieve his end. This is how I saw him then; that is how I shall always see him now – a tussling wisp of humanity, high overhead, and swirling with the slow swirl of the mast against a tumult of tempestuous sky . . .[17]

The closing days of the cruise were indeed hard going, as *Asgard* beat north again up the Kattegat to Oslo. The winds were again almost always against them, and the seas rough. A brief log entry, 'under way at 6.15pm . . . all ready for a heavy thresh to windward',[18] is typical, and happily recalls Davies, 'practising smartness in a heavy thresh'.[19] On 23 August they finally reached Oslo, where *Asgard* was to be laid up for the winter.

'We have had a most glorious cruise,' Childers wrote to his sister Constance, 'the best we have ever had.'[20] So indeed in many respects it was. At 2,500 miles it was significantly the longest; with the last 1,000 miles to Oslo spent beating against the wind, it was arguably the toughest; and some of the intricacies of navigation around Stralsund clearly placed great demands on those skills in which Childers, like Davies, abounded. As Hugh and Robin Popham wrote in their collection of Childers' nautical writings, it was 'one of the two or three [cruises] on which his claim to fame as an outstanding yachtsman most securely rests.'[21]

The Childerses returned to London by steamer at the end of August, to find that the Balkan war had been settled by a treaty signed earlier that month at Bucharest. It was not to last.

III

After the frustrations of the spring it must have been a considerable relief for Childers to escape the cares of his putative political career in sailing the Baltic. Nevertheless, given the nature of his crews – all good Radicals, as Shephard himself might have described them – the subject of Ireland and Home Rule can hardly have remained undiscussed. The summer had done nothing to ease tensions in Ireland; indeed, quite the reverse, with a strike at the end of August by the Irish Transport and General Workers' Union in Dublin and a reciprocal lock-out by the employers.

Childers' first duty on his return was to sort out the matter of his candidature, to which he had been giving much thought. He was by now less than absolutely confident of his potential as an MP, rightly in many respects. He patently lacked two qualities of the successful politician: pragmatism, and the skill of presenting himself attractively to the voters – there was that matter of the liquid 'charitable donations'. The upshot of his deliberations was his agreement in September with the local party chairman that he should abandon Devonport. The central party managers received the news with some surprise, but nevertheless thought sufficiently well of their high-minded candidate to offer him alternatives in Kidderminster and St Pancras. 'They evidently want to keep me,' Childers wrote to Molly, 'but I still have currently a strong feeling of resistance to embarking on another constituency. I think it is partly the money question and partly the impression that I could use such powers as I have better in other ways. I fear you will think it cowardice, but I believe it is not so.'[22]

The truth was that Ireland was again beckoning. Childers set off in the last week of September 1913 for Ulster, now clearly the most significant obstacle to Home Rule. Here he found Sir Edward Carson virtually at the peak of his energies in encouraging the Ulster Unionists in active resistance to the implementation of the Home Rule Bill. To many people, the emotional signing of the Solemn League and Covenant in September 1912 (to use all necessary means 'to defeat the present conspiracy to set up a Home Rule Parliament in Ireland'), the formation in January 1913 of the Ulster Volunteer Force (a militia as yet unarmed), and the Ulster Day ceremonial Childers himself witnessed later that year, would have been a sufficient indication that Carson and the Orangemen were serious in their intention that their 'Provisional Government' should seize power, in line with their various declarations. Yet Childers, writing to Molly, was still able to be dismissive. 'I am beginning to think it is true, what I have always suspected, that the Carson racket is a Belfast proposition only and that the Provisional Government is meant for Belfast only and could never gain any control outside a small radius.'[23] Of the great Ulster Day Parade he remarked, 'We counted about 8000, and you may discount all accounts purporting to give a higher figure . . . Not, I should say, temperamentally a *fighting* lot . . . I expected more fire and popular excitement from the men in the ranks. The quietness *may* be due to confidence and habit . . . or it may partly be due to weariness with a grand imposture.'[24] Like some (but not all) observers, Childers persuaded himself that the whole Ulster programme was a bluff.

It was also on this trip that he first met the enigmatic Sir Roger Casement, a man in whose story can be traced some parallels with Childers' own. A Dubliner of Ulster Protestant stock, he joined the British consular service in 1894, doing sterling work, mostly in Africa. His report of 1903 on the Upper Congo revealed the sort of colonial exploitation explored by Joseph Conrad in *Heart of Darkness*, the whole system of collecting rubber there being based 'virtually on unpaid labour, enforced by penalties of which mutilation was the most common'. The sensation this caused was to be surpassed only when his study of the Peruvian Amazon (1909) revealed comparable abuses. When he was awarded the KCMG for his services, he wrote to the Foreign Secretary that he found it 'very hard to choose the words with which to make acknowledgement of the honour done to me by the King.'[25] Such sentiments notwithstanding, he was from his youth an extreme Irish Nationalist, and had joined the Gaelic League as early as 1904. 'Casement is mad about Home Rule,' remarked Childers on this first meeting, possibly writing a more literal truth than he knew. 'He is a Nationalist of the best sort and burning with keenness but, I fear, unpractical.'[26] Casement was also somewhat unpractical in his private life, being a homosexual of extreme promiscuity.

The outcome of his visit to Ulster was to set Childers' heart on working more actively for the 'cause' in Ireland itself. 'These last days I have been more and more accustoming myself to the idea of giving up a political career in England,' he wrote to Molly after a morning spent with Casement discussing the Ulster stalemate. 'Oh how sad I felt as I . . . looked down at Belfast in the haze – the key to the whole of this terrible problem – and thought of its wonderful history way back and what a desperate pity it is that no resolute effort had been made for a century to win it back to Nationalism.'[27]

Since Molly has subsequently been painted as the real impetus behind Childers' passion for Ireland, it seems worth emphasizing how limited was her own enthusiasm for this move. From the practical point of view, she doubtless disliked the notion of uprooting herself (and her two young children) from the English life to which, over ten years, she had become thoroughly accustomed: Chelsea, her friends, the stimulating intellectual circle of Pollocks and Trevelyans in which she lived. Dublin in 1913 retained some of its Georgian elegance of appearance, but was otherwise neither particularly stimulating nor entirely salubrious. By comparison with London it was parochial, and the Dublin tenements (of which the dramatist Sean O'Casey would soon be writing) were some of the worst in Europe. Yet Molly was in certain respects quite as idealistic as her husband, and it may be that even now, more profound concerns about the wisdom of such a path for her husband were beginning to cross her mind. Despite Childers' belief that Carson was bluffing, there were many less partial observers of the scene ready to assure Molly that in reality Ireland lay on the brink of civil war. When Childers was in Belfast, Molly briefly visited the Bartons at Glendalough, where she was able to talk things through with Robert Barton, as fervent as his cousin, but by temperament perhaps more judicious. 'I have been talking to Bob who agrees with me that you might . . . come to Ireland later, not at a time when the old nationalist regime – by a pitiful necessity – becomes the first Government of Ireland,' wrote Molly. 'Moreover from a *wise* and I think, *right* worldly point of view, I do not think you should come here from what will look like failure . . . success would in no way hinder you from coming to Ireland in a few years and making it your home. It is a very big thing to do and I think we need more time to think it over . . . it may well be that you can help Ireland in England more at this crucial time than you could over here.'[28]

(In passing, Barton's own comments on the relationship between Molly and her husband are interesting; they were elicited by questions from Andrew Boyle, but were not published. Barton observed, 'Erskine was never "under Molly's thumb". He loved her supremely, trusted her judgement enough to seek it, and admired her intellect . . . but he would never have taken action against his own conviction, and his was the better-trained intellect.')[29]

To a couple who were and remained so devoted, a disagreement like this could not fail to be painful. Eventually, on his return to London, Childers decided to permit his name to remain on the list of potential candidates for seats to be contested by the Liberals, as and when the election should come; equally, the connection with Ireland was to be maintained. Writing to Flora Priestley at the end of November, Childers' old enthusiasm for practicalities and for action comes through – as does his continuing belief in an Ulster bluff. 'Things *are* certainly rather exciting,' he wrote. 'No one can foretell results, but I don't think there will be a "great revolution". The situation is amazingly tangled: Irish parties all mixed up . . . I am seeing a lot of Casement, Alan Wilson and Jack White, all Protestant Ulstermen who are working for Home Rule. You would love Casement – the Cunningham Grahame type.'[30]

Childers spent the winter of 1913 and the spring of 1914 shuttling between Belfast, Glendalough and London, and doing such work for the cause as he could find.

IV

In the meantime, events were moving on, the prospect of confrontation between North and South becoming more real.

To counter Carson's Ulster Volunteer Force, the Irish Volunteers had been established in the South towards the end of 1913 by two men who were soon to figure in Childers' story: the medieval scholar Professor Eoin MacNeill, one of the founders of the Gaelic League, and a Gaelic teacher named Padraic Pearse. In response, in Dublin towards the end of November 1913, Bonar Law in effect called upon the army in Ireland – largely Protestant Unionists – to disobey orders should they be called upon to disperse Carson's Provisional Government in Ulster on 'the morning Home Rule passes'. Asquith, still procrastinating, was patently being driven by events rather than dictating them. On 9 March 1914 it fell to him to move, for the third time, the second reading of the Home Rule Bill. Childers does not go into the finer points of the Bill in his letters at this time, though he must, given the circles in which he moved, have been aware of the general outlines. A recent amendment was that while the Bill would go forward for the whole of Ireland, as originally intended, as a temporary expedient counties within Ulster might be permitted to opt out of Home Rule for a period of up to six years. This offered a measure of reassurance to Ulstermen, and at the same time deferred the temptation of an immediate seizure of power by them; no doubt the assumption was that after six years the mere passage of time would have reconciled the Unionists to the reality of devolution. Whether there was wisdom in formally conceding the principle of the partition of the country was, and remains, another question. All depended on the extent to which what were undeniably two communities would be better or worse off (in every sense) if they could settle their differences. Nationalists like Childers believed strongly that Ireland was, should and could be an integrated nation in its own right.

Carson's own reaction was disappointing to the government, if not perhaps surprising: he rejected the amendment, declaring, 'We do not want a sentence of death with a stay of execution for six years.'[31] In the opposing camp, Childers was aghast at the compromising of the ideal to which he had devoted himself. Asquith, he felt, had given in to the 'Ulster bluff', had inexcusably abandoned the principle of national unity which he held dear, had in fact 'surrendered to Carson'.[32] At the time Childers was returning from a brief trip to Boston with his mother-in-law, and received the news on board ship. 'I was off Queenstown in a Cunarder,' he later wrote, 'and my heart sank really deep for the first time.' In London, at Liberal headquarters he asked for his name to be expunged from the list of candidates immediately. His days as a potential Liberal MP were over.

The situation was now fast approaching crisis. In the nature of

Parliamentary procedure, that Ulster 'morning' was now only six months hence. Some 58 officers stationed at the Curragh, in Kildare, in Ireland, no doubt incited by Bonar Law, took it into their heads to threaten resignation should they be ordered North – the so-called 'Curragh Mutiny' of 20 March. Churchill then initiated the movement of naval units from Spain to just off the north coast of Ireland, in an attempt to overawe the Unionists, 'a flamboyant order which Asquith countermanded'.[33] Churchill was also by far the most prominent member of the government to take a firm verbal stance against the Unionists, promising in a speech famous at the time to call Ulster's bluff, 'to go forward together and put these grave matters to the proof'.[34] Then came the Larne gun-running. The Ulster Volunteers, hitherto armed with possibly 6,000 rifles, were on the morning of 25 April provided with a further 30,000, courtesy of the steamers *Mountjoy* and *Millswater*, and under the auspices of Sir William Adair and Major McCalmont, MP. The initial consequence of this was obvious; the consequences of Asquith's failure to convince the Cabinet of the need to arrest McCalmont and Adair were arguably the more explosive, in so far as the implication was either that the British Government acquiesced in the affair, or that they felt powerless to punish its perpetrators. Simultaneously, the sporadic outbreaks of violence between the two sides that had begun in Belfast in 1912 became more serious.

For Childers, Larne and the submission to Carson were the last straw. Since removing his name from the candidates' list he had of course felt free of party-political constraints. Now something like the urge that had driven him to South Africa, the urge for action and adventure, was to drive him quite beyond constitutional political activity. His Home Rule friends both in London and in Ireland had been horrified by the events of that spring. What now, practically, could be done for the cause? Professor MacNeill of the Irish Volunteer movement in the South had made 'We must have rifles' his refrain. In some respects the position had been tenable, while the Ulster Volunteers, before Larne, were obliged like his own troops to drill with wooden dummies, broomsticks and the like; after Larne, a compelling need was felt to redress the balance. What was to be done?

One day a friend of the Childerses paid a visit at Embankment Gardens. She was Mary Spring Rice, daughter of Lord Monteagle of

Foynes – another highly respectable Ascendancy family. Taking off her gloves, she announced her brainwave: a committee should be formed to raise funds to buy arms for the Irish Volunteers.[35] The Childerses at once agreed. Besides them the committee comprised Alice Stopford Green, widow of the distinguished historian Richard Green, Mary Spring Rice's cousin Conor O'Brien, and Roger Casement – all Anglo-Irish Liberal intellectuals of Protestant stock. Joined with them were Darrell Figgis and MacNeill himself. John Redmond, now closely associated with the Volunteer movement, gave the project his blessing, as did the Committee of the Volunteers in Dublin.

The principles agreed, it was then merely a question of practicalities. Rifles might readily be procured abroad, but a boat to transport the booty would also be needed; a private yacht would be both free and unobtrusive. Given his experience, talents and temperament, it seems scarcely surprising that Childers should have volunteered. It was, after all, 'a chance to be useful'. Basil Williams later commented: 'It appeared that the Government was either powerless or unwilling to impose respect of law on Ulster, and that the rest of Ireland, unarmed and comparatively defenceless, might be at the mercy of the [Ulster] Volunteers. At least that is how it appeared to Childers . . . he came to the conclusion that the South should be provided with arms. Having so decided, he naturally chose to take the risk himself.'[36]

11

The Rousing of Mr Gordon

> 'Mr Gordon never attempted to get up till everyone else was at breakfast, except on the rare occasions when he shaved, and his food was kept hot as a matter of course.'
>
> Mary Spring Rice, 1914

I

At first there was no question of using the *Asgard.* Mary Spring Rice owned a fishing smack, the *Santa Cruz*, harboured on the Shannon, close to the family home at Foynes. 'A fine powerful smack – very old but sound enough for sea with certain repairs,'[1] Childers wrote home to Molly in May. But estimates of the cost of such work and uncertainty as to how long it would take to complete made the committee think again. Conor O'Brien had a small yacht, the *Kelpie*, that could be pressed into service. O'Brien was a fine sailor, if of explosive temperament; indeed, in his cousin Mary's view he was 'useless in a crisis'.[2] Childers was of course just the reverse, and it was thought the job might be done using *Asgard* and *Kelpie* together. The committee had raised £1,523 19s 3d; it was thought that the two craft would be just capable of shipping the number of rifles that might be bought for such a sum.

Then the arms had to be obtained. Childers and Darrell Figgis went shopping on the Continent, where their own identities and the ultimate destination of the guns would be easier to obscure. From the Magnus brothers of Hamburg they bought 1,500 elderly but serviceable Mauser rifles, pretending to be Mexicans to allay any suspicions that might

1. Trailing clouds of glory:
Erskine Childers (*right*) and his brother Henry

2. A pleasant seat: Glendalough, County Wicklow

3. Childers as a Trinity undergraduate

4. The *Johannes* and her skipper, Bartels, in 1897; immortalized in *The Riddle of the Sands*

5. Childers aboard *Sunbeam*, *circa* 1902

6. Molly on her wedding day

7. Two Erskines: Childers and his eldest son, *circa* 1912

8. The Volunteers at Howth

9. The 'harbinger of liberty':
Childers aboard *Asgard* at Howth, 26 July 1914

10. On guard: a Thorneycroft coastal motor boat of the type navigated by Childers

11. Cork, 1 November 1920: the funeral of Terence MacSwiney

12. De Valera consults Childers, *en route* to London, July 1921.
Arthur Griffith looks on

13. Churchill on his way to settle the Irish question, October 1921

14. A mission divided: the Irish delegates to the peace treaty at Hans Place, December 1921

15. Brother against brother: civil war in Dublin, July 1922

16. Shades of the prison-house:
an emaciated Childers towards the end of his life

have been aroused by the events at Larne (Mexico was then the scene of some unrest). Needless to say, this subterfuge pricked the conscience of the punctilious Childers, while his accounting for all expenses of the trip – receipts still to be seen in the archives of Trinity College, Dublin today – irritated Figgis, who had conceived for himself a high romantic role in the business. Together they planned that a tug bearing the arms should rendezvous with the two yachts close to the Ruytingen Bank lightship, between the Goodwins and Ostend; the arms would be transhipped, and *Kelpie* and *Asgard* would sail for Ireland. It seemed a fine scheme.

The arrangements made, Childers had to find himself a crew. Molly was acting as secretary to the arms committee, and would accompany her husband as a matter of course, and Mary Spring Rice was too much the inspiration of the affair to be left behind, although she was a novice sailor; but given the distance to be sailed, some rather sturdier assistance was clearly desirable. Childers therefore approached Gordon Shephard, fellow yachtsman and Home-Ruler, now a pilot in the newly formed Royal Flying Corps; and a friend of Shephard's, Colonel Robert Henry Pipon of the Royal Fusiliers. Over lunch in Embankment Gardens towards the end of June 1914 the plan was explained, with due cautions as to secrecy. Shephard, a great admirer of Childers and very much of his own heart, accepted immediately; Pipon thought the scheme absurd.

> Childers asked us both to come and help him on his yacht to meet a German ship off Terschelling where, at sea, cases of arms would be transhipped. He was then going to land them at Howth Bay for the Irish Nationalists to show they could do what the Ulster people had done. He promised us there was no intention of using them other than as a gesture of equality. I refused. I recognised Childers as a crackpot. Something always happens to crackpots. Something always goes wrong . . . Shephard and I knew the Childers[es] well . . . [They had] a little boy of nine whom they – chiefly she – wouldn't allow to be told any word of religion of any sort until he was old enough to decide freely which he considered the best religion . . . Poor little devil! Crackpot, of course. It always comes out somewhere.[3]

No spirit of adventure seems to have inspired the good Colonel; on the other hand, his opinion was not without prescience: as events were to prove, the gun-running scheme was equivalent to dousing a fire with petrol. It may be that the Childerses themselves regarded the scheme in the light of a gesture, but this would have been remarkably naïve. If they saw more in it than this, did they see as far as the logical outcome – the provocation of civil war? The responsibility of this question would have been a heavy burden to encompass, and perhaps Childers' habitual desire for 'action' here got the better of a conscience as a rule unusually refined. Alternatively, he may have supposed – and many would have considered him to be right – that the extremity of the situation justified the action.

Two Donegal fishermen, kept in ignorance of the purpose of *Asgard*'s voyage until the last moment, were co-opted to complete the crew. *Asgard* had been lying at a boatyard at Criccieth on the Welsh coast, having been returned there from Oslo the previous autumn, at the end of the Childers' Baltic voyage, by Shephard himself. Childers inspected her on 21 June, writing to Molly that 'the condition of the yacht was rather dispiriting – very behind-hand and everything done rather slackly'.[4] After a brief trip to Dublin to finalize details of *Asgard*'s reception, he returned to Conway. Here his crew were appearing in dribs and drabs; as a serving officer, Shephard adopted the *nom-de-guerre* 'Mr Gordon'.

After a false start, on 3 July *Asgard* began the voyage that would see her sail into the pages of Irish history.

It began badly. The plan was to rendezvous with O'Brien's *Kelpie* on 6 July at Cowes, some three hundred miles away. As they struggled down the Welsh coast against headwinds and rough seas, it soon became apparent that they would be late, and so at risk of jeopardizing the rendezvous off Terschelling; Childers cut a finger badly and it turned septic; one of the two hands was hit by a piece of tackle and retired to his berth; and everyone except Shephard was seasick. Mary Spring Rice, who had on the whole risen admirably to the challenge, was discouraged by Shephard's remark that 'it wasn't really rough',[5] and Shephard himself demonstrated a firm commitment to getting an adequate amount of rest. Mary's light-hearted account of the voyage, which breathes the amateur enthusiasm of the whole venture, notes on 6 July that 'All efforts to rouse Mr Gordon proved in vain until a tin of golden syrup was got out.'[6]

That day they at last turned across the mouth of the Bristol Channel, and close to St Ives the sun broke through. Shephard was in favour of stopping for lunch, going so far as to plan the dishes he would consume, but Childers insisted on pressing on, and slowly Cornwall and Devon were put behind them. Now the wind quickened and veered, and across Poole Bay to the Needles they managed eight knots, reaching Cowes shortly after one o'clock in the morning of 9 July. Already two days late, they had barely breakfasted when they were hailed by O'Brien, who met them with 'a torrent of abuse'.[7] Accurately bearing out his cousin's predictions, he fell into a paroxysm of complaint. 'If all Cowes and Dublin, not to say the Castle, do not know of our destination, it is a miracle,'[8] wrote Mary.

Awaiting them was a letter from Darrell Figgis, postponing the rendezvous at the Ruytingen lightship until Sunday the 12th. They were therefore able to finalize details with O'Brien, carry out some essential repairs, and both lunch and dine at the Marine Hotel, where Mary so overspent herself as to have to borrow two shillings from 'Mr Gordon'.

Kelpie slipped anchor the following morning, Friday 10 July, *Asgard* in the afternoon. They had a hundred and fifty miles to go. The wind was at first a fresh and contrary easterly, and *Asgard* bucketed along with her topsails set. By Sunday, the day of the rendezvous, the winds were light and changeable, the sun making it a glorious English summer's day. 'We were keeping right inshore,' wrote Mary, 'and I saw Folkestone beach within a stone's throw, full of the "smart set" parading their best clothes in the brilliant sunshine, while on the starboard side lay four or five warships with their bells ringing for Church.'[9] So slow was their pace that they had to forgo stopping at Dover, where a letter might have awaited them, postponing or cancelling the operation. Despite a freshening wind, it was going to be tight. As evening fell a dense haze settled; Shephard busied himself sawing up bunks to make room for the rifles. There was the Goodwin fog signal, then the Sandeltie. Molly, with the best eyesight, peered ahead into the gloom. The lightship! But no *Kelpie*. A fishing smack. Then 'A cry from Molly:

"Conor and the tug! Do you see? A steamer and a yacht mixed up – lying close to one another – now the tug is coming towards us."'"[10]

O'Brien had just finished loading, finding he could fit in only 600 rifles, rather than the 750 he had expected, and not half the ammunition. That left *Asgard*, a 27-tonner, to take all of 25,000 rounds and 900 rifles. For Childers, there could be no question: his one thought was to take everything.[11] There followed hours of hard labour. 'Darkness, lamps, strange faces,' wrote Molly to Alice Stopford Green:

> The swell of the sea making the boat lurch, guns, straw everywhere, unpacking on deck and being handed down and stowed in an endless stream . . . the vaseline on the guns smeared over everything; the bunks and floors of the whole yacht from the sole filled about 2 feet 6 inches high even from side to side . . . A huge ship's oil riding light falling down through the hatch, first on my shoulder and then upside-down on a heap of straw, a flare up, a cry, a quick snatch of rescue – the lamp goes out, thank God, work again, someone drops two guns through, they fall on someone; no room to stand save on guns, guns everywhere. On and on and on.[12]

Asgard was loaded by half-past two in the morning, now drawing eighteen inches more than usual. The Hamburg tug towed her towards Dover. Then, early on the bright Monday morning of 13 July 1914, they were cast off. They were on their own now, committed.

Again the winds were against them as they beat up past Beachy Head, Portland Bill and the Lizard, racing for the rendezvous in Dublin. 'Below decks we sleep, crawl over, sit on, eat on guns,' wrote Molly. 'Guns everywhere, lying everywhere save in odd corners where they stick up on end. They catch us in our knees, odd bolts and butts and barrels transfix us from time to time, but we are all so happy and triumphant, so proud of ourselves that we swear we are comfortable.'[13] After brief but – considering their cargo – frightening encounters with British warships, first off Folkestone and then again off Plymouth, they reached Milford Haven on Sunday the 19th. There was a last-minute panic caused by the departing Shephard. His leave was up, he was due to report back to his base in England, and he did not know whether he would be able to rejoin *Asgard*: he had misplaced not only his hat, but his boots. With a week to reach Howth, *Asgard* could well afford a couple of nights in harbour; but a favourable easterly blew up early on the Monday morning, and this Childers could not miss. Needless to say, no sooner had they put to sea than it dropped, but rose again on Tuesday night. By Wednesday they were in Holyhead, where they brushed off some inquisitive coastguards. They had only the short trip across the Irish Sea before them: they were due in Howth Bay, just to the north of Dublin, on Sunday at midday, and might have rowed across and still made it. Then the wind got up, and showed every sign of remaining so. On Friday they were obliged to set sail; returning to harbour briefly to mend a tear in the mainsail, they plunged again into gale-force winds. Childers was now the only sailor of real experience on board, and on him rested the success of the whole venture. 'It was an awful night,' wrote Mary. 'Erskine stayed on deck the whole time; the waves looked black and terrible and enormous and though everything was reefed one wondered if we should ever get through without something giving way.'[14] But *Asgard* was as well-found as she was well-handled, and by dawn on Saturday the Irish coast was in sight. It was tempting to seek shelter in Dublin's harbour, Kingstown; Childers felt it would be too much of a risk. That whole day and the following night they beat about just north of the city. Daybreak on Sunday revealed a bright, still windy day. At ten o'clock a boat should appear to signal that all was well.

Two hours passed, and still no boat came.

Their contact was a man named Bulmer Hobson. Although Casement had done a certain amount of liaison work between Dublin and London, he and the other Irish Volunteer leaders were too prominent to be involved in the details of such an operation on a day-to-day basis; Hobson, of Ulster extraction and with a wide experience of various strands of the Nationalist movement, ingenious and enthusiastic, was the ideal 'fixer'. Two of the details he stage-managed were very clever, and vital to the success of the whole operation.

The comparatively small number of guns involved meant that their greater worth lay in their propaganda value, so this run must be 'better' than the Unionist run at Larne: the landing would be in daylight, and members of the IVF would collect the guns themselves and march off with them. Hobson accordingly arranged that the Dublin Volunteers should assemble and drill at Howth on the three Sundays immediately preceding the 26th. On the first occasion the police were much in evidence, on the second less so, on the third not at all, having completely lost interest. He also managed to lure the Naval patrol boat HMS *Porpoise* south, by hinting to an 'ancient solicitor . . . not noted for his reticence'[15] that guns were to be run into Wexford. In the matter of the boat he had organized to signal to the *Asgard* he was, however, less fortunate; its passage up from Bray on the far side of Dublin having been rough, the men refused to put to sea again. Gordon Shephard, having reported for duty at the end of his leave, had again absented himself, and managed to reach Howth by half-past ten. He spotted *Asgard* in the middle distance and, horrified by Hobson's failure with the signal boat, tried unavailingly to find a substitute. The situation was becoming serious: Howth was a drying harbour, which *Asgard* could enter and leave for only a few hours before and after high tide; if she did not come in soon, she might be unable to get away once the job was done. Childers aboard the *Asgard* was as aware of this as Shephard on shore – but every bit as aware that to come in without waiting for the signal-boat was to risk sailing straight into a trap. To be caught would mean public exposure at the very least, probably the confiscation of the *Asgard*, almost certainly the end of any hope of a conventional political career. With a courage worthy of his own fictional heroes, at noon he turned to Molly and said, 'I am going to risk it.'[16] With Molly at the helm, *Asgard* headed for the harbour.

From that moment it was forty-five minutes before they berthed. Almost until the last minute, Childers could not be sure of the wisdom of his decision, for the 800-odd Volunteers were hidden from his sight behind the mass of the Howth breakwater: not until *Asgard* rounded the point did the Volunteers, and Shephard, come into view. Professor MacNeill himself was among the group on the quay, as were two other figures who were to play momentous parts in Irish affairs in the coming years, and indeed in what remained of Childers' own story: Arthur Griffith, and Éamon de Valera.

Shephard directed the berthing of the yacht, and within moments the guns were being unloaded. The Volunteers, who had been kept in ignorance of their purpose until the last moment, now broke ranks in their excitement. Childers held up the operation until order had been restored. Then a coastguard cutter was seen approaching; guns were instantly raised by the Volunteers, and the cutter's crew, conceiving caution to be the better part of valour, restricted themselves to firing rockets to alert the somewhat distant HMS *Porpoise*. 'Molly and I and Mr Gordon stood by the mizzen,' Mary Spring Rice wrote, 'and looked at the scene; it seemed like a dream, we had talked of this moment so often during the voyage.'[17] Within half an hour the unloading was completed, and the Volunteers formed up to cheer the yacht out of the harbour. A few days later, *Kelpie*'s cargo found its way to Kilcoole in County Wicklow.

So the job was done, history was made, and *Asgard* might be dubbed, somewhat poetically, the 'harbinger of liberty'.[18] In a sense this was true. In the words of the foremost scholar of the incident, Father X. Martin:

> History may be seen as a pattern of 'movements', but the role of the individual remains of supreme importance for it is the individual who at a crucial moment deflects or thwarts a movement, or carries it forward to victory. Childers, from the moment he accepted Mary Spring Rice's invitation to run the guns to Ireland until he warped the boat beside the pier at Howth, showed mastery of practical detail, persistent courage, and a visionary sense of the ultimate achievement. The guns from Hamburg were to be of greater importance than he could foresee. The foundation of the Irish Volunteers in November 1913, the landing of the guns at Howth and Kilcoole, the rising of 1916, were three steps which led logically but not inevitably one to the other. From the Easter Rising came the Declaration of Independence by Dáil Éireann on 21 January 1919 and the emergence of a separate Irish state in 1922.[19]

Yet the gun-running was not without further incident – relatively minor, but a presage of things to come. On their way back to Dublin the Volunteers were accosted at Clontarf by the police and a battalion of the King's Own Scottish Borderers. Ordered to surrender arms, the leaders argued while the men melted away one by one into the fields with their weapons, saving all but nineteen of the guns. The battalion withdrew towards their barracks in Dublin, followed by a growing, jeering crowd. At Bachelor's Walk on the Liffey quays, the soldiers suddenly took a stand and – without orders – fired randomly into the crowd, killing three and wounding thirty-eight: Howth had become more than a symbolic gesture. The Childerses were certainly shaken by the news when they heard it; but as events at Sarajevo prompted Austria to declare war on Serbia that same day – Tuesday, 28 July – there was dismay enough in the air anyway.

Two days later the gun-runners, to all appearances the same civilized and well-connected couple they had always been, were taking tea at Westminster. 'Erskine and I were sitting on the terrace of the House of Commons, having failed to obtain seats to hear Grey's speech,' wrote Molly. 'We were deeply anxious, and dreading war. After a time of waiting . . . suddenly we heard wild cheering from the House. I said to Erskine "thank God, that means there will not be a war." And Erskine replied, "Darling, when men cheer like that, it means war." '[20]

III

Until almost the end of July 1914, the Commons and the Cabinet had certainly been concerned with war, but with war in Ireland, not in continental Europe.

As the Lords' delaying period on the Home Rule Bill drew to its end, so too did the threat that the Unionists would seize power in Ulster draw nearer. A conference had been called at Buckingham Palace in a final attempt to find a solution before the further eruptions of violence the Larne gun-running seemed to bode. The principle of some form of partition, temporary or otherwise, having been tacitly agreed, the immediate issue was determining the precise area in the North which was to remain under direct Crown rule. Simple enough in the areas in which Protestant Unionists comprised a sizeable majority, it was altogether less so in those with more substantial Catholic and – loosely – Nationalist populations, Tyrone and Fermanagh in particular. At the Palace, it proved impossible to reach any agreement on the two counties. Churchill, at the heart of these talks, was their chronicler. On 21 July, the Foreign Secretary Sir Edward Grey told him privately that he doubted whether a course could be devised acceptable to both the Irish Nationalists and the Ulster Unionists; Churchill commented, 'Of course the contending Irish parties may think it worth a war and from their point of view it may be worth a war, but that is hardly the position for the forty millions who dwell in Great Britain; and their interests must, when all is said and done, be our first care.'[21]

The following day the Cabinet met again, again to discuss Ireland. 'And so, turning this way and that in search of an exit from the deadlock, the Cabinet toiled around the muddy byways of Fermanagh and Tyrone,' wrote an exasperated Churchill.

> One had hoped that the events of April at the Curragh and in Belfast would have shocked British public opinion and formed a unity sufficient to impose a settlement on the Irish factions. Apparently they had been insufficient. Apparently the conflict would be carried one stage further with incalculable consequences on both sides . . . The discussion reached its inconclusive end, and the Cabinet was about to separate when the grave quiet tones of Sir Edward Grey were heard reading a document which had just been brought to him from the Foreign Office. As the reading proceeded it seemed absolutely impossible that any state in the world could accept it, or that any acceptance, however abject, would satisfy the aggressor. The parishes of Fermanagh and Tyrone faded back into the mists and squalls of Ireland, and a strange light began immediately, but by perceptible gradations, to fall and grow upon the map of Europe.

So, in one of his finest passages, did Churchill record how the opening salvoes of the Great War were first heard in England.[22]

IV

The document Sir Edward read to the Cabinet was the ultimatum issued by Austria to Serbia, and as Churchill makes clear, it came as something of a surprise.

There was no question but that events over the previous twenty years had amply demonstrated the gradual erosion of the 'Pax Britannica': indeed, *The Riddle of the Sands* itself had played a part, in emphasizing the fragility of the European balance of power. War had long seemed to be threatening, and in pursuing an ambitious naval building programme and modernizing the army – here again, Childers had played his part – both the major British political parties could be said to have made due practical preparation. Crisis after crisis had more than once brought Europe to the brink of war. Yet whether this current *démarche* constituted a sufficient reason for a general war was another matter. The Austrian ultimatum followed the assassination by a Bosnian revolutionary student of the heir-apparent to the Austro-Hungarian Empire, Archduke Franz Ferdinand, and its far-reaching consequences arose out of the established relationships between the various European powers of the Triple Alliance and the Triple Entente. Germany, usually seen as responsible for the escalation of the crisis, sided with Austria-Hungary; Russia initially with Serbia, ultimately with France. From a British point of view it was all most regrettable but not, strictly, British business. Churchill, as late as 31 July, voiced the widely-held opinion that 'Balkan quarrels are no concern of ours',[23] and Asquith felt similarly. Balkan quarrels became a British concern because of Belgium, sandwiched between France and Germany, whose neutrality Britain had guaranteed in a treaty dating from 1839 – the notorious 'scrap of paper'. Since France's short border with Germany was heavily fortified, the Germans wanted to cross Belgian soil to strike at France along a less well-defended front (they described it as anticipating French activity) – a clear violation of Belgian neutrality. More broadly, there was also to be considered the increasingly close relationship established over the last ten years between England and France, stemming from the Entente of 1904. Did the turn of events justify Britain in enforcing the treaty of 1839, guaranteeing Belgium neutrality and, in effect, declaring war on the country that had become her leading rival for global power – Germany?

At the height of the crisis, in the few days between Childers' return from Howth and the declaration of war, debate was intense. Both the Liberal and the Labour parties were strongly in favour of maintaining a neutral position and, on a purely practical level, so too were half the Cabinet, most vociferously Lloyd George; the same has been said of the City, and of the North of England. Although they obviously could not know of the horror to come, men were nevertheless vividly alive to the responsibility of plunging Britain into war in a Europe now armed to the teeth, war on what would patently be a hitherto unprecedented scale. Childers and the majority of his radical friends took the view that the abandonment of Belgium was a reasonable price to pay to avoid being drawn into what was essentially a continental squabble. Childers being Childers, he was also irritated by the failure to debate the matter appropriately and fully. 'I myself was against our intervention as long as it was an open question,' he wrote a little later. 'In the meantime it is enough to see that the merits of the question are absolutely ignored and red herrings poison the air – improvised pretexts having nothing whatever to do with long-standing causes.'[24]

But there *was* debate, and the turning-point for some came in that following the speech by Sir Edward Grey that Childers had sought to attend. Fired by patriotism, John Redmond made the remarkable proposal that the Irish Volunteers should join forces with their Ulster counterparts to defend Ireland, so releasing tens of thousands of English garrison troops for France; many people found this moving, not least in the Dominions and the United States. For most, it was the German invasion of Belgium in the early hours of 4 August that finally tipped the balance. The violation of Belgium, and the consequent threat to France, conjured up the prospect of 'the subjection of Europe to an Empire better calculated to survive and rule than ever Napoleon's had been'.[25] For the vast majority this was enough, and it is said that when Britain finally declared war, the country was largely united.

For Childers the issue even then was complicated by his activities at Howth, activities that might be – and later were – construed as an effort to dismantle that very country for which he was again about to risk his life. Yet in the August of 1914 a paradox so dramatic did not exist. He still regarded Home Rule within the Empire as a reasonable and desirable ambition for Ireland, his quarrel with the British government at this stage being merely as to the means by which it might be achieved. The Empire in itself remained an institution in which he placed much faith, and he was still prepared, quite literally, to do battle on its behalf. The fact that the technical *casus belli* was the violation of Belgium's neutrality was providential, since it eventually enabled Childers – and many others – to persuade themselves that the conflict was in essence a war fought by Britain on behalf of the independence of small nations; by extension, every reasonable man with an interest in the matter could assume that the war's outcome – doubtless both rapid and favourable – would have satisfactory consequences for Ireland. Thus Childers reconciled his ever-active conscience to war. Yet how far was the Childers of 1914 from the simpler man who declared on the eve of the Boer War, 'Don't you think it would be splendid to do something for one's country?'[26]

On 28 July Austria declared war on Serbia; Russia mobilized. On 2 August Germany reciprocated by declaring war against Russia, on her eastern flank, and on 3 August against France, to the west. On 4 August the British Ambassador in Berlin was instructed to inform the German Chancellor that unless German troops were withdrawn from Belgium's borders by midnight of that day, the two countries would be at war. The deadline passed, and to no one's surprise, Germany declined to bow to Britain's ultimatum. As Sir Edward Grey declared, 'The lamps are going out all over Europe. We shall not see them lit again in our lifetime.'[27] Lloyd George was in Downing Street that evening when Churchill burst in to announce that he had sent signals to units of the Admiralty to begin hostilities against Germany. As the Chancellor commented, 'Winston dashed into the room, radiant, his face bright, his manner keen, one word pouring out after another how he was going to send telegrams to the Mediterranean, the North Sea, and God knows where. You could see he was a really happy man.'[28]

V

Now that war had finally been declared, Childers returned to Dublin. There were a number of loose ends to be tied up with the Volunteers following Howth, such as the inquest into the Bachelor's Walk incident, a proposal that he should write a series of articles on the Irish crisis for the *Chicago Tribune*, and various schemes for repeating the running of guns. Indeed, at this time any number of madcap notions were bubbling up in a chaos that the punctilious Childers found infuriating. To Molly he admitted that he had been sucked into 'arguments with all sorts of people', largely as a consequence of 'their total weakness and utter lack of organisation and money of their own . . . the position is simply pathetic, comic if not tragic.'[29]

Comic in certain aspects it may well have been, but behind the chaos lay matters a good deal more serious than Childers realized. Part of the problem was the double-dealing in the background between the more straightforward Nationalist Volunteers like Eoin MacNeill, in favour of a political solution, and the more impatient hot-headed members of the Irish Republican Brotherhood with whom they were intermingled. In general, this was to have results which some would argue were in themselves sufficiently unfortunate. More specifically, it was unfortunate for Childers that some members of the IRB should have been in the Volunteers' office when a telegram arrived for him from no less a person than the Director of Naval Intelligence. As Andrew Boyle has speculated,[30] this may well have sown the first seeds of the utterly fatuous notion of duplicity in respect of the cause on Childers' part. Why, the IRB may have wondered, was the DNI enquiring after the author of a famous spy novel, who had just spirited guns into Howth?

Why, indeed? Churchill, keen for action as we have seen, had proposed to the Cabinet as early as 9 August the seizing of one of the Dutch Frisian islands, a project his staff deemed impracticable; it was for a scheme such as this, or something similar, that Childers' name had first been mentioned, supposedly by his old friend Edward Marsh, still Churchill's private secretary. The Admiralty began to make enquiries as to his whereabouts (there was in any case a general call for capable men, and Childers was patently one such). The Frisian expert having removed himself from London to Dublin, the DNI eventually tracked him down and requested his return. In the Volunteers' office, 'a hornet's nest of conspiracy',[31] it would have been more surprising if this telegram had *not* been misconstrued. 'Received wire from Admiralty that my offer of service was accepted and I must return at once,' Childers scrawled in his diary of 17 August. 'Took the night boat and arrived in London at 7.30 a.m. Molly met me at the station . . . and with marvellous efficiency had everything packed for me in case of an immediate start. At 10.00 I was at the Admiralty . . . I saw the 4th Sea Lord who sent me to Captain Sueter of the Air Department who told me I was appointed to HMS *Engadine* as Lieutenant in the RNVR, as an ancillary, to provide any assistance I could from my knowledge of the German coast.'[32]

So began Erskine Childers' second war. After due deliberation he had volunteered to serve King and Country in the way he felt he best could, and did so at an age when he might very reasonably have supposed his martial obligations to be over. As Basil Williams wrote, 'he was nearly fifty [*sic*: he was 44] when he entered the service, and for the first two years he was doing exactly work for which men are generally chosen in the very prime of life.'[33] For Childers it was again a 'chance', a chance for adventure and a chance to be useful. And he saw it as a chance, too, if only indirectly, to fight for Ireland.

PART THREE

The Irish Airman

I know that I shall meet my fate
Somewhere among the clouds above;
Those that I fight I do not hate,
Those that I guard I do not love;
My country is Kiltartan Cross,
My countrymen Kiltartan's poor,
No likely end could bring them loss
Or leave them happier than before.
A lonely impulse of delight
Drove to this tumult in the clouds;
I balanced all, brought all to mind,
The years to come seemed waste of breath,
A waste of breath the years behind
In balance with this life, this death.

W. B. Yeats

12
An Incalculable Experiment
1914–1916

'It will be months before the North Sea is safe for yachting.'
Commodore Reginald Tyrwhitt, 1914

I

The war in which Childers was to fight contained all the elements with which we are now only too familiar: the aerial dispensation of death; tanks, poison gas and submarines; casualty figures among the armed forces running into millions; indiscriminate and wholesale attacks on civilian populations. Yet to the bright-eyed generation of 1914 all this was new. Even more pertinent than when he first made it was Churchill's observation that 'Instead of a small number of well-trained professionals championing their country's cause . . . we now have entire populations . . . pitted against one another in brutish mutual extermination.'[1] Childers was very much one of the pioneers of this world of what came later to be described as total war.

Nominally a member of the Royal Naval Volunteer Reserve, at the beginning of the war Childers was in practice attached to the RNAS, or Royal Naval Air Service, the air arm of the navy, and very much in its infancy. Military aviation in England had been tentatively begun by way of balloons and airships well before Bleriot's cross-Channel flight of 1909, but developed apace thereafter. Not unnaturally, it was first regarded as an adjunct to the existing land and sea forces, primarily used to provide intelligence on the disposition of enemy forces; such information being as valuable to Admirals of the Fleet as to generals in the field, in 1911 the navy accordingly arranged for four of its officers to be initiated into the mysteries of flight, at Eastchurch on the Isle of Sheppey. The record of their experience provides a glimpse of the sophistication of aviation at the time:

> Instruction in those days was no easy matter; the machines were pushers; the pilot sat in front with the control on his right hand, the pupil sat huddled behind catching hold of the control by stretching his arm over the instructor's shoulder, and getting occasional jabs in the forearm from the instructors' shoulder, as a hint to let go. Mr Cockburn weighed over fourteen stone, and Captain Gerrard only a little less, so the old fifty-horse-power Gnome engine had all it could do to get the machine off the ground. In straight flight along the aerodrome the height attained was often no more than from twenty to thirty feet; then the machine had to make a turn at that dangerously small elevation, or fly into the trees at the end . . . fortunately the training was completed with only two crashes, neither of them very serious.[2]

Those little machines were something like today's microlights, only less safe.

The Royal Flying Corps was formed in 1912, to act as handmaiden to the army; one of its early recruits was Gordon Shephard. Its naval arm formally became the RNAS in July 1914 and, naturally enough, came under the direction of Churchill at the Admiralty. He took a close interest in the service, himself coined the term seaplane, and was on the point of qualifying as a pilot when his wife forbade him to do so. The love of risk and adventure was indeed a quality he shared with Childers; he later remarked that seaplane service was 'the most dangerous profession a young Englishman can adopt.'[3] In the circumstances, it was perhaps not surprising that at the beginning of hostilities the RNAS was relatively small: in the summer of 1914 Churchill had at his disposal only sixty machines and seven hundred men; Childers was soon to be one among the hundred officers.

HMS *Engadine*, the ship to which he was appointed, was as experimental as aviation itself. Built to carry cross-Channel passenger traffic for the South-Eastern and Chatham Railway, she was small at 650 tons, and at 23 knots not especially fast. Commandeered by the Admiralty at the beginning of the war, she had been hastily converted to an aircraft-carrier by the provision of hangars on her after-decks, in which the three seaplanes she carried could be sheltered, and a crane by which they might be deposited on and retrieved from the sea. As might be supposed, these launching and landing arrangements were in themselves hazardous, and it was 1917 before a successful landing was made directly onto the deck of a ship especially adapted for the purpose. The seaplanes themselves were also primitive. Quite apart from their very limited range and speed, one of their minor drawbacks was an inability to break free of the water when it was either unduly calm or unduly rough. Nor were they very reliable. As Childers was soon noting ironically in his diary, 'Captain D. is understood to have sternly prohibited breaking down. "I do not *want* you to break down," he declared, to the amusement of the pilots who wished he could have known more (1) of the weaknesses of the 160 HP Gnome engine (2) of the amenities of breaking down.'[4]

Childers joined *Engadine* at Chatham on 18 August, and spent a few days settling in to his new life. By the 21st the ship had been coaled, and was setting sail. 'We steamed slowly down the peaceful river,' wrote Childers in his diary, 'which I had not seen since the old *Vixen* days in 1898, full of memories of her, and William [Le Fanu] and the *Mad Agnes* and happy threshes down sea reach and through the swatchway.'[5] Along with two other vessels liberated from the Chatham Railway, *Empress* and *Riviera*, *Engadine* was to join the Harwich destroyer flotilla.

The group's task was to patrol the North Sea, keeping the area south of a line between the Humber and Heligoland free of mine-layers and torpedo craft; it was commanded by Reginald Tyrwhitt, hawk-nosed, keen of eye, and one of the great naval leaders of the war. Tyrwhitt's ships were the first in the Navy to see action, sinking a German mine-layer in the Thames estuary on the day war began. Soon they were to be involved in the action off Heligoland that saw the destruction of three German cruisers, and in 1915 played a vital part in the battle of Dogger Bank. Tyrwhitt's aggressive activities soon came to be engagingly described as 'creating the right atmosphere'.[6] One of his contemporaries recalled the occasion when, on returning to harbour one day and berthing, 'The Commodore was slightly annoyed at our stern persisting in swinging to windward. He does not like nature to defy him!'[7] Here was a man of action after Childers' own heart.

II

Childers' task was to instruct the pilots of *Engadine* and her two sister-ships in the arts of navigation, and soon he was embroiled in a laborious compilation and marking-up of charts such as would have delighted Arthur Davies. A man who preferred to be more rather than less busy, he also volunteered to act as intelligence officer, a task that demanded a comprehensive understanding of codes and signalling practices – then, Morse and semaphore. He was also made ship's censor, and got himself added to the rota of the ship's Officers of the Day:

> This is a function that arises when the ship is in harbour. One has to keep a general eye on all that goes on on the ship, see that the decks are tidy . . . and in the middle of the night make one round of the entire ship. I rather enjoy this pilgrimage through the silent sleeping ship, picking one's way among sleeping forms of men in the lower deck mess-rooms, through the engine room with its 'purring dynamos' and the grim stokehold, along dim alleyways and saloons stacked with coalbags down deep to the magazines, right aft where the propeller shafts run, and right forward to the workshop of the air-mechanics.[8]

From a literary perspective, this is a return to Childers' style at its vivid best, and it is interesting to know that initially the diary was intended for publication; later, he came to feel that he had included too much personal criticism for it to be suitable, and also that it was 'not funny enough, for my heart was too heavy to be funny about the small amount of fun'.[9] Quite apart from the exigencies of war, Childers was desolate at the separation from Molly, as Molly was at being parted from him. Childers later wrote to his wife's sister of this separation, and of how they contrived a semblance of communication. 'I do not know how I stand this parting from Molly, save that by a paradox we are so absolutely one that in a sense we never part, but talk to one another and watch one another and commune night and day, and grip fast the same ideals. The North Star is our only meeting place, in this manner. We both look at it every night.'[10]

Although it might be against regulations, Childers would hardly have been Childers if he had not felt obliged to discover at first hand the difficulties his pilots would face, so he soon seized an opportunity of flying in one of the ship's planes. It was a memorable experience:

> At first I found my observing duties extraordinarily difficult, my glasses being perpetually clouded up with oil splashed from the engine, my neck cricked with the strain of holding my head braced against the hurricane of wind from the propeller, and the deafening noise of the engine. I had no compass, the only one being in the pilot's seat, and I could only take accurate account of the course whenever we made turn-about.[11]

The fragility of the aircraft was underlined a few days later, when the machine in which he was accompanying Lieutenant Gaskell suffered engine failure some twenty miles from the coast. Landing on the sea, they drifted for some hours on that most fragile of platforms. As dusk approached and with no sign of rescue in sight, Childers scribbled a farewell note to Molly. 'You must forgive me if I was wrong to fly. You must trust me that I decided that it was my duty as the only way of making real use of myself . . . it is for our country and we are happy to think that in this great crisis we have tried to do something for the fatherland.'[12] Eventually they were spotted by a Swedish cargo ship, and towed into port.

Despite such disturbing experiences, Childers was stimulated by the novelty of his role, noting that 'the atmosphere on board is one of cheerful optimism. Of course, it would be ridiculous though more accurate to call it pessimism, so sanguine and jovial is the anticipation of certain doom at the hands of the Germans in our jim-crack [*sic*] pleasure boat with its pop-guns and delicate butterfly planes. But indeed no human being can forecast destiny, because the whole enterprise is new in war: an incalculable experiment.'[13]

III

Engadine's first important mission was to try to deal with the problems posed by mines, a threat as indicative as were the seaplanes themselves of the startling technological challenges this war was producing.

Mines had been used in the Baltic as early as 1855, but first to any effect in the Russo-Japanese war of 1904–5. Yet before 1914, the Admiralty was not disposed to take them very seriously. As the official historian noted, 'We despised the mine, we considered it was a weapon that no chivalrous nation should use, and acted accordingly.'[14] This gentlemanly attitude was not shared by the Germans: no sooner had war begun than they laid mines all the way down the east coast. On 6 August the light cruiser *Amphion* stuck one and immediately sank, at the cost of 150 lives. Then a new dreadnought, *Audacious*, met a similar end. This was serious, making it plain that the weapon threatened not merely an occasional loss, but the entire fleet.

Such was the importance of the fleet in 1914 that, as Churchill later graphically remarked, its Admiral was the only man who could lose the war in an afternoon.[15] It would be one thing for the fleet to engage with its German equivalent in a second Trafalgar – quite another for its ships to be picked off one by one – either by mines, or by that other new threat, the submarine. As early as September 1914, the fleet felt itself vulnerable. 'The Grand Fleet was uneasy . . .', Churchill commented. 'Conceive it, the *ne plus ultra*, the one ultimate sanction of our existence, the supreme engine which no one dared brave, whose authority encircled the globe – no longer sure of itself!'[16] Action was required: E. F. B. Charlton[17] was appointed Admiral of Minesweepers. Tyrwhitt was also involved, having described the mining as 'distinctly barbaric' and complained – in those early days when a short war was still anticipated – that 'It will be months before the North Sea is safe for yachting.'[18]

It was in this connection that *Engadine* and her seaplanes were sent north, to locate and destroy as many mines as they could. The ship settled herself close to the mouth of the Tyne, and for some weeks in the early autumn of 1914 it became Childers' task to plot suitable patrol areas for the seaplanes in their new role as mine-seekers. As often as not he flew as an observer himself. 'It is eerie work, this mine-hunting,' he wrote, 'and not much use I should think, in proportion to the work involved to a ship of this size . . . Nevertheless, the work must be done somehow and by someone. This one minefield has wrecked twelve vessels all told, and every day adds to the tale of mine-sown areas and disasters to shipping.'[19]

It was as Childers supposed: Charlton was soon reporting that the seas were too thick with mud and sand for mines to be spotted effectively from the air. The experiment had to be abandoned.

Returning to Harwich, *Engadine* transported a party of seventy naval ratings to Ostend – where Childers had his hair cut – and then went back to Sheerness. A plan to attack Heligoland with the seaplanes was mooted on 11 October, but the following day deemed 'too risky', and *Engadine* was sent instead to the Isle of Wight, to give the planes some bombing practice. With his desire for action, Childers had little complaint to make of this regime. Enormously though he missed Molly, he was beginning to settle into service life, declaring to her mother, 'I am very well and having a fairly interesting time – though alas! the censorship forbids me to tell you a single word that you would be interested to hear! Being shot with volcanic suddenness into the Navy at an hour's notice is a queer experience, but I am beginning to get used to the life and forget I ever had a moustache or tweed suit!'[20]

IV

Nevertheless, this sort of work was by no means what Childers had volunteered for: forays up and down the east coast made little use of his intimate knowledge of the Frisians. There was however a certain poignancy in a rumour he recorded in his diary for 2 November: 'The sensation today is an unofficial report to the effect that thirty steel barges, bullet- and machine-gun proof, have been built in Germany. Is *The Riddle of the Sands* going to come true? Log pontoons and barges filled with cement are also spoken of. Also, the Germans have bought a fleet of powerful tugs in Amsterdam, but the Dutch will not let them leave.'[21] Better yet, a plan had lately been hatched in England which was to return Childers to the setting of his novel.

A few days earlier *Engadine* and her sister-ships had been escorted out of Harwich and across the North Sea to a position not far from Heligoland. From there the German coast was (theoretically, at least) within reach of the seaplanes, and the plan was that they should bomb some zeppelin sheds believed to have been recently built a few miles south of Cuxhaven. The relative merits of lighter- and heavier-than-air machines had yet to be resolved, and the zeppelins and the bombs they might carry were seen as posing a significant threat to England's civilian population. Enthusiastic though Childers invariably was about action of almost any sort, even he had doubts about a scheme apparently planned in some haste. He noted that 'the total distance to be traversed was practically fifty miles direct as the crow flies – great for seaplanes which can never make anything but an approximately correct course.'[22] Nevertheless, he threw himself into the preparation of the airmen's charts, and as usual provided moral support for his young charges. 'I cannot say that the wardroom was very cheerful,' he wrote of the night before the raid. 'Perhaps there was some foreboding of tomorrow . . . However, Ross played after dinner and we sang songs and did our best to be gay.'[23]

On this occasion his concern was misplaced, as various mechanical mishaps with the seaplanes led to the cancellation of the raid in the early hours; soon *Engadine* was back in port. It was decided to repeat the exercise, but with the benefit of rather more careful planning, and with an interesting change of purpose. Intelligence reports had indicated a build-up of German battleships in the Weser and Elbe estuaries. Churchill accordingly wrote to Jellicoe, then Commander-in-Chief of the Grand Fleet, suggesting that 'the aerial attack on the Cuxhaven sheds, which we had previously thought desirable in itself, might easily bring on a considerable action in which your battle-cruisers and the Grand Fleet might take part without undue risk . . .'[24] With this in mind a larger operation was planned, involving the Grand Fleet as Churchill had proposed, the intention being to lure the Germans into what might prove a decisive naval battle. On 18 November Childers wrote of his idea 'to show clearly every sea-mark that could be sighted and identified by the seaplanes *en route* to their objective with a very wide margin for error on each side . . .';[25] three weeks later the old complaint resurfaces, of 'how difficult it is to get at the most recent details of marks etc.' Frantic work followed, and on 18 December Childers noted, 'A cypher message from the Admiralty warns us that Y plan (Cuxhaven sheds) will take place when the weather improves.' On 23 December, 'The plot thickens. Two telegrams in succession from the Admiralty. Are we ready? And are we ready for Y? Reply yes. A little after 3 p.m. definite order came.'

An attack which would for the very first time involve a combination of air, submarine and surface vessels was finally 'on'. Known subsequently as the Cuxhaven Raid, it is now regarded as having been the prototype of modern naval warfare.

It was Childers' task to give the pilots a final briefing on how they were to reach Cuxhaven. Warming to the subject he knew so well, Childers gave a fine exposition; in the middle of it, one of the pilots, Flight Commander Kilner, declared, 'Childers, you ought to be flying with us.' The slight, greying, bespectacled figure in his forty-fifth year replied, 'I am longing to do so, and have asked to, but I understand no passengers are allowed.' At the end of the briefing Kilner said, 'I have a 200 HP Canton Short which will carry both of us with ease. Get leave from your skipper and come with me.'[26] The pair were to lead the raid.

In a personal echo of the human touch that had added so much to *The Riddle of the Sands*, Childers overslept the following morning, Christmas Day 1914:

> I began the day badly, waking with a guilty start at 6.00 a.m., an hour and a half late. I shall never forget my horror and despair. The quartermaster was abject. He had forgotten to call me before – on this of all days . . . I leapt into my boots, trousers and jackets, tumbled all my gear, lying ready laid out, into my bag, donned helmet and goggles, seized charts and rushed to the upper deck . . . The dinghy was lowered. The sea was calm under a heavy swell. *Engadine* towered above my cockle-shell. The dark shapes of *Riviera* and *Empress* could be seen not far away . . . and at intervals on the surrounding sea the dim, spidery forms of planes at rest, expanding their wings and preparing for the flight . . . I strained my eyes for Kilner. The hoarse hum of an engine was heard in the direction of *Empress*. 'Row like blazes,' I shouted to my men and out we went to meet the plane . . . 'Is that you, Kilner?' I called. 'Is that you, Childers?' was the reply. We sculled up to the port-side float and I jumped on to it saying, 'Happy Christmas'.[27]

They might have been Davies and Carruthers.

At first, all went well. The task-force was then some twelve miles north of Heligoland, the Grand Fleet in the middle of the North Sea. Six of the eight planes succeeded in taking off, and set course for the coast. The day was fine and clear, and soon Childers spotted the 'grim grey cliff' of Heligoland. As they neared the coast, Childers asked Kilner to fly lower to pick up two important landmarks; having done so, they turned for Cuxhaven, when visibility began to fail as they ran into frost-fog. One of the planes had already ditched, and the little squadron had been spotted from the shore; the carriers, steaming to a fresh rendezvous point with the planes some twenty miles north of Norderney, were under attack from four German aircraft and two zeppelins; and just as Kilner and Childers approached Cuxhaven, their engine began to fail. 'In any ordinary light we should, by this time, have easily sighted the sheds,' wrote Childers. 'We now circled for a bit searching for a clue, but then Kilner turned south-west . . . Engine trouble rendered it imperative to return to open water.'[28] The remainder of the squadron similarly failed to locate the sheds – the very existence of which Childers now began to doubt. Their engine failure was only intermittent, and as they returned to the carrier they spotted in the Schillig roads[29] 'a quite considerable fraction of the German fleet', and were briefly under fire. The carriers, meanwhile, had beaten off their attackers, and indeed scored a hit that eventually destroyed a zeppelin. By eleven o'clock Kilner and Childers were back in *Engadine*'s wardroom 'for Bovril, sherry and a biscuit, though indeed I was not and I had not been conscious of any hunger.' The historic raid was over.

From a strictly military point of view the operation, as Childers fulminated in his diary, could not be regarded as a success. The ostensible target had been neither located nor destroyed, and only three of the planes returned. Neither had the secret objective of luring the German fleet into action been achieved. It was true that the action was technically interesting, marking, as Childers observed, 'a new era in war, the first regular battle between the ships of the sea and the ships of the air. We are fortunate to have witnessed a remarkable event, which is but a foretaste of a complete revolution in warfare.'[30] This was also the line the Press took, calling it the 'Most Novel Combat of the War of Surprises – zeppelins, seaplanes, submarines and warships engaged.' The Admiralty, too, was pleased with the operation, regarding it as invaluable experience. Childers was later personally thanked for his participation, and was described by Churchill as having displayed 'daring and ardour against the Germans on the Cuxhaven Raid'.[31] The Admiralty also marked Childers' contribution by sending a copy of *The Riddle of the Sands* to every ship in the navy.

January saw two more raids on the German coast planned, and postponed. Then, more happily, came rumour of a new ship, HMS *Ben My Chree*.[32]

V

The advent of this larger and marginally faster craft marked a significant change in Allied war strategy. It was by now apparent that the war would not be over by Christmas, and that in the absence of any decisive sea-battle, the issue would be settled on the Western Front, in France. Here deadlock had already been reached. Following several preliminary battles, the two sides had established themselves in trenches running intermittently from the Swiss Alps to the sea; military commanders on both sides were faced with a form and scale of combat for which they were virtually untrained and to which – it can be seen with the benefit of hindsight – they applied little imagination. As Lloyd George later observed, 'since they were engaged in a new sort of war, the ordinary staff officers had little to their credit except a certain familiarity with out-of-date technique'.[33] The first consequence was one of the great and terrible set-pieces of the war, the Battle of Ypres. While the losses on both sides were modest by comparison with what was to come, by the standards of the time – in British eyes, the Boer War – they were horrifying. 'Are there no alternatives to sending our armies to chew barbed wire in Flanders?' asked Churchill.[34] There were, and in such plans both Childers and Churchill were becoming intimately involved.

Just before he joined *Engadine* in August, Childers had been set the agreeable task of preparing a paper headed 'Seizure of Borkum and Juist', in essence a child of his modest proposal of 1906 for the invasion of Germany by way of her North Sea coast. Noting that these two islands commanded between them the branches of the Ems estuary, Childers' notion was that their seizure should act as a prelude to:

(a) A close blockade of the German North Sea coast.
(b) 'Digging-out' operations by air sea and land against naval and military strongholds.
(c) Invasion on a grand scale.

It was a measure of the esteem in which Childers was held that he should have been asked to write the paper. It was quite a plan, and culminated in a very characteristic request on the part of its author, 'that he may have the honour of being employed, if the service permits, whether in aeroplane work or in any other capacity, if any of the operations sketched in this memorandum are undertaken.'[35] Disappointingly, silence was the official response to the scheme, and no prodding on Childers' part, either official or unofficial, elicited anything further. Yet in reality a good deal was happening, for the plan was under consideration as one of two likely alternatives to the chewing of barbed wire.

The Borkum scheme had existed in the Admiralty files in one form or another from as early as 1907 – a year after Childers' first proposal. As Churchill later wrote, 'In my earliest meetings with Lord Fisher in 1907 he had explained to me that the Admiralty plans at that date in the event of hostilities with Germany were for the seizure as early as possible in the war of the island of Borkum as an advanced base for all our flotillas and inshore squadrons blockading the German river mouths. I was always deeply interested in this view.'[36] Churchill was more than interested; he positively advocated it in a letter to Asquith in December 1914, and went so far as to obtain agreement to it in principle from the War Council in early January 1915. He did, however, accept that it was not without risk. 'Everyone . . . realized the momentous character and consequences of such an operation. They could hardly have been less than the immediate bringing on of the supreme battle. Within a week at the latest of the island being in our possession, much more probably while the operation of landing was still in progress, the whole German Navy must have come out to defend the Fatherland from this deadly strategic thrust.'[37] It was the level of danger involved that ultimately led the Cabinet and the War Council to look elsewhere, finally to the shores of the Mediterranean and the peninsula of Gallipoli, where the Straits of the Dardanelles act as a narrow gateway to Constantinople. This scheme mooted the city's seizure, as a 'back door' into Germany, a pressure which would also relieve England's allies the Russians, embroiled as they were with the Turks in the Caucasus.

The fact that Borkum and Gallipoli were the two chief alternatives is intriguing. Churchill emphasized that 'Both plans were expressive of the same idea and rested upon the same foundation. Both were based on the conviction that the fronts in France would undergo no decisive change for an indefinite period. Both aimed at turning a hostile front. Both held out a hand to Russia.' In the end, the view of the Cabinet was that in Gallipoli 'the difficulties [were] less baffling, the stakes smaller, the risk less.'[38] In view of the outcome of the campaign in the Dardanelles, it is fascinating to speculate what might have happened had it rather been decided to invade the Frisians in 1915. Would the Allies have been defeated? Or might they have won a rapid victory that would have shortened the war, saved millions of lives, and changed the course of history? Either way, it would have been a curious consequence of that voyage in the *Vixen* so lightly undertaken in 1897.

Early in 1915 the *Ben My Chree*, an Isle of Man steamer, was in Barrow-in-Furness, being readied for the fray. Childers was then sent to supervise the fitting-out of his quarters. He was surprised both by the size of the ship – some 2,500 tons – and by the relatively generous amount of space allotted him for navigational tasks which had hitherto been carried out in circumstances mildly reminiscent of those aboard *Vixen*. By the end of March he had been formally transferred to the new ship at Harwich, where she was engaged in trials. He took the opportunity to install Molly and the children in a nearby Felixstowe hotel. Molly, now increasingly involved in charitable work on behalf of the thousands of Belgian refugees who had flooded into the country, was also beginning to suffer from a chronic intestinal disorder that was to plague her and worry her husband for the rest of the war. Their reunion was therefore only as joyful as these circumstances permitted.

Meanwhile, Tyrwhitt was as busy as ever. In April his flotilla made its first attempt to destroy the wireless commando station at Norddeich from which German zeppelins and U-boats took their bearings. Norddeich was the coastal town opposite the largest of the Frisian islands, Norderney, in the very heart of *The Riddle of the Sands* country. Several further attempts were made while *Ben My Chree* was working up her trials, and she was eventually assigned to the operation in early May. But the results were no better: it was the old problem of seaplanes being unable to take off from choppy waters.[39]

The Second Front had finally opened in February of 1915 with the bombardment by British and French ships of the Turkish forts on the Dardanelles. It was soon discovered that naval batteries were less than effective against their shore-based equivalents, and the Allied forces also lost ships to mines. The original scheme of seizing the Straits by naval force alone had to be abandoned, and by the end of April troops had been landed. A month later, when *Ben My Chree* received her long-awaited orders to sail for the Mediterranean, something of an impasse had been reached. British, New Zealand and Australian troops were pinned down by the Turkish reinforcements that had poured into the peninsula. When *Ben My Chree* arrived on 12 June, Childers noted little improvement. Moreover, as he was himself vividly aware, there was superficially little logic in the presence in the Dardanelles of a man expressly commissioned on the basis of his knowledge of the north German coast. Childers had occasionally holidayed in the western Mediterranean, but was entirely ignorant of its eastern shores, more particularly the Aegean. However, his qualities as an observer, an increasingly expert aerial navigator, and a first-class instructor in both disciplines were recognized, and he was highly regarded both by his captain, Cecil L'Estrange Malone, and by those above him, such as Roger Keyes;[40] Keyes had been in charge of the submarine force in the Cuxhaven Raid, when he was 'particularly impressed'[41] by both L'Estrange Malone and Childers.

The initial task of the carrier seaplanes, working under the chief of the RNAS in the Middle East, Colonel Frederick Sykes, was reconnaissance. The rocky terrain of the peninsula made the disposition of enemy troops and lines of communication difficult to discern, the location of enemy batteries and mines even more so. Based at first in Jero Bay at the south east of Mytilene, the job of *Ben My Chree*'s seaplanes was to act as spotters for the British naval batteries. This kept Childers busy in the early part of the summer. The Turks continuing to prove stubborn in defence, a new initiative was soon required, and on 6 August 20,000 fresh troops were landed at Sulva Bay. The element of surprise was vital to this operation, so the seaplanes were used to provide a diversion by way of a bombing raid on port installations at Sighajik, some twenty miles away; this marked a small step in the progression of air power from a mere adjunct of the traditional forces to a force in its own right. A few days later came another such step. By 1915 the value of the torpedo as used in both submarines and torpedo-boats was acknowledged, and it was clear that the weapon's usefulness would be greatly increased if it could be launched from the far faster platform of an aircraft. On 11 August Childers' star pupil, Charles Edmonds, became the first man to sink a ship by torpedo from the air, his victim a 5,000-ton Turkish steamer.[42]

This was good news, as was the success of the Sulva Bay landing. Unaccountably, this latter success was not exploited to the full, and when Bulgaria declared war on the Allies in September, the whole initiative of the Second Front came under threat. One of the results of the Bulgarian action was the reopening of the railway line from Berlin to Constantinople, which was now used to supply the Turks. Colonel Sykes was therefore ordered to attack a vital railway bridge across the Maritza River. Childers ignored regulations in order to take part in this attack, which involved a round trip of 120 miles – a substantial distance at that time. The raid badly damaged the bridge, but thereafter defeat loomed. It seemed to be impossible to make further progress into the peninsula, leaving evacuation as the only sensible alternative, the wisdom of which was apparently confirmed on a visit from Kitchener in November. With no progress whatsoever having been made in France, evacuation would be a major strategic blow, one against which Churchill fought tooth and nail – but to no avail. Even evacuation was sufficiently hazardous; as the official historian reported, 'It was an operation which no one concerned could contemplate without the gravest of misgiving. Nothing of a scale so great or under conditions so formidable had ever been attempted before.'[43] Yet it proved an almost miraculous success: 90,000 troops and two hundred guns were removed from the beaches without the loss of a single life. In this precursor of the heroic failure of Dunkirk, the role of *Ben My Chree*'s aircraft, successfully carried out, was to prevent the incursion of enemy planes. Childers took part, of course, observing that it 'was melancholy to realise through maps, charts, trench diagrams etc. the prodigious amount of time, money, labour and the like wasted over the attempt to force the Dardanelles.'[44]

There was one very prominent casualty to be added to the more than 200,000 dead claimed by the Gallipoli operation – its prime mover, Churchill, was obliged to resign. After a period as Chancellor of the Duchy of Lancaster, he went off to fight on the Western Front himself, in the Queen's Own Oxfordshire Hussars, accompanied by a portable bathtub and a water-boiler – sensible precautions in that inhospitable area. He was there for six months.

VI

With the evacuation of Gallipoli complete, *Ben My Chree* was ordered to sail for Port Said, where she arrived on 12 January 1916. Childers found the city little to his taste, 'a nondescript place, without character, a discordant medley of buildings of East and West, aping both and satirising both, with its ugly hybrid buildings and crude colours, part American, part Parisian, part Egyptian.'[45] As Port Said was already sufficiently equipped with a French squadron of seaplanes, it was less than clear to Childers what his ship's role there was, never mind his own. However, it soon became apparent that the strategic issue was that of a possible Turkish invasion of what in 1916 was still British-occupied Egypt. Asquith and the War Cabinet took the threat seriously: a quarter of a million men guarded the Suez canal, and the Arab tribes were being induced to revolt against the Turks by a young Anglo-Irishman, T. E. Lawrence. Childers regarded the threat to Egypt as remote, but the remainder of the winter was duly spent reconnoitring the approaches to Egypt using yet another infant technology, that of aerial photography. Initially developed by the French, this had proved its worth on the Western Front as a means of recording the position of forces with unprecedented accuracy, and in Gallipoli such photographs had constituted the only good maps available. Childers was as quick as its most energetic English advocate, Churchill, to recognize its potential, and rapidly became an expert photographer.

On one such mission, on 11 February, Childers and his pilot failed to find the carrier on their return and had to ditch two miles from the coast, with a strong off-shore breeze. The incident brought forth all Childers' customary coolness in trying circumstances: 'We had no anchor and no possibility of making one. We could do nothing in fact but wait for our ship. The machine lay nearly head to sea and seemed fairly comfortable, but the elevators broke almost at once and then the tail crumpled. However, we appeared to be all right and I smoked a cigarette with great enjoyment.'[46] Eventually they were rescued by a fishing boat, but Childers was irritated by the loss of what he was sure were some first-class negatives. Another mission took him over the biblical town of Beersheeba, which fell to the British a year later. Here he noted with characteristic precision that 'the approaches to the town from Gaza are entrenched for many miles out; that three hitherto unreported bridges exist, two of them near to the Gaza road, one of them being broken or uncompleted as well as one of the deviation bridges on a loop at this point, so that traffic is blocked [then . . .] We flew back very low over Gaza and I gazed in rapt admiration at a beautiful mosque and courtyard, showing an exquisite pale green colour, with delicate fretted arches and porches. Wright made, as always, a beautiful landing.'[47]

Although Childers was manifestly good at his job, he was not the only one beginning to wonder whether this was entirely the best way for a man of his temperament, age and talents to be serving his country. His commanding officer, Colonel Sykes, regarded him as a 'brilliant officer and utterly fearless', but also observed that he found it difficult 'to prevent him taking flights out of turn. On two occasions when he crashed into the sea it was found he had no business there at all . . .'[48] The truth was that Childers, though much liked and admired, was too much of an individualist to fit easily into military life. In the circumstances, his recall at this time to England was fortunate – initially for what were nebulously termed 'intelligence duties in the Air Department'.[49] This left Childers not much the wiser, but he assumed, as did his colleagues, that an extension of his existing intelligence task was indicated. As L'Estrange Malone put it on his departure, 'You can help us better than anyone. You know our needs.'[50] On 4 March Childers gave his last lecture, and on the 10th prepared to leave the ship:

> The boat was alongside at ten minutes to twelve. In hurrying round the ship saying goodbye I heard an unusual sound and a 'clear lower deck' for no apparent reason. Now as I came to the gangway I found all the officers drawn up and I shook hands with each, last with Barber . . . The motorboat shoved off . . . and three cheers were given by the whole ship's company standing on the upper deck. It was utterly unexpected and I felt quite overcome. I cheered back and waved my cap. We rounded the bow of a French carrier, and I saw the last of *Ben My Chree*.[51]

It was a gesture expressing the great affection felt for this idiosyncratic man.

Childers might now, not unreasonably, have expected a period of rest and relaxation. He had pitched himself into the war at the shortest notice some seventeen months previously, and had been sufficiently hard at it since to have taxed a man of twenty-six rather than forty-five. He had seen action in two of the main theatres of war, had planned and participated in a number of daring aerial missions, and had been frequently under fire. Above all, he had manifested dedication to the job in hand, superlative skill in a novel form of navigation, and a lion-hearted courage that had won him widespread respect. It was not surprising that, steaming home on a P&O liner, he should record 'No work; no worry; an ecstatic relaxation of mind and body.'[52] Reaching London, he found Molly busy in her work with the Belgians. After a few days' leave, he reported to the Admiralty.

Then, on Easter Monday 1916, only a month after his return, Childers heard the news of the republican rising in Dublin. He was horrified.

13
Neurotics, Dreamers and the Claims of a Republic

Easter 1916

> All changed, changed utterly:
> A terrible beauty is born.
>
> W. B. Yeats

I

Since the outbreak of the war, events in Ireland had as usual followed a tangled course.

A settlement of a sort, probably involving the partition of the North and the granting of Home Rule to the South, had been imminent in August 1914. As Churchill had observed – perhaps, as a sequel, so too had civil war. The outbreak of the European war further complicated the issue because of the extreme nationalist sentiments it naturally evoked, as exemplified by John Redmond's proposal that the Irish Volunteers should join forces with their Northern Protestant counterparts in defending the country to enable Britain to withdraw her troops for use in France. Nothing came of this generous gesture – indeed, it was effectively spurned: the Ulster Volunteers were permitted to form their own regiment, under their own colours and officers; the Irish Volunteers were not – were, indeed, obliged to march under the Union Jack. Moreover, to salt the wound, the immediate political consequence of the war was that the whole question of Home Rule was shelved until continental hostilities should have ended. While this was not particularly irksome so long as a speedy outcome was anticipated, it began to seem less and less satisfactory as the war dragged on. Childers' friend Professor MacNeill likened the Home Rule Bill to a continually post-dated cheque. Then the replacement of the Liberal government, in May 1915, with a coalition that included unreconciled Unionists made it seem more unlikely that the cheque would ever be honoured. Many of the Irish Volunteers had found their way to France to join the fighting there, but those who remained continued to parade, and drill, and generally represent themselves as ready and willing to fight for the Nationalist cause. And soon there loomed conscription. Losses on the Western Front needed constantly to be made good, and the supply of voluntary recruits was fast diminishing. In January 1916 conscription was introduced in Britain, and its extension to Ireland seemed merely a question of time. Needless to say, it aroused the bitterest of feelings across the Irish Sea amongst those opposed to the British presence. Ultimately, indeed, it would prove the spark that would ignite Childers' personal fire.

What might be done about all this was a different matter. In one of the paradoxes of war, high agricultural prices meant that the economic circumstances of the majority of Irishmen were a good deal more satisfactory than they had been in 1914; as a consequence, the electorate stood fairly solidly behind Redmond's National party seeking Home Rule, while support for Sinn Féin and republicanism remained small. Similarly, there was no real enthusiasm for anything so radical as insurrection among those of the Irish Volunteer leaders with whom Childers was familiar, such as Bulmer Hobson and Eoin MacNeill, who was the Volunteers' Chief-of-Staff. They were reasonably content to bide their time. But for the more enthusiastic, committed, perhaps fanatical republicans within the Volunteer movement, this patience would not do. Not caring whether they had general public support, it was their intention to follow in the tradition of the risings of 1641, 1798 and 1848, and declare a republic, believing that the time had never been riper.

The details and the personalities involved are of concern here only in so far as they are germane to Childers' story. Mooted as early as September 1914, the insurrection was actively planned from the end of 1915, its leaders the Volunteers' Padraic Pearse, the veteran republican

Thomas Clarke, and the labour leader James Connolly. Others more or less closely involved included de Valera and Countess Markievicz. The men Childers had most contact with, Hobson and MacNeill, were kept in ignorance of the scheme. Sir Roger Casement (whose common sense Childers had doubted from the first) was sent to canvass the Kaiser's support and to raise an Irish battalion from among prisoners-of-war in Germany; Clan-na-Gael, the Irish republican movement in America, was prevailed upon to provide funds; and elaborate plans were laid for the rising itself, to be led by the Volunteers in all the principal centres in the south. Set initially for Easter Sunday, 23 April, it was subsequently changed to the following day, when the military would, as a matter of course, be amusing themselves at the Fairyhouse Races.

Admirably planned though it might have seemed, in execution the rising proved less satisfactory. The Castle, in the form of the Chief Secretary, Augustine Birrell, knew from various quarters that there was something in the air. One source of information was Casement's compromising correspondence with Childers' friend Alice Stopford Green – broken off by her when the extremity of Casement's intentions became clear, which caused Birrell to observe, 'I do not know where she stands in the hierarchy of treason, but I should put her *low*.'[1] Casement had in any case found it difficult to persuade the Germans to take him seriously, and had recruited only 52 prisoners to the cause. Eventually he induced the Germans to send the steamer *Aud* with 20,000 rifles to the republicans' aid, but nothing by way of trained troops. Supposing that this would all be insufficient, and desperate to postpone what promised to be a disaster, Casement was put ashore on the Kerry coast on 21 April from a German submarine, and immediately captured. On the same day MacNeill got wind of the whole scheme and cancelled all Volunteer activity for the day – activity under cover of which the rising was to take place. The British, better informed than MacNeill, had already arranged for the capture of the *Aud*. The final rising, intended to be undertaken by tens of thousands of ardent republicans countrywide, in the end involved fewer than a thousand, mainly in Dublin itself. Half a dozen strategic positions were seized, and the republic was proclaimed at the main post office in O'Connell Street:

> We declare the right of the people of Ireland to the ownership of Ireland and to the unfettered control of Irish destinies, to be sovereign and indefeasible. The long usurpation of that right by a foreign people and government has not extinguished the right, nor can it ever be extinguished except by the destruction of the Irish people. In every generation the Irish people have asserted their right to national freedom and sovereignty: six times during the past three hundred years they have asserted it in arms. Standing on that fundamental right and again asserting it in arms in the face of the world, we hereby proclaim the Irish Republic as a Sovereign Independent State, and we pledge our lives and the lives of our comrades-in-arms to the cause of its freedom, of its welfare and of its exaltation among the nations.

Matters then became serious. The unarmed Dublin police force could scarcely be used to dislodge the rebels, but troops are not a delicate instrument, and neither was the Fisheries Patrol Boat *Helga*, moved up the Liffey to shell James Connolly's Labour headquarters in Liberty Hall. Some two hundred British troops died in a frontal assault on Mount Street Bridge, and the young Éamon de Valera distinguished himself with one of the republican detachments. The fighting continued intermittently for a week, at the end of which the surviving rebels were smoked out by setting fire to the central buildings they occupied. When all was over, almost two hundred buildings had been gutted, and some thirteen hundred people wounded or killed.

The majority of Dubliners, however, 'were indifferent to the aims of the rebels and the effort that was being made, allegedly on their behalf.'[2]

II

Matters would have been difficult enough if they had ended there, but what followed made infinitely worse a situation which was in some respects still simply absurd. General Maxwell, in charge of the British forces, arranged for the summary court-martial of the ringleaders and – with the exception of Countess Markievicz because she was a woman and de Valera because of his American parentage – had them all shot. While such a response to such a situation was considered less extreme in 1916 than it would be today, and while it is true that Britain's fullest attentions were legitimately directed elsewhere, Asquith's view that 'on the whole . . . there have been fewer blunders than might have been expected with the soldiery for a whole week in exclusive charge'[3] nevertheless seems wide of the mark: as common sense might have suggested to the General, the executions had the effect of animating public feeling. Hitherto remarkably indifferent to the rising in their midst, the whole country was now galvanized by the extremity of the British response. In the weeks that followed sympathies veered rapidly to favour those 'martyred' by the British, in what Childers himself later described as 'a strange psychological reversal of opinion'.[4] The republican movement and Sinn Féin received a stimulus they were not to lose for six years, and Yeats's 'terrible beauty' was born.

Both Childers and Molly were profoundly shocked by these events. Childers, like so many others, had by choice, since August 1914, largely sacrificed personal interests and ambitions to the larger ones of King and Empire. Nevertheless, his thoughts had rarely been far from Ireland, he had actively considered standing as an MP there,[5] and in his absence Molly had herself become something of a lobbyist for the cause. In a way, they must also have felt a degree of responsibility, for the guns and ammunition they had landed at Howth had helped to arm the rising – an outcome which, in their sometimes rather naïve way, this decent, conscientious, highly intelligent couple seem not quite to have conceived of. They were certainly very far from approving of it. Although they were moving gradually, perhaps inevitably, towards republicanism, before the rising they were as yet advocates of little more than the devolution proposed in *The Framework of Home Rule*. Even had he felt some sympathy for republicanism, it is hardly possible that Childers would have supposed an armed insurrection and the declaration of independence a reasonable procedure. 'The rebellion itself was pitiful, in some respects hateful – in calling in Germany,' he wrote dismissively a few weeks after the event. 'But that is not the real point. The typical rebel is often half-crazed and half-starved, a neurotic nourished on dreams. We shoot a decent number – again a venerable convention, probably justified seeing the nature of man, and the wisest then say "Yes, but we must now *do* something", and Asquith goes over to try to set up Home Rule! Terrible paradox. Why wait till now? I pray for success, but have never hoped much . . .'[6]

It was the time of the British naval failure at Jutland, and the second anniversary of the declaration of war was approaching. Night had fallen.

14
The Irish Airman

1916–1918

> 'I feel profoundly that England must in the long run stand or fall by her treatment of Ireland – a supreme test – and in her whole attitude towards the cause of the war and her intervention in it.'
>
> Erskine Childers, 1917

I

Returning to England had its compensations. Separation had been wretched, and with Childers based in England he and Molly could be together again on a fairly regular basis – as indeed they were, for much of the remainder of the war. Similarly, Childers' abilities had been increasingly recognized by his superiors, and they now had in mind for him something which seemed promising professionally.

His old friend Commander Tyrwhitt at Harwich had a new toy. As Childers had already seen in Turkey, the torpedo was becoming a weapon of some versatility, although conventionally it was but an ancillary weapon on large ships, only primary on some smaller ones. The present idea was to build a very small, very high-speed boat more or less around a torpedo, with the idea of it being able to skim *above* the minefields in the Heligoland Bight to attack the German fleet. In the summer of 1915 the Admiralty approached the famous boat-builders John Thorneycroft, who in 1873 had created the very first torpedo-boat. By the beginning of 1916 it had been decided to build twelve experimental 40-foot boats. These had been constructed under conditions of great secrecy at Thorneycroft's works on an island on the Thames, and by the early summer of 1917 the flotilla was established at Harwich, close to the railway pier at Queenborough, under the supervision of Barry Domvile.[1] All that remained was to try them out, and who better to supervise the navigation side than the man originally recruited for his intimate knowledge of the German coast – and who Domvile himself later described as a 'quiet little man with the courage of a lion'?[2]

The whole project is so reminiscent of the role of torpedo boats in the lee of the Frisian Islands as outlined by Childers in *The Riddle of the Sands* that it seems likely he helped to inspire the idea, in one way or another; in a newspaper article entitled 'The Battle in the North Sea', written just after the outbreak of war, Childers had remarked of the Frisians that 'the shoal area described above would be a tempting base and theatre for small torpedo craft.'[3] Having become increasingly frustrated with the role of mere observer in the air, Childers welcomed the prospect of change, and by the end of June he was formally attached to the Coastal Motor Boat (CMB) squadron. It was a very satisfactory arrangement domestically, as preparing the flotilla for action and in particular – the old story – extracting appropriate and accurate charts from the Admiralty would take Childers to London on most days of the week; otherwise Molly could conveniently join her husband at the hotel in Felixstowe she had used before. At the end of August she came down to stay for some weeks with the two boys, now five and eleven, inspiring her husband to lyricism: 'Darling precious, all the world here seems utterly changed with your coming, the people look different, familiar objects strange – all very drab and queer and chill. I have grown so used to having you near and your spirit is so strong.'[4]

Nevertheless, it was not altogether an agreeable summer. On the Western Front, the Battle of the Somme had claimed 19,000 British dead and 57,000 casualties on its first day alone. At home, it was inevitable that Childers should follow Roger Casement's trial with close interest, although he now had little sympathy with Casement himself. 'Casement is to be executed on August 3,' he wrote to Molly at the end of July. 'It is hard to believe that more than half the nation cannot realise that our policy towards Ireland is the reverse of our whole war policy and our whole national ethic. A dogfight or a holy war? A scramble for power, territory or trade, disguised under hypocritical pretences, or a crusade for right?'[5] With the human cost of the war ever more apparent, and the passing of the second anniversary of its outbreak, these were questions that liberals everywhere were asking. Soon would come revolution in Russia, and an armistice between the Bolsheviks and the Germans.

II

The situation in Ireland in the autumn of 1916 was such as might induce gloom in the most reasonable of minds.

The rising had been suppressed with unintelligent ferocity, but Asquith, in his dilatory way, now did what he could to salvage something from the wreckage. He took over from Birrell as Chief Secretary for Ireland, and made a fresh attempt to achieve a settlement based on Home Rule. Lloyd George was asked to open negotiations with the antagonists Carson and Redmond. Under his clever handling, added to the pressure of the circumstances of the rising and the war in Europe, some measure of agreement was achieved: Home Rule for the twenty-six counties of the South should be brought into operation 'as soon as possible', Ulster to remain part of the United Kingdom until after the war, when an Imperial Conference would be held to resolve all outstanding problems. Then, in a move painfully illustrative of the complexities of the Irish issue, this flowering of common sense was crushed by Unionists, not from Ulster but from the South, led by Lord Lansdowne. When Redmond could come to no compromise with Lansdowne, it spelled the end of the initiative, the effective end of his own moderate Nationalist party, and the victory of the extremists and of force.

Childers read great significance into this further failure of British statesmanship in Ireland. Writing to his mother-in-law in the autumn of 1917 he remarked,

> I feel profoundly that England must in the long run stand or fall by her treatment of Ireland – a supreme test – and in her whole attitude towards the causes of the war and her intervention in it. We stand, or ought to stand (I think we do stand) for the liberties and the rights of

> small nations. That being so it was a disaster that Ireland's claim should not have been granted before war broke out. Rebellions alas are the invariable result of a denial of freedom, and rebels half-crazy with long denial are not particular about the moments they choose or the helpers they call . . . it is all hideous and hateful to me but I have to recognise history and human nature and get down to the ultimate responsibility. I can only long – and expect – a wonderful and complete change of heart when the great settlement comes and principles are seen in perspective.[6]

Childers' continuing attachment to Britain, his lofty expectations of her behaviour, and the optimism he felt about the outcome, once European peace was achieved, are all manifest here. They were not unique to him, but part and parcel of conventional liberal thought of the time. Yet all too soon these illusions would be dispelled.

In the meantime, service life was currently proving less satisfactory than Childers had anticipated. On *Engadine* and *Ben My Chree* he had been stimulated by constant action and the opportunity of playing a significant and – when it could be managed – dangerous part in the progress of the war. In theory the motorboats too should have provided all this: in practice, they did not. The early boats were slower than had been anticipated, and seemed to Childers no more reliable than the seaplanes he knew so well. Moreover, there was some ambivalence about using them. Adventure and initiative were the things that captivated Childers' imagination, but by this time caution was the watchword in the war, and he was constantly disappointed by the postponement and cancellation of operations. It was not Tyrwhitt hanging back but the Admiralty, insisting that if the raid in the Schillig Roads was to go ahead, a reconnaissance should be made to ensure there was no boom guarding the fleet. Childers, established at Harwich in an office once an old bathing-hut, had of course been involved in the planning: now he would fly on the reconnaissance. On 29 October the carrier *Vindex* took two seaplanes within reach of the Roads but, as at Cuxhaven, the operation was frustrated by the weather – thick fog inshore prevented either seaplane spotting a boom. Childers and his pilot actually landed inside the harbour to consider the situation, but sadly concluded that nothing further could be done.[7]

Then, by way of a diversion, Childers started looking up old friends and acquaintances from his *Engadine* days, now at the naval air station at Felixstowe. They were soon persuaded to take him on informal reconnaissance flights, and then – doubtless wondering why he had not done so before – he tried flying himself. Rather curiously, though he was in many respects so eminently practical and dexterous, so at home in a boat, he found the skills required beyond him. 'I am rather low today,' he wrote to Molly on 22 November 1916. 'Not been doing well at flying – don't know why. I was getting on so splendidly once. I daren't ask them to give me much more if I don't get on well enough. They have been awfully nice about it.'[8]

So it was that Childers once again began intriguing to get himself moved – either within the service, or without.

On 7 December 1916 Lloyd George had replaced the ageing Asquith as Prime Minister. Looking forward to the end of the war, the new PM was quick to set up various bodies for the promotion of post-war reconstruction; and, decidedly with an eye on American opinion, made a renewed initiative regarding Ireland, which culminated in General Smuts's suggestion of a Convention along the lines that had proved so successful in South Africa in the years immediately after the Boer War, when the South Africans had themselves settled their differences. Both projects seemed promising to Childers. 'This imperial conference sounds interesting – that is if it settles Ireland,' he wrote to Molly at the end of December. 'I wonder if that is what Lloyd George is aiming at. Darling, have you sent that letter to the Reconstruction people? I think you ought to. It is possible that this change of government may have thrown the work – or is in the course of throwing work – into new hands!'[9]

At the same time, it seemed likely that he would be returning to the RNAS in one of two or more jobs, both to do with intelligence. On 1 January 1917 Childers wrote of 'contradicting orders for me but I *think* I shall probably be staying here.'[10] A month later he heard that he was 'definitely' to return to *Engadine*. Two weeks later it was all off. 'Jellicoe quashed my appointment himself – not on personal grounds I don't suppose – but on the ground that no officers are to be taken from this establishment.'[11]

With spring came progress. The original 40-foot motor boats having proved unsatisfactory, Thorneycroft had produced a 55-foot variant, twice as powerful, for the flotilla to test. This was an improvement: in March Childers recorded a successful speed trial at 34 knots, and the expectation was that six craft would be ordered, on the lines of the prototype. Hopes were raised. Abruptly, the flotilla was relocated to Dunkirk, close to the port of Zeebrugge, held by German forces. Night-bombing of the port in the spring of 1917 had forced the German destroyers based there to put to sea by night and anchor off the mole; this had been observed from the air, and a combined attack was planned in which aircraft from Dunkirk were to act in a diversionary capacity while motorboats attacked the destroyers. On 8 April Childers recorded in his diary: 'I was shaving when Jackson came from his bath. I suggested enquiry as to Beckett's enterprise. Result, a signal saying that two destroyers had been torpedoed at Zeebrugge. Our boats all returned safely!! So at last the CMBs have justified their existence! Hurrah!!'[12]

Subsequently it emerged that one of the destroyers had been sunk by submarine action, but the new boats could claim credit for the destruction of G88. Here was something to celebrate, and within twenty-four hours came the news of the major Allied advance on the Western Front at Arras: Childers wrote simply, 'The success at Vimy Ridge seems wonderful.'[13] Vimy was not to prove all that it seemed, but with the American entry into the war later that month, the promise was still of the beginning of the end.

III

At Dunkirk Childers was quartered at the Hôtel Chapeau Rouge. 'I have room 22,' he relates in his diary. 'Small, fairly comfortable, but needs a fire, which is extra. *Pension* is 13 francs, paid by the government for us. A horrible little dark "*fumoir*" and no other sitting room whatever. People very civil. I strolled after supper. What a city of the dead . . . Not a single shutter unbarred. Shops all shut. An unrelieved gloom.'[14] He was saddened to be separated once more from Molly, but at least Dunkirk was likely to provide some opportunities for action. Inevitably, he soon inveigled himself up in an aircraft – a

Sopwith – to get the lie of the land. Then he busied himself preparing charts of the area. Bad weather caused the postponement of two operations, but finally, on 19 April, he enjoyed the briefest of actions off Zeebrugge. He noted, 'So, at last after thirteen months I have been on a war enterprise with the CMBs.'[15]

A couple of weeks later, he reflected that 'the past month has been fairly satisfactory, though we have got only one destroyer to our credit . . . much hard work: no breakdowns at sea and only one casualty. But the enemy is thoroughly aroused, and it will be increasingly difficult for us to obtain results. One thing is certain: the mere fact of obtaining hard action after a year's inactivity has cheered everybody and put an end to many grumblings, though things are not altogether satisfactory yet.'[16] Typically, there is no mention in this little review of the decoration that had been announced on 17 April. 'In recognition of his services with the Royal Naval Air Service for the period January–May 1916', Childers was to be awarded the Distinguished Service Cross. The citation continued: 'During this time he acted as observer in many important air reconnaissances, showing remarkable aptitude for observing and for collating the results of his observing.'[17] It was a just accolade, as was his promotion at the beginning of the year to the rank of Lieutenant-Commander.

As spring turned into summer in 1917, Childers continued to keep a close eye on the various irons he had put in the fire at the turn of the year. As usual, it was a matter of rumour and counter-rumour, order and counter-order. At the end of April he managed to get himself on an RNAS refresher course for observers at Eastchurch, only to have his attendance vetoed at the last moment. A few days later he wrote with confidence that he was to be appointed to the new seaplane carrier *Furious*; by 22 May it transpired that he would not. On 5 July he wrote, 'I am to be transferred to the RNAS under Clark Hall.'[18] The following day it was known that the transfer was still on . . . but not under Clark Hall. Childers remarked, 'Which is worst, the impudence or the inefficiency of the thing, I cannot say.'[19] Finally, he found himself appointed Observer and Intelligence Officer at the seaplane base . . . at Dunkirk, scarcely a mile from his colleagues in the CMBs – a posting that was to last less than three weeks.

* * *

General Smuts's idea for an Imperial Convention on Ireland had been gathering favour as 1917 progressed. Childers had expressed interest as soon as it was mooted, and by the spring his friend Sir Horace Plunkett was campaigning to have him appointed to lead the secretariat that would record the Convention's proceedings. In some respects this would have been just right for Childers: it had of course been his job for fifteen years in the Commons; his expertise in Irish affairs was well known; and he could not be a delegate, having no constituency to represent. It is indicative of his reputation at the time, however, that he was denied the secretaryship, being considered a partisan of the Dominion Home Rule side. Eventually, Sir Horace achieved provisional agreement that he might approach the Admiralty to have Childers seconded to act as secretary and adviser, not to the Convention as a whole, but to those who favoured Home Rule.

On 21 July, as Childers was patrolling off Zeebrugge for submarines, the Convention, sitting for the first time, elected Sir Horace its chairman. The following morning Childers received orders to report immediately to the Admiralty. On 27 July he recorded, 'Saw Sir Graham Greene and Commodore Payne, the Fifth Sea Lord, at the Admiralty, and was told I was to go to Dublin as an assistant secretary to the Convention. To receive my pay as before. To wear civilian dress if I wished. I asked Payne to be sure to send a relief for me . . . I left by 8.45 night mail for Ireland full of hope and joy at the prospect of being useful to Ireland in this crisis.'[20] Characteristic of the man were his insistence that a replacement should be sent to Dunkirk, and his pleasure at the thought of 'being useful'. Gordon Shephard, now a Brigadier-General in the RFC, commented in his diary, 'It is a very good thing that Erskine Childers has got a job to which he is most eminently suited.'[21]

In principle, there was something to be said for the Convention. British initiatives had failed, so surely it was not unreasonable to get the Irish, in their various factional manifestations, to settle the matter themselves? As Lloyd George put it, 'Ireland should try her hand at hammering out an instrument of government for her own people.'[22] A hundred delegates were invited, roughly representing the major political forces as they then stood. Half were Nationalists, a quarter Ulster Unionists, ten Southern Unionists, and there was a sprinkling of others. Crucially, however, Sinn Féin chose not to attend. Five members of the party had been invited, an accurate reflection of their parliamentary constituency; but there had been no general election since the rising and, on the basis of these recent, sweeping by-election victories, the party argued that the figure of five was markedly unrepresentative of their real political importance. Whether this justified their abstention is another matter, particularly in the light of subsequent events. As Childers observed to Molly on 5 July, even before he had become officially involved, the 'Sinn Féin abstention is crippling. I understand their point of view too well to waste time blaming them. In essence they are right and they fail only in the worldly wisdom which is so rare in extremists.'[23] Later events were to lend irony to the last of these words.

Childers' own position on the spectrum of opinion between Redmond's Nationalists and Arthur Griffith's republicans is here implied, and at least in the early days of the Convention he would still have argued for Home Rule. By early August he was established in the home of Diarmid Coffey, whom he had met as one of the crew aboard fellow gun-runner Conor O'Brien's *Kelpie*. Here he also encountered Edward MacLysaght,[24] who had been sent by Sinn Féin, not as a delegate, but as an official observer. To MacLysaght, Childers was 'an Englishman who showed an intelligent and sympathetic interest in Ireland. None of us thought an Irish Republic to be a realistic aim – the British Empire, after all, was at its zenith – and Childers obviously favoured his own solution of Dominion Home Rule.'[25]

In these circumstances the Convention began. It was to last nine months, a very reasonable period for gestation.

IV

Childers was as content that summer and autumn as he had been for several years. He was at long last concentrating on work which he considered of value, and in which his expertise was respected. Equally importantly, Molly had managed to escape from her work with the refugees to bring the two boys out to Dublin. They were often able to visit Glendalough, still presided over by Childers' elderly aunt Agnes and her son Robert Barton; and he even had *Asgard* brought over to the Shannon, so they could sail. It almost seemed possible to forget the war. 'We are having a lovely time together, peaceful and happy after the anxieties and perpetual separation of the last three years, and in touch with work we both love – important work at this great crisis in Anglo-Irish history,' Childers wrote to his mother-in-law on 8 September. 'I can never be grateful enough to Plunkett for applying for my return from the Navy for assisting at the Convention.'[26]

Childers was also taking to the agreeable task of getting to know his children. In the first three years of the war he had seen little of them, at an age at which their personalities were developing fast. Young Erskine was doing well at Gresham's at Holt in Norfolk, an old-established public school that had recommended itself to the Childerses because of the liberal views of its headmaster, G. W. S. Howson. By October, Erskine was back at Holt, but Bobby was still at Glendalough. 'It is lovely to have Molly and Bobby here,' Childers wrote to his sister Constance. 'I have just been digging an underground dwelling with him – with tunnels, chambers, stable etc. I was not thinking of the war but I suppose some instinct made me do war work!'[27]

Meanwhile the affairs of the Convention proceeded. At first all went well. Lloyd George had arranged for the release of the remaining Easter rebels to coincide with its opening. There was an atmosphere of some goodwill. The delegates had accepted Plunkett's proposal to visit parts of Ireland with which they were unfamiliar, and sittings in Cork enabled Belfast Unionists to discover something of the South, as sittings in Belfast informed Southerners about Ulster. Lavish hospitality oiled the wheels of reconciliation. Of one of the dinners at the Vice-Regal Lodge, Lady Diana Manners recorded, 'Forty to dinner – Convention men, Labour ones and peers – red ties, diamond studs and stars. The table and its pleasures a treat – all gold and wine and the choicest of fruit. One conventioner said he had never tasted a peach . . .'[28]

Behind this sufficiently pleasant façade there remained, however, the customary complexity and intransigence of Irish politics, something which Sir Horace himself in his final report to Lloyd George called 'the most complex and anomalous political situation to be found in history – I might almost say in fiction.'[29] Here, as the winter of 1917 approached, in the fine committee room the Convention had secured in Dublin's Trinity College, Childers heard rehearsed *ad infinitum* the old arguments of a society divided by race, religion and class – to say nothing of money. From the beginning it was apparent that Ulster's reluctance to compromise her prosperity within the Union was as important as any more philosophic issue of Liberty. Childers noted in his diary as early as 2 November, 'The crux came on the fiscal question, Ulster refusing any concession to fiscal autonomy, declining to put forward any constructive suggestions or even to state roughly how far they would be willing to go.'[30] Increasingly no stranger himself to dogma and intransigence, he could still reasonably complain to his mother-in-law at the end of that month that 'No spark of high imagination seems to illuminate statesmanship.'[31]

To this disinclination of any of the parties round the table to compromise was added the small matter of Sinn Féin, its failure to participate actively in the Convention, and its activities elsewhere. On the constitutional front, de Valera's by-election victory at East Clare on a Sinn Féin ticket was unfortunate for the Convention, leading as it did to nationwide rejoicing 'unprecedented in the history of Irish political contests'.[32] Simultaneously, the Volunteers were becoming sufficiently active again to merit repression and arrest. When such prisoners struck back by going on hunger-strike, martyrs were soon provided. The funeral in Dublin for the first, Thomas Ashe, on 30 September 1917, conjured up 30,000 or 40,000 mourners. 'Folly of the government inconceivable,' commented Childers. 'Difficulties to convention very great.'[33] In the circumstances it was inevitable that he should find himself increasingly drawn into the argument over Ireland and her affairs, and it was individuals as well as events by which he was influenced.

Childers had always been close to his cousin Robert Barton – closer, in fact, than to his own brother Henry. Robert's father Charles had been very much a surrogate father to him, and when he died Childers had in turn become something of a father-figure to Barton. It was with Barton and Horace Plunkett that he had undertaken the motor-tour of southern Ireland in 1908 that had converted the cousins to the cause of Home Rule – and Barton had now gone rather further. Like Childers he had volunteered on the outbreak of war, and as a lieutenant in

Dublin in 1916 had seen the ferocity with which the Easter rebels were treated; feeling it to be incompatible with the uniform he wore, he sent in his resignation. Childers remarked idly at the time that the only worse thing that might happen would be his conversion to Sinn Féin – and converted he was. Childers, visiting him at Glendalough in the snowy early December of 1917, observed that 'Bob is still a very keen Sinn Féiner.'[34] And the pair had long talks.

V

Over Christmas of 1917 the Convention was in recess, and Childers returned to London, where he looked up old friends, such as Basil Williams. He had persuaded himself to be mildly optimistic. With the American entry into the war, and some signs of progress on the Western Front after the disaster of Passchendaele in the summer, he even seems to have thought the war might be over before the Convention. To his mother-in-law he wrote, on 22 December, 'We are all four together for a longer time since the outbreak of war – Molly is better, children flourishing. It is lovely to be all together for Christmas.' He continued, 'The Convention is not yet over – no agreement reached yet but one is expected in the new year.'[35] Returning to Dublin early in 1918, he remained in good spirits. The Convention seemed to be edging forwards, and he was able again to spend time at Glendalough, where he found his aunt Agnes ageing rapidly. 'I have been frequently to Glan lately,' he wrote to his sister Constance at the end of January. 'I am so happy about Aunt Aggie who seems peaceful and quietly happy. Infinitely softer and more tolerant on most subjects . . . seems to take Home Rule quite naturally, and to regard even "independence" with complete philosophy though detesting Sinn Féin and all its works. Odd!'[36]

Childers was also cheered by President Wilson's famous Fourteen Points, addressed to Congress on 8 January 1918. This public commitment to the principle of self-determination, to the 'undictated development of all peoples',[37] was not surprisingly greeted with enthusiasm by nationalist groups everywhere, not least in Ireland. To the idealist Childers, they became virtually articles of faith. The French leader,

Clemenceau, more pragmatic, restricted himself to remarking that 'The Lord God has only ten.'[38]

In early February, though, it became clear that impasse, so long threatening, had now been reached. It was the old story in new form, Ulster on the one hand, customs duties on the other. As Sir Horace put it, 'the Ulster difficulty the whole world knows'.[39] Nationalists and those inclined further towards republicanism were not going to be satisfied by an arrangement which meant that the most prosperous quarter – Ulster – remained part of Great Britain. On this occasion the focus of this issue was customs duties. To retain the economic integrity of the country, the Nationalists demanded the power to levy customs duties and to have unrestricted fiscal control. This was a point against which the Southern and the Ulster Unionists were united in opposition. As Sir Horace observed, they were 'both apprehensive that a separate system of customs control . . . might impair the authority of the United Kingdom over its external trade policy.'[40] At its simplest, the Unionists feared that trade with Britain – virtually Ireland's sole trading partner – on which such wealth as the country had was based, might be threatened. It was deadlock.

Lloyd George, warned in February by Sir Horace that a breaking-point had been reached, invited a group of the delegates to Downing Street in an attempt to resolve the issue. For Childers, who accompanied Sir Horace, it was altogether a depressing time. It had become known that John Redmond was mortally ill, and although Childers had begun to drift towards more extreme counsels, this was felt by him to be little short of a tragedy. Then there was Gordon Shephard. At the end of January, he had been killed making a routine flying tour of the squadrons under his command. Molly, writing to Lady Shephard, remarked, 'I can't find words to tell you what this will mean to Erskine and myself. If Gordon had been our own son or brother, I don't think the blow could have struck harder.'[41] And finally, with the Convention clearly on its last legs, Childers, with his future to consider, was obliged to write to Commander Tyrwhitt in search of another job. Day-to-day life merely added to the gloom as London, after almost four years of war, began to feel the effects of Germany's successful U-boat campaign. 'Food very scarce, controls and ration cards on meat, sugar, butter and coal,'[42] Childers discovered. The war on the Western

Front was going particularly badly, under a major German assault that marked its worst crisis and inspired Haig's cry that 'with our backs to the wall and believing in the justice of our cause, each one of us must fight to the end.'

With matters at such a pass, it is understandable that Lloyd George should have felt a degree of impatience with the comparatively parochial issue of Ireland, and with the intransigence displayed by the Convention delegates. His cabinet's most pressing problem now touched on Ireland only in the sense that there were urgent demands for the conscription that was to find the 150,000 recruits needed for France to be extended to Ireland. When his appeal to the delegates for concessions on all sides fell on deaf ears, it was clear the Convention was dead, and it finally adjourned on 5 April 1918, issuing no consensus report, merely majority and minority documents. 'Perhaps', declared Plunkett, apparently without intentional irony, 'unanimity was too much to expect.'[43]

A scholar of the conference comments:

> Its convening could be considered a declaration of faith in the principles of nineteenth-century liberalism. Liberals believed that the free exchange of opinion should lead to the triumph of the truth; that if men of goodwill got down together and discussed rationally their political differences, by conversion and compromise they could reach agreement . . . [yet in practice] the convention failed to answer the Irish question. The gaps were too wide, or, to put it another way, the main groups clung too tightly to their prepared positions. Moreover the majority of the convention's members were constitutional nationalists who were rapidly losing the confidence of the sections they were supposed to represent. For the most part responsible, established, middle-aged men, they were plainly and pathetically out of touch with the new nationalism. The war had encouraged the feeling that direct action was the most efficient solvent for political problems. In Ireland the rising of 1916 had kindled widespread admiration for bold action.[44]

Childers' own reactions are also revealing, not least as regards the compulsory conscription about to be forced on Ireland:

> I thought the war might be over before the Convention ended, but subsequent events destroyed this hope and for some time past I have

> roughly estimated October 1919 as the end . . . It is a terrible thing to say but the hopes of Ireland now as for the last 700 years depend on the pressure she can exert on England. The crisis is approaching now and the English Government is characteristically pursuing an insane and criminal course in trying to coerce Ireland even at the moment when it is offering Home Rule . . . Alas, a large part of Ireland is in a grave condition under military law, with opinion stifled; the young men almost hopelessly estranged from Britain and not merely willing but anxious to die – not on French battlefields but in Ireland for Irish liberty.[45]

As a broad analysis of the situation, this was not far wide of the mark, though whether the government's course could appropriately be described as 'insane and criminal' is perhaps a different matter. Childers was far too intelligent and well-informed not to realize that a German victory – at the time, a very real prospect – was likely to mean what his friend George Trevelyan later described as 'the permanent slavery of Europe'.[46] Thoroughly ill-timed though it might be, the extension of conscription to Ireland in an attempt to avert such a catastrophe could be seen as balancing the freedom of Ireland against that of the whole of western Europe. It was significant that Childers considered her young men to be 'anxious to die' for the cause of Irish freedom: the leader of the Easter Rising, Padraic Pearse, had supposed that the republican ideal might be achieved through a baptism of blood; he declared chillingly that 'We may make mistakes in the beginning and shoot the wrong people . . . but bloodshed is a cleansing and satisfying thing and a nation which regards it as the final horror has lost its manhood. There have been many things more horrible than bloodshed; and slavery is one of them.'[47] Childers' diary entry is the first indication that he himself was beginning to find such a position comprehensible.

So the Convention ended. It had failed, and Childers could take no pleasure in either his own role, or the result. Inevitably, perhaps, it had the effect of embroiling him further in the affairs of Ireland, as the inclination grew in him to seek his future there. Later, in a document prepared as a justification of his actions when under threat of execution in 1922, he wrote: 'The collapse of the whole Convention, and the attempt to enforce conscription, convinced me that Home Rule was dead, and that a revolution, founded on the rising of 1916, was inevitable and necessary, and I only waited until the end of the war, when I had faithfully fulfilled my contract with the British, to join in the movement myself.'[48] It must be appreciated, however, that this is a statement which over-simplifies and glosses over the facts, prepared for propaganda purposes by a republican preparing to sacrifice himself – or to be sacrificed – for the cause. He was too committed to Molly to have made such a decision independently, and she was at this time highly ambivalent both about settling in Ireland and about the whole republican movement. Yet it does give a broad outline of the path that Childers was taking.

VI

Technically, throughout his service at the Convention Childers remained attached to the RNAS; coincidentally with the collapse of the Convention came the amalgamation of the naval flying service and the Army's Royal Flying Corps into the Royal Air Force, which was to operate under the auspices of a new department of state, the Air Ministry, with Lord Rothermere at the helm. Hugh Trenchard, then a major-general, was to be Chief-of-Staff.

As has already been noted, and as its earlier organization implied, operations in the air were initially regarded as ancillary to the work of the two other services, helping them do a better job. In reality, already in 1915 air power had become a force to be reckoned with its own right; as Childers' commanding officer in the Mediterranean, Frederick Sykes, remarked in his memoirs, the RNAS operation in the Dardanelles, with its bombing and torpedo work, was essentially independent.[49] The formation of the Royal Air Force indicated political recognition of the validity of arguments put forward by its advocates, that major strategic aims could be achieved through the use of air power. In view of the carnage on the Western Front, the prospect of bombing Germany into submission from the air was highly attractive to the government. General Smuts was a prime mover behind this notion, as he had been of the Irish Convention.[50] An 'epoch-making document,' wrote A. J. P. Taylor ironically of Smuts's paper containing this recommendation. 'There stem from it all the great achievements of our contemporary civilisation: the indiscriminate destruction of cities in World War II; the nuclear bombs dropped on Hiroshima and Nagasaki; and the present preparations for destroying mankind.'[51] Childers' last service to Britain was to be involved in forwarding the plans that were to lead to Bomber Command – and beyond.

For the present, there was other business to be attended to. His aunt, Agnes Barton, was growing increasingly weak, and at the end of April Childers returned to Glendalough to be with her. 'How long she may last no one knows – looks rather stronger than I expected,' he wrote to Molly. 'I gave her your message of tender love and she loved it and was very sweet to me. She whispered, "you have always been like a son to me".'[52] Her death when it came inevitably revived many memories: of his father's death and his mother's removal to the sanatorium; of the migration of the young Childerses to Glendalough to be cared for by Agnes, his mother's sister, and her husband Charles; of his mother's death when he was twelve. 'Aunt Aggie's dying ends a long chapter,' he wrote to Molly a few days later. 'Muddled happiness and sorrow.'[53]

Soon Childers was busy once again. His first move as an officer – now a major – in the new Royal Air Force was a return to Felixstowe, where he was to be the Intelligence Officer at the seaplane base close to the pier from which the CMBs had operated. He found everything 'higgledy-piggledy, a big job to get it in order.'[54] No sooner had he begun to do so than he was caught up in the political in-fighting which soon beset the establishment of the new force. Hugh Trenchard, the first Air Chief-of-Staff and himself very much a man of action in the mould of Churchill or Childers, resigned after a squabble with his political master Lord Rothermere, and was replaced by Frederick Sykes, now a major-general. Well aware of the various strings to his bow, Sykes responded to Childers' letter of congratulation by proposing that he might turn his hand to a history of the new service – or rather, of its component parts. To Childers, however, the diligent scrutiny of the past military activities of others seemed to lack point; convincing Sykes that he would be more profitably employed on something more practical, he won a posting to the new long-range bomber group being established in Bircham Newton, not far from King's Lynn, where he was ordered to report on 4 September. 'Strange arrival,' he wrote to Molly. 'Lost half-built hangars and silent as the grave. No one about. Found an office and a young orderly officer. Didn't even know the name of my CO, much less me. At last found a friendly officer who had *heard* of Mulock (my CO) in France, and after kindly giving me his tent for the night, disappeared on weekend leave.'[55]

Soon things began to drop into place. Trenchard had found himself a berth at the headquarters of the newly-formed Strategic Bombing Command at Château Autigny, near Nancy. Childers, squeezed into a corner of one of the group's giant new four-engined Handley Page bombers, flew out to be briefed by Trenchard. 'Paris looked gorgeous from the air, the Sacré Coeur a great landmark with its fine façade high up Montmartre, while of course the Eiffel Tower could be seen long before any sign of the city was visible.'[56] Childers found Trenchard 'a bluff man, unintellectual I should think, but with great driving power and energy.' Something of a visionary himself, he responded to the same quality in Trenchard, to whom distant Berlin appeared an eminently reasonable target for aerial attack, and who 'seem[ed] to think the machines will rise to 12,000 feet *with bombs*'.[57] Trenchard's plans were for activity in November at the earliest, the first objectives Childers noted being '(a) metropolitan towns and (b) Wilhelmshaven and Kiel' – back to *Riddle of the Sands* territory yet again.

The programme was then hurriedly brought forward. Following the desperate repulsion of the German spring initiative, there were real signs of imminent success in France after four years of stalemate. Trenchard was eager to demonstrate the practicality and merit of the new Air Force, and on 18 October Childers was called to the Air Ministry to be told of 'a special stunt . . . to bomb Berlin with the first two machines. I am to do maps and intelligence here.'[58] Enthusiastic as ever at the prospect of action, Childers was nevertheless shocked by the proposal to fly over neutral Holland *en route* to Berlin. 'To my great regret Mulock and of course the pilots were strongly in favour of it. I hoped Trenchard would turn it down but not so. The answer was a "smile". It is utterly unsportsmanlike and immoral.'[59] Given the more obvious questions of principle raised by aerial bombardment, this was a somewhat quixotic concern.

In the days that followed, Childers busied himself with the familiar task of preparing large-scale maps for the pilots and their navigators, having discovered (to his considerable chagrin, despite his misgivings about the violation of Holland's neutrality) that he himself was not to be permitted to fly on the raid. At last all was ready, and not too soon: orders came through from the Air Ministry that Berlin was to be attacked that same night. On 10 November 1918 Childers conducted a final briefing of the crews, only to learn shortly afterwards that, because of bad weather, what would have been an historic operation had been postponed. History was in the making, nevertheless, for as Childers recorded in his diary, 'The orders were for a start in the afternoon, but at eleven o'clock we were called to fire stations and addressed by the colonel who said the war was over and the armistice signed.'[60]

After four years of turmoil, Childers found it difficult to respond to the occasion. 'I cannot see the war yet whole,' he wrote to Molly. 'I ought to be exultant, I know, yet I am very sober, and hardly dare look at the papers.'[61] The conflict often spoken of as the war to end war was finished, yet among thoughtful people a restraint like that felt by Childers was not uncommon. The western world had changed immeasurably in five years. As John Buchan later observed, 'victory dawned upon a world too weary for jubilation, too weary even for comprehension. The crescendo of the final weeks had dazed the mind. The ordinary man could not grasp the magnitude of a war which had dwarfed all earlier contests, and had depleted the world of life to a greater degree than a century of the old barbarian invasions.'[62] It was the equivalent of a great revolution, and one of its many victims was the old liberal ideal – shared by Childers – of a world increasingly prosperous, peaceful, and civilized. It seemed that ahead now lay challenges as great as those that had been faced in war, or greater. 'I am steeling myself to acquire a new noble and strenuous outlook,' continued Childers, 'and to throw out the tendency to brood.'[63]

PART FOUR

On the Breaking of Nations

'Then came the Great War. Every institution, almost, in the world was strained. Great Empires have been overturned. The whole map of Europe has been changed. The position of countries has been violently altered. The modes of thought of men, the whole outlook of affairs, the grouping of parties, all have encountered violent and tremendous changes in the deluges of the world, but as the deluge subsides and the waters fall short, we see the dreary steeples of Fermanagh and Tyrone emerging once again. The integrity of their quarrel is one of the few institutions that have been unaltered in the cataclysm which has swept the world.'

Winston Churchill

15
Sorcerer's Apprentice

1919–1920

'Propaganda, propaganda, propaganda. All that matters is propaganda.'
Adolf Hitler

I

The saddest irony of all was the influenza epidemic that spread across the world in the autumn and winter of 1918. Sixteen million died in India, more than the total casualties on all sides in the war. In England, something like three-quarters of the population were said to have been affected, and 150,000 died. Childers was nearly one of those victims. When the war ended he was given the interesting task of assessing the effect of Allied bombing in Flanders, which meant a busy six weeks, flying to and from the various sites, and producing one of the earliest studies of the effects of bombing. He seems to have picked up the germ in Belgium, and on returning to London in January 1919 was sufficiently ill to be hospitalized. Then complications set in. 'It really was touch and go,' wrote Molly, 'and the pleurisy very nearly killed him.'[1]

At forty-eight, Childers took a long time to recover, and was eventually sent by his doctors to Glendalough to convalesce. There his strength gradually returned. 'I am very well – nothing left but a slight shortness of breath – no fever, very little cough,' he wrote on 23 March to Molly in London, where she was experiencing the privations of post-war life. 'I am ashamed by the way we live. Cream four or five times a day – with porridge – sweets at lunch and supper – and in tea and coffee. Fresh butter and eggs and wonderful mutton and meat and home-made brown and white bread. It seems wicked to eat it with you not here.'[2] It was natural enough that he should have gone to the old house full of happy memories to recuperate; but his return to Ireland inevitably reopened for him the question of his future involvement in Irish affairs.

In a sense, as Churchill later observed,[3] nothing in Ireland had changed since 1914, and certainly its complex problem remained unsolved. Yet the landscape was scarcely recognizable, politically. In 1914 the majority of the Irish seats in Westminster were held by Nationalists who espoused Home Rule, a mere seven by Sinn Féiners. The general dislocation of the war, the Easter Rising, and the conscription issue had caused a dramatic shift in public opinion, and the general election of November 1918 roughly reversed the position of 1914: Sinn Féin took 73 seats, the Nationalists 6, and the Unionists remained much the same, with 26. This did not represent, however, quite the overwhelming vote for republicanism it might suggest: nearly a third of electors did not vote, 485,000 were cast for Sinn Féin, but a far more substantial minority than the number of seats suggests – 237,000 – voted to retain the links with the Crown. Nevertheless the results had a profound effect, not least because the elected Sinn Féin representatives followed the by now established custom of abstaining from taking up their seats in Westminster; they called instead their own convocation, the Dáil Éireann, or Assembly of Ireland, and adopted the Irish form, TD (*Teachta Dála*, Member of the Dáil), rather than MP. *All* elected members, of whatever party, were invited to attend the Dáil Éireann, but the invitation was ignored.

The first session of the Dáil, held in Dublin on 21 January 1919, was attended by those free to do so; nearly half the TDs were in prison, including the party president, de Valera, and the vice-president, Arthur Griffith. They had been arrested the previous May on the pretext of their involvement in treasonable conspiracy with the Germans – the so-called 'German plot' – and in July the Volunteers, the Gaelic League and various Sinn Féin organizations had been pronounced 'a grave menace' and their meetings declared illegal. Despite the leaders' absence, the Dáil session was important because it reaffirmed the Declaration of Independence of Easter 1916, pledging the assembly and the people 'to make this declaration effective by every means at our command'. Coincidentally, as violence was being threatened, it was manifested that very day, at Soloheadbeg near Tipperary. Here, a section of the Volunteers now known as the Irish Republican Army seized some gelignite being transported to a local quarry, and shot dead its police guard: the two constables – MacDonnell and O'Connell – were Irish members of the Royal Irish Constabulary. In a sad presage of the bitter 'Troubles' to come, Irishmen had begun to kill Irishmen, in order to free themselves of the English.

Notwithstanding the spasmodic violence that followed this incident, Sinn Féiners held in English and Irish gaols had been released before the Dáil's second session opened, on 1 April 1919. Here the TDs determined to pursue Arthur Griffith's policy of establishing a parallel and rival government to that of Dublin Castle, with its own system of administration, including courts of law. De Valera, who had escaped from Lincoln gaol in February, was elected President of the Dáil; subsequent Cabinet nominations included Arthur Griffith, Michael Collins, Eoin MacNeill, and Childers' cousin Robert Barton. Thus it was that Childers, convalescing in Glendalough in the spring of 1919, found himself in the midst of Irish affairs.

Whether or not he should become closely involved was scarcely a new question; he and Molly had been discussing it as early as 1912. Now it seemed his inclination was to move from London to Dublin, and there devote his still considerable energies to 'the cause'. In many ways this was not difficult to understand. From 10 March he was formally demobilized, and though never one to be at a loose end, might thereafter technically be construed as unemployed. He felt a need to be engaged in some work that both he and Molly thought to be of high moral worth – and this at a time when, if there had been Irish crises before, it was apparent that this was the greatest yet. The prize of freedom was, conceivably, within Ireland's grasp. What better time could there be to help her? So long as a constitutional solution arrived at in Westminster still seemed possible, and so long as he was 'under contract' to the Westminster government, it was reasonable to stay in London. When it began to seem increasingly likely that events in Ireland, not in England, would dictate the country's fate, then it was there, in the land of his mother's birth, that Childers wished to be; for surely it was there that he might best take action, and seize another 'chance'.

Urged on by Molly, at the end of March Childers consulted his friends George Russell and Alice Stopford Green: 'I talked of the question of living in Ireland or England with AE and Mrs Green, of course coupling us together as one problem (how could I dream of doing otherwise). They both feel inclined to think that Ireland would be best on the ground that steady creative thoughtful work is required – utterly lacking here owing to the political violence . . .'[4] Molly was as unenthusiastic as she had been in 1912, and for the same reasons. In her mind she compared their close circle of London friends with those they might find in Dublin, and replied: 'On the subject of natural freedom we should be close comrades with them . . . [but] . . . nationalism being solved, . . . should we be content, at ease, and comrades with them in other ways? This is only one of many things which need to be studied by both of us together. I want to be *convinced*. You would not want me to make such a change until you had shown me your reasons.'[5] She was equally firm in questioning where her husband, whose background, education, temperament and manner were decidedly more English than he later portrayed them, might *best* work for the 'cause'. Playing a Trevelyan against a Stopford Green, she next wrote: 'This decision should and must be made in the light of cold reason and a wish to be efficient. I still think it possible that you may find that you can do far more good here than in Ireland. I discussed it with George Trevelyan and he said . . . you could be more helpful to the cause here without doubt . . .'[6] She was particularly quick to pick up on Childers' comment that living in Ireland would be 'far the less easy course in every way and it is for this reason that I think I feel impelled towards it.' She had long ago detected his inclination towards self-sacrifice, and noted in particular 'how untrustworthy it has proved'. Continuing, she reminded him how 'This very thing very nearly made our marriage impossible. You thought the harder way the right way and that you must deny yourself me.'[7]

Years later Molly was to comment that the period was one of

'tremendous mental and spiritual development for us both as we gradually became ready to give ourselves to Ireland.'[8]

Meanwhile, Childers was nevertheless involving himself, willy-nilly, in the cause.

His first step was to rebuild his contacts with the leaders of the republican movement, first established at Howth, revived at the time of the feeble Convention in the winter of 1917–18, but subsequently fallen again into abeyance. Despite its proscription, Sinn Féin managed to keep an office open in central Dublin, and here Childers presented himself in March, armed with a note from Robert Barton reminding Sinn Féin of his *bona fides*. A young journalist working in the propaganda section, Robert Brennan, later described Childers as having made the following declaration: 'I want to tell you straightaway that after a good deal of thought, I have decided that Sinn Féin is the right policy for Ireland. I have come over to give a hand any way I can help.'[9] It is open to question whether these were quite the words Childers used, and whether they are an accurate reflection of his political stance at the time; there is, however, no doubting the enthusiasm they convey, or the suggestion that Childers should help with propaganda.

Though not the force it is today, by 1919 public opinion was something of recognized importance in political affairs, not least in the matter of Ireland. Much as Westminster might wish it otherwise, Britain's handling of the Irish question was being closely observed elsewhere in the Empire. It was inevitable that the war should have subtly altered the relationship between Britain, at the hub of Empire, and her galaxy of dependent states, several of which might have been considered – or might justifiably consider themselves – as having in a sense 'come of age' by virtue of their contribution to the common cause. A number of dominions had achieved autonomy, albeit under a common Crown, and autonomy at least was certainly the aspiration of countries such as India and Egypt. To them, Ireland was the weathervane, and merited the closest observation. Events in Ireland were also of interest in the United States, drawn into the European war in 1917 and inevitably to be involved in the Peace Conference in Paris. American sympathy for a country trying to follow the same republican course as she had chosen in 1776 was strong, and there were also the matters of the substantial war debt of Britain to America, and the American-Irish vote. International press coverage of the Irish situation had hitherto had what might be described as an Anglo-Saxon bias, representing Ireland, in Childers' phrase, 'as a stab-in-the-back rebellious province which didn't help in the war';[10] the other side of the story was barely and rarely told. Sinn Féin had therefore been quick to establish a propaganda section, and concerted efforts to influence public opinion were increasingly made by both sides.

The first Sinn Féin Director of Propaganda, Lawrence Ginnell, had to be replaced almost immediately, following his arrest in May 1915, and the operation was placed under the control of Desmond Fitzgerald.[11] Fitzgerald, one of the founders of the Imagist group of poets in pre-war London and a man of intelligence and wide learning, initially found Childers sympathetic; through him, Childers was introduced to the various republican leaders, in particular Arthur Griffith. The Sinn Féin vice-president welcomed Childers' approach, and it was tentatively agreed that he should play some part in helping with propaganda, though quite *what* part remained uncertain. For Childers it was undoubtedly a 'chance to be useful': as Griffith remarked to Brennan, Childers had 'the ear of a big section of the English people'.[12] And, for the moment at least, the integrity and reputation of Major Childers, DSC, were unimpeachable.

Perhaps to demonstrate the seriousness of his commitment, Childers also involved himself in a peculiar legal affair. In February the Royal Irish Constabulary had arrested the witness to what appeared to be a republican armed robbery, and were holding him incommunicado – a reasonable course of action, compromised by the fact that the witness – Connors – was a boy of eleven. Sinn Féin felt it inappropriate to appear directly in the case, so Childers, ostensibly acting on his own initiative, instructed lawyers to seek a writ of *habeas corpus*. This was secured in early April, and his temporary success was noted by Dublin Castle, Sinn Féin, and his friends in England: his new colours had been run up the mast. Success turned to misfortune, however, as Childers' subsequent attempt to bring a civil action for damages proved less satisfactory. 'I fear there may be difficulties,' he noted in his diary. 'The boy is not all there.'[13]

II

At the end of April Childers returned to London, his health largely but not entirely recovered, to busy himself in lobbying on the Irish question. Articles appeared under his name in various newspapers, and MPs among his friends were carefully informed of the Connors case, and of conditions in Ireland generally. These were deteriorating. The incident at Soloheadbeg heralded a concentrated republican campaign directed chiefly against the most obvious manifestation of British authority, the RIC, and led by the youthful and charismatic Michael Collins,[14] once a post-office clerk in London. The RIC, seen as traitors, were a handy and accessible source of the guns and ammunition with which the republicans were at this stage still very poorly supplied. This guerrilla war was waged without the specific authority of the Dáil, and therefore lacked even a pretence of political respectability; Childers was curiously silent on these activities in his diaries and correspondence. However, enthusiast as he was for some form of Irish independence, it is difficult to believe that either he or Molly, at least in the spring of 1919, would or could have condoned this approach. Neither, it must be presumed, did they know of – or if they knew of them, condone – the more imaginative schemes being hatched, to blow up or individually assassinate the British Cabinet.[15]

Rather was Childers, at this stage, looking towards the Paris Peace Conference, which in marking the legal end of the war would also lead – theoretically – to the implementation of the hitherto suspended Home Rule legislation for Ireland. Childers was not alone in pinning hope on this long-deferred objective. He and many others of liberal persuasion had believed that in the last analysis they were fighting for the freedom of small nations; having roundly defeated the enemies of such freedom, the victors would naturally grant and guarantee that self-determination for the principle of which they had fought and for which so many had died. The nightmare was over; it was time to begin anew.

At the end of May Childers was summoned to Dublin, where he was interviewed by Collins, Griffith and Desmond Fitzgerald, and asked to go to Paris to publicize the Sinn Féin case. In January the

Dáil had appointed de Valera and Griffith as two of its three delegates, but because the party was proscribed, not all the efforts of the Sinn Féin lobbyists Sean O'Kelly and Gavan Duffy had been able to secure their formal admission to the Peace Conference. O'Kelly and Duffy were left to do what they could to rally support for the republican cause but, though talented and energetic, they were essentially politicians, with little experience as publicists and few of the press and Establishment contacts Childers could boast. There was thus much sense in adding him to the party, and he was overjoyed by his inclusion.

By the beginning of July Childers was settled in Paris, where he found the French, conforming to national stereotype, were taking advantage of the opportunities offered by the Conference and charging the Irish party at the Grand Hotel 'the huge price of 35 francs a day'.[16] He quickly established congenial relations with O'Kelly and Duffy; the latter had been a defending counsel in Casement's trial. All three were much entertained by the Irish-American delegate whom, Childers wrote, 'between ourselves we called the Connecticut Hoo-Hoo or the Bellamy Buffalo, from the names of the clubs he belonged to whose cards he generously offered for our admiration.'[17]

The Conference itself could not have been construed as a success for the Irish. The approach agreed upon was to demonstrate that 'the whole solidity of the American–French–English alliance depended on the settlement of the Irish question by self-determination', but while on the face of it there was sense in linking what was (in international terms) the small problem of Irish independence with the larger one of the strength or weakness of that alliance, in practice Childers found it was like pushing water uphill.

The problems were various, beginning with the delegation's unofficial status, Ireland's 'independence' having received no international recognition. Secondly, amid the manifold complexities of agreeing terms for peace with Germany, Austria, Hungary, Bulgaria and Turkey, and adjusting to a relationship with what was now an entirely 'new' ally, Soviet Russia, it was difficult to persuade anyone to devote much time to the Irish case. Thirdly, there was the eminence of Great Britain's position to contend with: having just defeated her most dangerous rival, Britain was firmly established in Paris as one of the Great Powers. And the Great Powers, embodied in the triumvirate of President Wilson, Clemenceau of France, and Lloyd George, now settled themselves to dividing the spoils, rather in the manner the Four Powers at the Congress of Vienna. Any little difficulties in Britannia's back yard were surely no one's business but her own. Childers, whose main responsibility was to lobby politicians and journalists, should not have been surprised to find them 'nervous as old women about offending England'.[18] He suspected counter-propaganda on the part of the British: a letter to Molly written at the end of July recounts one of his meetings. 'Then to Janvrain of *Débats*. Talked from four till 5.45, exhausted, as he knows no English and it is a great strain to talk and *think* in French for too long. Used every argument in my power. Useless I think. He is old and set and nervous and ignorant of the subject. Someone – the hidden hand I detect – has been poisoning his mind with mares' nests about bitter Irish hostility to France on account of anti-clerical policy . . .'[19] The only real progress made was with *Le Temps*, which in August came out in favour of a British withdrawal from Ireland – an achievement Duffy did not hesitate to credit to Childers.[20]

Naturally the delegates were particularly interested in lobbying the Big Three themselves. On two occasions Childers got as far as a meeting with someone from Clemenceau's office, but his attempts to see the man himself were fobbed off with the promise of a written response – 'a reply which of course never came'.[21] Then there was Wilson, who in the Fourteen Points had so publicly affirmed his belief in the principle of self-determination for nations small as well as large. The President proved as elusive as Clemenceau, remarking of his refusal to meet the Irish:

> You have touched the great metaphysical tragedy of today. When I gave utterance to those words I said them without the knowledge that nationalities existed which are coming to us day after day. Of course, Ireland's case, from the point of view of population, from the point of view of the struggle it has made, from the point of [view of the] interest it has excited . . . is the outstanding case of a small nationality. You do not know . . . the anxieties I have experienced as a result of these many millions of people having their hopes raised.[22]

Like Childers himself, Wilson was experiencing difficulty in reconciling high principle with the practical and political realities of the fallen world.

Childers would scarcely have been human if he had not occasionally reflected on the wisdom of the cause he was following. As he remarked to Molly (when asking her to send him out half a dozen copies of *The Riddle of the Sands*), there was a certain paradox in his discovery that in Paris the novel was his 'only passport – ironical as it seems'.[23] Perhaps, too, he recalled a letter written to Molly some two years previously. He had been re-reading Dickens, and found himself sufficiently impressed to declare, 'He must I think have effected more by his books than the noblest politician and legislator.'[24] Childers' own creative gifts were not those of Dickens, nor were his ambitions confined to literature. Yet he must again have wondered whether he was using his talents appropriately.

In the circumstances there seemed little point in remaining in Paris; Childers returned to London in early August. It is difficult to see how anything definable as 'success' would have been possible of achievement, and in terms of concrete results, the envoys must be said to have failed. On the other hand, Childers had established a number of contacts among the international press community who were to prove useful over the next two years; Churchill later noted that those present in Paris comprised 'the most able, competent writers in every country, representing the most powerful newspapers and the largest circulations.'[25]

He had also very clearly signalled to Sinn Féin his enthusiasm for the cause.

He may have signalled enthusiasm, but his real feelings towards the republican movement seem to have been rather more ambivalent at this time than his actions suggested. Indeed, he seems to have been uncertain about his support for the objective of total independence from the Crown, and – presumably – about the means by which that might be achieved. In a letter to Molly from Paris just before his return he explored these ideas, and the particular strategies it might be wise to adopt: 'As to compromise I foresee no vital difficulty. To *advance* it, to *propose* it would be fatal – Sinn Féin is the only vital force in the whole thing, and even the DRs [Dominion (Home) Rulers] who depend on Sinn Féiners to go to prison for their (? our) panacea would drop dead. But to *accept* it, under compulsion, is another matter. Of course they would have to accept that DR, acquiesce in it, even perhaps a modified DR. Is there anything wrong about this attitude, my darling?'[26] This seems to cast Childers in the somewhat unusual role of pragmatist. He sees Sinn Féin – his efforts on its behalf – not as a means to the end of the stated Sinn Féin objective of a glorious republic, but as a means by which the more realistic goal of Dominion Home Rule might be achieved. As an intelligent propagandist, however, he realized that public acknowledgement of the limited objective would be catastrophic.

Soon these views would change. He was, of course, still embroiled in the Peace Conference when these words were written, and the full substance of its settlements – or the absence of any – had yet to become entirely clear. Certainly his opinions were affected by the Irish failure there, although Williams seems to overstate the case when he comments that Childers 'was bitterly disappointed by the results of the peace negotiations of Paris, where he vainly tried to get Ireland's case heard by the assembled plenipotentiaries.'[27] Either way, by the summer of 1919, with or without Childers, there were a sufficient number of people in Ireland whose patience with the sonorities of statesmen had now run out. These were people who became determined to seize what they were clearly not going to be given.

III

Childers spent the six weeks following his return to England in Worthing. The little seaside town was gradually recovering from the effects of war, and much the same might be said of Childers. It was the first real holiday he had had with his family since 1914, and he relished the company of Molly and the two boys. The young Erskine was then fourteen, Bobby eight, both bright, lively children, with their father's slight frame, and their mother's auburn hair. Childers bathed and walked over the downs with the boys, and escorted Molly when she drove out in a pony and trap. 'A happy and healthful time,'[28] he recorded. Molly had by now become to some extent reconciled to the notion of moving to Ireland, although her enthusiasm was still some way from Childers' own. As idealistic as her husband she was nevertheless, apart from any other consideration, understandably doubtful of the wisdom of moving closer to ever-increasing violence. Yet in her devotion to Childers she observed his growing enthusiasm for the cause: despite the frustrations of Paris, her husband's heart was plainly set. It seemed only right that they should be prepared, together, as she said, 'to give ourselves to Ireland'.[29]

At the end of September Childers returned to Dublin, leaving Molly in Chelsea to set about tidying up their affairs. He had already prepared written reports on Paris for Sinn Féin, but also wanted to report in person. De Valera was now in the United States, on a fund-raising trip among the American Irish. On 5 October Childers met first Michael Collins, then Arthur Griffith, who urged him to return to Paris to see out the end of the Conference. This could be construed as an accolade, but in reality concealed an ambivalence felt by Griffith which was later to crystallize into animosity and play an important part in Childers' fate.

Griffith – short, thickset, myopic, argumentative – was a Dubliner of working-class origins. Like Childers, he had spent some time in South Africa, although as a miner rather than fighting the Boers. Returning to Dublin, he founded the radical newspaper *United Irishman*, then, in 1905, Sinn Féin. Yet his vision was not of an independent republic achieved by means of violence, which the party in 1919 seemed increasingly to represent; on the contrary, Griffith advocated independence under the Crown, and his idea was that Sinn Féiners should copy the methods of the Hungarians, who in the 1860s boycotted the Austro-Hungarian parliament, thereby paving the way to Hungarian independence. A man of considerable personal courage, and as selfless as Childers himself, in the treaty negotiations of 1921 Griffith won the admiration of men of the stature and judgement of Churchill and Lloyd George. Even at this early stage it was Griffith's view that Childers could be made best use of outside Ireland.

With this Childers disagreed.[30] He had set his heart on Dublin, and to him it seemed more useful to work on the propaganda sheet being produced by Desmond Fitzgerald and Robert Brennan, the *Irish Bul-*

letin. He eventually persuaded Griffith to let him discuss the idea with Fitzgerald and Brennan, whom he discovered, at the end of September, trying to rescue their office from the aftermath of a British raid. Falling into the language of a John Buchan hero, Childers remarked: 'It is a dastardly dodge to silence legitimate propaganda and business. It makes me howl.'[31] But little could be firmly settled until he had sorted out his domestic affairs.

As a temporary measure Alice Stopford Green had found him some rooms in Harcourt Street in central Dublin, but they were not suitable for Molly and the boys, and Childers had to find himself a house. For the next month he remained in Ireland, visiting Belfast, going out to Glendalough, meeting a number of the republican leaders, and gradually getting drawn further into the cause. He was particularly active in lobbying the MP Wedgwood Benn,[32] who had succeeded him as Intelligence Officer on *Ben My Chree*. In Childers' eyes Benn, like many English MPs, underestimated the strength of the Sinn Féin movement, and Childers did what he could to correct this impression. In the intervals of his other activities he was preparing material for the *Bulletin*, the launch of which was timed for 11 November, the first anniversary of the Armistice. Having found no suitable house, he returned to London for a week. Here he helped Horace Plunkett with a speech, and also encountered the *Engadine*'s former captain, Cecil L'Estrange Malone, now an MP. Malone was just back from Soviet Russia, and his tales of the revolutionary government must have stirred Childers to his bones. Certainly his political thinking was now developing rapidly, and soon he was to publish an important personal statement, 'Might and Right in Ireland'.

In this passionate, vehemently argued piece Childers begins with a consideration of the War, noting that 'the evil thing fought against was described in many ways . . . all of which meant the same thing, the selfish use of national force by the strong against the weak.' The aim, he states, was 'to defeat this evil, to protect the weak against the strong, and to preserve the freedom of small nationalities . . . this aim was declared by the world and by none more solemnly than Great Britain.' To complement this 'solemn declaration' came the 'brilliant and ardent propaganda of President Wilson', which Childers quotes approvingly: '"Our message is to all imperialists . . . we are fighting for the liberty, the self-government and the undictated development of all peoples . . . a principle of justice to all peoples and nationalities and their right to live on equal terms of liberty and safety with one another . . ."'

If one accepted this, where lay the justice in the fact that Ireland was 'the only white community on the face of the globe where the "government by consent" which President Wilson summoned the "organised opinion of mankind" to sustain is not established.' Where, indeed?

In conclusion, Childers faces the British public with a decision, whether to support Imperialism, or self-determination:

> It is for the British people to help forward one force or the other, and it is impossible to believe that in this crisis in the world's affairs, with all the evidence of their eternal failure in Ireland staring them in the face, they would consciously decide to give fresh impetus to the evil but weakening force. Great issues turn on the decision . . . To make the right decision would be to transform and purify the politics first of the British Empire, then of the world, to put an end to the scandalous succession of risings and repressions now making that Empire a by-word in Europe, and to give its statesmen and those of America the power they do not now possess of insisting on international morality and justice.[33]

This was a clear description of his new political philosophy, and provides an explanation for much that was to come.

Since his various sallies in the press that autumn were committing him so publicly and irrevocably to the Irish cause, it was perhaps fortunate that his plans for leaving England were nearly complete. Embankment Gardens had been disposed of, and having failed to find a suitable house to buy in Dublin, Childers had rented one for six months, in Wellington Road. Then he made a discovery which surprised and pleased him: 'What do you think has happened?' he wrote to Molly. 'Our Chelsea friends, all your friends and my friends and all my work friends . . . are planning a big fête or rather Chelsea party to say goodbye to us. Basil [Williams] came to tell me, and his description of the way people feel about you made me nearly cry with joy . . . old Lady Courtney is one of the plotters – and Lady Lyttelton . . . It's to be at Crosby Hall because no other place is big enough.'[34]

The party was held on 11 December; among the guests were William Le Fanu, Logan Pearsall Smith, Lady Scott-Moncrieff, and General Sir Neville and Lady Lyttelton. A week later the whole Childers family, including a nurse for the boys, finally left for Dublin.

Their English friends – and, as Basil Williams later wrote, the Childerses had many devoted English friends – undoubtedly regarded the move as quixotic. High-minded as they knew them to be, with England struggling to regain her feet after a devastating war there was surely a great deal of valuable reconstruction work to be done in London by the likes of Erskine and Molly Childers. In his memoir Williams notes a change in Childers at about this time, observing that he had 'lost much of his humour, his tolerance, his breadth of vision, even something of his gentleness'.[35] There may have been elements of truth in this, but the two men were no longer as close friends as they had been, the war itself, age, and political outlook having driven them in different directions. It seems likely that the move to Dublin arose out of that 'continual process of change' that Molly was to recognize. It was of course true, as Michael McInerney noted in his short, sharp study of Childers, that here was a man leaving 'not only a country, but an intimate social circle, his closest friends and a political and social philosophy, to embrace the revolutionary life'.[36] Yet it is difficult to imagine someone of Childers' temperament taking any other course now. A man committed to the devolution of power to Ireland since 1908, who had fought constitutionally for the cause for several years, then run guns into Howth, then given four years of his life fighting for the freedom of small nations, he could scarcely at this time of crisis wish to be anywhere but at the heart of the struggle – whatever the consequences. Ireland and her freedom had become his *raison d'être*, his articles of faith, his creed.

A hard course it was, perhaps the hardest. And there was doubtless something in Molly's observation of her husband's inclination to take the hardest course; how she must have prayed that it was also the right one.

IV

Circumstances in Ireland were now rapidly worsening. In December 1919 Lloyd George had introduced a Better Government of Ireland Bill, child of the suspended Home Rule Act of 1914, and full of complex provisions. It proposed the setting up of two Home Rule parliaments, one in Dublin for the twenty-six counties of the south, one in Belfast for Ulster. There was also to be a Council of Ireland, drawn from the two Irish parliaments, to be responsible for cross-border issues. Both parliaments were also to retain a level of representation at Westminster and, importantly, control of finance remained with the Westminster parliament. Divorced from political reality as it was, the Bill was doomed: Ulster would refuse to recognize the Council, Sinn Féin the Southern parliament. Before the end of the War, the Bill might have been accepted; before the Easter Rising, positively welcomed. Now its proposals would solve little, and violence was growing apace.

In September 1919 a party of Volunteers had ambushed a squad of the King's Shropshire Light Infantry, seized their guns and escaped, killing one soldier. A local jury refused to convict them, and in retaliation the Shropshires wrecked their homes. The business of reprisals had begun. The very day of the Childerses arrival in Dublin in December saw an assassination attempt on the Viceroy, Lord French. By the following spring, violence had become a commonplace. One of the worst incidents occurred when the Lord Mayor of Cork, a prominent republican, was shot dead, almost certainly by members of the RIC. At the subsequent trial the jury brought in a verdict of wilful murder against the British Government and its agents. It was at about the same time that the Black and Tans first arrived in Ireland. The inspiration of Lloyd George and Churchill's friend General Tudor, the Black and Tans were a body far removed from the more creditable traditions of British police institutions. Drawn for the most part from servicemen unable to settle down or find work after the war, they were inured to violence, brutal, much given to drink, and barely under the control of their own officers. They had been recruited to augment the ranks of the RIC but equipment was short so they were clad in a motley outfit of khaki and dark green, reminiscent of the coats worn by a famous hunt in the south of Ireland. They soon acquired a fearsome reputation, and were scarcely advertisements for British rule. Such, indeed, was their impact that, by June, Asquith was declaring that 'Things are being done in Ireland which would disgrace the blackest animals and lowest despotism in Europe.'[37] What on earth had the two Chelsea liberals got themselves into?

From Childers' point of view, of course, it was precisely the barbarity of the situation that made their presence necessary and valuable. Although Lloyd George's Bill was in some ways defensible, the means chosen by the Government to maintain law and order – in A. J. P. Taylor's words, 'a policy of murder and terrorism'[38] – were precisely the reverse. When coverage of events in the British and English-speaking press gave only the British point of view, a more accurate representation of the activities of the Black and Tans and their like was a laudable objective, for which Childers, with his reputation and his now very substantial array of press contacts, could scarcely have been better placed. He was soon hard at work. 'Take a typical night in Dublin,' he wrote in the most famous of his pieces on the troubles:

> As the citizens go to bed, the barracks spring to life. Lorries, trucks and armoured cars muster in fleets, lists of objectives are distributed and, when the midnight curfew order has emptied the streets – pitch dark streets – the weird cavalcades issue forth to the attack. Think of raiding a private house at dead of night in a tank whose weird rumble and roar can be heard miles away . . . A thunder of knocks: no time to dress . . . or the door will crash in. On opening, in charge the soldiers – literally charge – with fixed bayonets and in full war kit. No warrant is shown on entering, no apology on leaving if, as in nine cases out of ten, suspicions prove groundless and the raid a mistake.[39]

This was the first major exposure of the behaviour in Ireland of forces acting in the name of the Crown; in the days before radio and television, its effect was to horrify the British public.

Soon, half a dozen such articles were published in pamphlet form, as *Military Rule in Ireland*. They were as vivid as the best of Childers' fictional writing, and garnished propaganda with a degree of factual accuracy then unusual. Childers had said of *The Riddle of the Sands* that it comprised only 'what is meant to be convincing fact'.[40] Unpalatable though the information conveyed in *Military Rule* might be in England, it was, similarly, all too full of convincing fact. *Freeman's Journal*, one of the most authoritative of the Irish papers, said of the pamphlet that

> No more formidable indictment has been drafted of the plan devised by Dublin Castle for what is accurately and vividly termed, 'the sabotage of a nation', and the charges made are the more damning because of the studied moderation with which the author states his case. Unlike the government apologists, whose defamatory propaganda is drawn up with a contemptuous disregard of names, dates and details that might enable independent investigators to check the conclusion, Mr Childers gives chapter and verse for all his statements, and though the space at his disposal necessarily entailed the summary treatment of the various episodes and incidents, full evidence is available for those who would test his conclusions.[41]

But for Childers, propaganda alone was insufficient. Robert Barton was a wanted man, lying low at Glendalough, when the Childers family spent Christmas with him. Imprisoned again, for making a seditious speech at the hustings, he had escaped courtesy of Michael Collins, leaving the prison governor a note that he was going because the service was unacceptable.[42] He was recaptured at the end of January, and on 22 February was sentenced to three years' penal servitude, in an English gaol. Childers returned briefly to England, to do what he could for his cousin's welfare. At Portland prison he interviewed the governor, then saw Barton himself: 'He wore his usual cheery smile, was in Prison clothes – khaki and broad arrows and a khaki forage cap.'[43] Thus the master of Glendalough.

His cousin's incarceration led to Childers playing a part in the setting up of the Land Bank, for which Barton was responsible as the Agriculture Minister in the Dáil. This was a scheme Barton had created with Michael Collins, the Finance Minister, to help fund the reoccupation of untenanted agricultural property. At the same time, Molly was asked by Collins to become a trustee of the Republican Loan; another Collins initiative, this was to help fund the establishment of the republican state, and subsequently involved the management of very large sums of money. Molly's war work (for which, ironically, she had recently been decorated by the King)[44] fitted her ideally for administrative undertakings of this nature. Both husband and wife were touched by the faith and trust being placed in them, which went some way to assuaging the concerns they – particularly Molly – had felt about their commitment to Ireland. Childers also took on the job of temporary magistrate in one of the courts of the republic's parallel administration. These courts had proved a surprising success, and as Roy Foster has noted, in the pages of the *Irish Bulletin* Fitzgerald, Brennan and Childers in turn 'made the most of this astonishing fact, so much more palatable for international and home consumption than the killings of policemen'.[45]

Childers' diary entry of 4 March 1920 gives a sense of him then, busy very much at the forefront of the Irish struggle:

> Met Monteagle and T. Spring Rice about Ulster maps. Saw Plunkett and worked at his speech – urged reference to Bob's case. Discussed publicity about Bob with Brennan. Finished and dispatched round robin letter to Bob in Portland; also letter to governor requesting information about his treatment. Alex Williams called for Mrs AE [George Russell's wife]. Worked on article about Bob. Plunkett spoke at Dominions dinner. Arranged with D. Coffey to have private dinner for SFs [Sinn Féiners] and others who could not go to public dinner. King's health *was* drunk.[46]

This was the life – or so at least it seemed.

16

The Necessary Murder

1920–1921

> Today the deliberate increase in the chances of death;
> The conscious acceptance of guilt in the necessary murder;
> Today the expending of powers
> On the flat ephemeral pamphlet and the boring meeting.
>
> W. H. Auden, 'Spain'

I

By the summer of 1920, the situation in Ireland appeared infinitely vexing, as seen from Westminster. The political solutions proposed by the Better Government of Ireland Bill had been a success only in so far as they were being grudgingly accepted in the North. The Bill, in acknowledging the highly debatable principle of partition, had played a part in fuelling the sectarian outrages flourishing in Ulster, and had been utterly rejected in the South. Simultaneously, law and order seemed a thing of the past, throughout Ireland. The RIC had been reinforced by an eventual total of 10,000 Black and Tans, and the British military commander General Macready had 50,000 regular troops at his disposal. Yet they were not enough. The problems of fighting in Ireland were not those of the Western Front, where the enemy and his territory were clearly defined. In Ireland there were no safe areas, no trenches, no no-man's land. All was nebulous, inchoate, vague. The republican forces seldom wore uniform, and could therefore materialize at any time, in any place, and melt away again. 'An apparently innocent group of bystanders could suddenly be transformed into a detachment of armed men who could strafe an RIC patrol and then slip away quickly and quietly to mingle with the local populace.'[1] A general lack of local knowledge, an absence of local information, made matters worse. Dublin was an armed camp, Cork scarcely better, and on 19 July four days of sectarian rioting began in Belfast which left fifty wounded and nineteen dead.

What was to be done? Lloyd George set up a Cabinet Committee (including Winston Churchill, now Secretary of State for War) to consider the problem of Ireland. Conciliation seemed scarcely on the agenda, and indeed, it is debatable whether it would have been a possible policy even if Ireland could have been dealt with in isolation. But Ireland was not an isolated problem – it was one all too closely paralleled in Egypt and in India, both in the throes of increasingly militant nationalist campaigns. In India the unrest had recently culminated in the Amritsar riots, in which troops under General Dyer had shot dead three hundred unarmed Indians. Churchill deplored Amritsar: 'Frightfulness is not a remedy known to the British pharmacopoeia.'[2] Nevertheless, it seemed clear to the government that it would be fatal to display weakness in any dealings with nationalist movements in the colonies. As Lloyd George put it in a letter to Churchill on 10 May, 'De Valera has practically challenged the British Empire. Unless he is put down the Empire will look silly.'[3]

From the British point of view, the case in Ireland was one of armed insurrection against Crown forces representing law and order. Churchill proposed the identification of IRA units from the air: 'I see no objection from a military point of view . . . to aeroplanes being despatched with definite orders in each particular case to disperse them by machine-gun fire or bombs, using of course no more force than is necessary to scatter and stampede them.'[4] It was also apparent to the Cabinet Committee that the RIC and Black and Tans were in need of further reinforcement; from July onwards this took the form of what was called the Auxiliary Division of the RIC, known as 'the Auxis'. These troops, as tough and experienced as the Black and Tans, were equipped with lorries and intended to be a more mobile force than the RIC. Acting in concert with the aeroplanes, their job was to counter the new tactic the republicans had adopted, of moving about the country in daylight, avoiding towns – the so-called 'flying columns'.

Inevitably, this influx of Crown forces had some effect in due course. Republican courts were broken up, areas in which republicans had been particularly active were aggressively patrolled, and their sympathizers were harassed, rounded up and arrested. 'We are going to break up this murder gang,' declared Churchill at a speech in Dundee on 16 October. 'That it will be broken up utterly and absolutely is as sure as that the sun will rise tomorrow morning . . . Assassination has never changed the history of the world and the Government are going to take good care it does not change the history of the British Empire.'[5] In view of the situation elsewhere in the Empire, a case could be made for this sort of action; the same could not be said of reprisals sanctioned by the Crown.

It was doubtless inevitable – witness the bloody aftermath of the Howth gun-running incident – that violence would beget violence. A sufficiently typical example occurred at Balbriggan in County Dublin, when Head Constable Burke was shot dead by the republican forces. He was a popular Black and Tan instructor, and his former charges ran amok, terrorizing the inhabitants of the village in search of the culprits, 'shooting and bayonetting two citizens to death in their nightshirts'; an eyewitness described the corpses as looking 'as if they had been killed not by human beings but animals'.[6] To such events the British government's response was ambivalent: while it was not considered politic to condone 'official' reprisals, the government appeared unable – or unwilling – to control *unofficial* acts of retaliatory violence, and by September 1920 reprisals had become commonplace. 'The murder of policemen', Lloyd George told Churchill, 'can only be met by reprisals.'[7] Churchill agreed.

While government reprisals, officially sanctioned or otherwise, were modestly successful from a military point of view, politically they were in the end catastrophic. Although feeling generally in Ireland was perhaps overwhelmingly in favour of the republican movement, the shooting of – usually Irish – policemen and similar activities commanded, in so far as it is possible to judge, only sporadic popular support. Furthermore, it called forth the condemnation of the only remaining institution of any real moral authority in the country, the Roman Catholic Church. At the same time, what support could His Majesty's Government expect for its policy of at best condoning and at worst sponsoring the reprisals? 'The violence was after all the product of the government's failure to solve the political problem in a manner acceptable to the majority of the Irish people. Having chosen simply to assert its authority, it was intolerable by any recognised standards of civilised government that that authority should itself be asserted by lawless methods.'[8]

II

By this time Childers and his family were very close to the centre of these terrible events. In March of 1920 they had finally found a satisfactory home, 12 Bushy Park Road, in the suburb of Terenure to the south of Dublin, a prosaic red-brick house looking out to the Dublin Hills. By July they had moved in – 'Margaret and Eileen are installed as servants.'[9]

Once settled, Childers began to display a capacity and appetite for work astonishing even for him. Robert Barton's welfare in Portland Prison remained one concern; he was chairman of the republican justices of Rathmines and Pembroke, and a director of the Land Bank; he was also now involved in the White Cross movement.[10] Predominantly, however, he worked with Fitzgerald and Brennan on publicity, either at an office in Dublin – the office led a somewhat peripatetic existence, on account of police raids – or at home at Terenure.

At 12 Bushy Park Road there gradually grew up something which was partly an office, and partly what can only be described as a salon. The office was intended for Childers' personal use, but came to be used as a post-office and sorting-house for Dáil interdepartmental material.[11] At the same time, Molly was establishing a cuttings and information service for the press. Now suffering increasingly from her disability, she would hold court from a couch in the drawing room, presiding over unofficial meetings between members of the press and the republican leaders. Here she would beguile the many correspondents, both English and foreign, sent to cover the disturbances. To the French correspondent Henri Beraud she would talk in his own language most fluently 'of French literature, of Paris, of the Russian ballet'.[12]

And she urged the dashing young Michael Collins, scourge of the Black and Tans, to read her favourite books. In the chaos that was Dublin in 1920, Bushy Park Road, presided over by that high-minded couple, the Erskine Childerses, must have seemed an oasis of civilization. If it had been in England, surely there would have been honey still for tea?

In the course of 1920, Childers seems to have become a little like a man possessed. For a man whose 'creed was in his own conscience', as his wife would observe, this was a time of tremendous soul-searching. As it was in so many of his generation, the notion of patriotism and nationalism was immensely strong in him. He had once declared that 'one can set no limit to the possibilities of an alliance of English speaking races';[13] he had remarked to his sister early in the Boer War, 'Don't you think it would be splendid to do something for one's country?';[14] twice he had volunteered to fight for his king and his country, and many times had risked his life. A 'fire of pent-up patriotism' gripped his soul, as it did that of 'Arthur H. Davies'. It had been hard for Childers to grapple with what he saw as British iniquity over the claims of small countries at Paris; three years earlier he had written, 'I feel profoundly that England in the long run must stand or fall by her treatment of Ireland – a supreme test – and her whole attitude towards the causes of the war and her intervention in it'.[15] It was worse for him to know that Britain was sponsoring the policy of repression in Ireland, condoning the reprisals; worst of all was that they should be carried out in the name of that Empire to which he had once been so devoted. As his fellow journalist Desmond Ryan recalled, 'A burning faith and noble indignation were implicit in every line of his denunciation of military rule in Ireland.'[16]

And the problem for his conscience and for his heart went even beyond this. In one of the essays in *Military Rule in Ireland* Childers, after detailing some particularly gross RIC behaviour, reminds his English readers that 'All this is in your name.'[17] But what of the outrages being perpetrated by republicans in the name of what Childers held so dear? That spring occurred the case of Alan Bell. Bell was a Resident Magistrate, who signed an order requesting information from the banks about the Republican Loan (the fund Molly was managing). On his way to work one morning Bell was pulled off his tram by armed men. They told him that his time had come. Then they shot him dead.

There followed the cases of Mrs Lindsay and Kitty Carroll. Mrs Lindsay was a Unionist who warned the RIC of a planned ambush; seven republicans were executed as a result; Mrs Lindsay, aged seventy, was subsequently kidnapped and shot as a spy (Childers was kept in ignorance of her fate by Michael Collins for some time). Two months later republicans shot Kitty Carroll because she had disobeyed (republican) orders to stop distilling illicit whiskey. Both incidents, understandably, received unfavourable press coverage, and a response from the republican *Irish Bulletin* was clearly required. Childers enquired of Collins: 'Shall we say (a) the execution of women spies is forbidden, and that Kitty Carroll was not killed by the IRA? or (b) Kitty Carroll was killed in contravention of orders by the IRA, and that (c) Mrs Lindsay is now in prison for giving information to the enemy?'[18] He was making a very nice point – particularly as Mrs Lindsay was actually dead. It was perhaps, for him, an even nicer point to distinguish between the highly questionable activities of the Crown on the one hand, and of the republicans on the other, however unflinching might be his belief in the justice of the Irish cause. Flesh began to drop from a frame that had never fully recovered from the influenza of 1919; his hair was rapidly greying, and he had a persistent cough; 'his worn features and searching eyes [were] alight with an other-worldly fire.'[19] He had just over two years to live.

III

In the autumn of 1920 events in Ireland began to move towards the first of several climaxes. While a fresh infusion of Crown troops had put the republicans on the defensive, public opinion both in Ireland and abroad had begun to turn decidedly against Britain. Sentiments were heightened by the fate of Terence MacSwiney, another republican Lord Mayor of Cork. Arrested in August, he had at once begun a hunger-strike in protest against the government's interference with his legitimate duties. He was deported to Brixton gaol, where his slow decline over the following months provided a very awkward and very public symbol of Irish defiance. On 9 November Lloyd George announced that he had 'murder by the throat',[20] yet it seemed that he was wrong. Michael Collins had long been masterminding both undercover and more overt republican military activity; the Castle had its own counter-terrorists, but by this time all were at least known to Collins – if not in his pay; various of the Castle's men had been picked off from time to time, but now Collins planned a larger gesture. In Dublin on the morning of Sunday 21 November, twelve men believed to be British officers were shot, most of them still in bed, some in front of their wives. Two Auxiliaries passing the scene of one of the shootings were also killed.

Feelings ran high. That afternoon there was a Gaelic football match between Dublin and Tipperary. Members of the RIC and the Auxiliaries present, on the lookout for the IRA, opened fire, killing twelve civilians; later they claimed there had been shooting from the crowd. That night two of Collins' Dublin Brigade leaders were shot in the guard room at the Castle, 'trying to escape'. This was the first notorious 'Bloody Sunday'. A week later, two lorry-loads of Auxiliaries ran into a republican ambush close to Macroom in West Cork. Three IRA men and seventeen of the eighteen British were killed; some of the wounds were inflicted after death. What price Lloyd George's claim?

In the light of these events, it is not altogether surprising that both sides should already have begun to seek some more satisfactory way of settling their differences. In October, an Irish businessman named Moylett had taken the initiative and, acting as liaison, opened tentative negotiations between Arthur Griffith and Lloyd George. These broke down after Bloody Sunday. As Robert Kee remarks, the mood of the times is conveyed all too well by a piece of contemporary doggerel:

> On the 29th day of November
> Outside the town of Macroom
> The Tans in their big Crossley tender
> Were hurtling away to their doom
> For the lads of the column were waiting
> With hand grenades primed on the spot
> And the Irish Republican Army
> Made shite of the whole fucking lot.[21]

What the government was obliged to admit had become a 'small war' now redoubled in ferocity. Up to November 1920, British casualties amounted to 125 killed and 235 wounded; from November to the following July, the figures were 400 and 700. Civilian casualties were more difficult to assess, partly because republicans, fighting as they did without uniforms, were often included in the figures. Some 700 killed and a similar number wounded is a tentative estimate for the first half of 1921.[22]

This was only one aspect of the war. The battle was not just about numbers killed on either side: the battle was for the hearts and minds of the electorate and, in the community of nations, for the hearts and minds of international leaders. Here Childers came more and more to the fore, orchestrating with Desmond Fitzgerald a publicity campaign which placed increasing pressure on the British government, from opinion both within the country and outside it. In February 1921 Fitzgerald was arrested, and Childers became Director of Propaganda. A report that he prepared for de Valera indicates the scope of his activities at the time.

> Since the last report was submitted by this Department . . . the Director of the Department has been arrested. A new Director has been appointed and the work of the Department in all its services has been carried on as usual. The *Bulletin* is circulated daily to two hundred English newspapers and public men, and weekly to three hundred other persons including many Continental and Colonial newspapers and journalists. The Enemy Government have made repeated endeavours to prevent the circulation of the *Bulletin*. They have been successful in a minority of instances. The *Bulletin*, however, still reaches the greater number of those for whom it is intended and is used with effect by many of its recipients . . . The interviewing of foreign journalists has been somewhat disorganised since the arrest of Mr Desmond Fitzgerald, but it is hoped shortly to rectify this. Letter communication with foreign countries and colonies is being arranged, and preparations have also been made to extend the work and the production of the Department. Steps have been taken to maintain closer touch with the Irish Press and to supply it, as far as can be safely done, with information of an authoritative character.

Childers closed with a terrible appeal. 'This Department would suggest to all members of the Dáil to arrange in their constituencies for the collection of signed statements from the victims of enemy aggression, especially in the case of murders, floggings and attacks on women.'[23]

It could be argued that Childers did no more than step into Fitzgerald's shoes; in practice, both contemporary and later estimates of Childers' work were a good deal more positive. Childers' fellow-journalist on the *Bulletin*, Frank Gallagher, noted that while it was under Fitzgerald the paper 'grew to such importance', it was under Childers that it 'came to full maturity'.[24] This comment reflects on Childers in his editorial role; as journalist in his own right, it was Griffith's view that he had 'the ear of a big section of the English people'.[25] This was also the opinion of Douglas Hyde, the Gaelic scholar who was later to become President. He wrote of Childers' 'great services' during the guerrilla war, noting that 'I had the opportunity of observing how very much his writings at that time impressed the British people.'[26] Subsequent scholarly estimates take a similar view. Dorothy Macardle described Childers as 'an advocate of genius who possessed an unequalled knowledge of the mentality to which Ireland's advocates had to appeal';[27] Roy Foster has written of Childers' 'tersely efficient propaganda machine'.[28] Likewise, Arthur Mitchell isolates as being of particular importance the change in strategy instituted by Childers in proclaiming that the republican military forces constituted a legitimate army, rather than an isolated collection of fighters.[29] In Childers' eyes the failure to have done so earlier was 'a fatal failure, because the propaganda of the enemy was that the Army was a "murder gang" and it was only by insisting that it was waging a legitimate war and basing it on that principle that one could meet the torrent of defamation.'[30] Mitchell credits Childers with a sensible change in the name of his department, from the pejorative 'propaganda' to the neutral 'publicity', and sees the 'reports on the administrative achievements of the Dáil government', edited and partly written by Childers in 1921 – *The Constructive Work of Dáil Éireann* – as his 'most important work'.

An anecdote of Gallagher's illustrates the powers of concentration that Childers brought to his job. 'Erskine was one of the most extraordinary workers I have ever met . . . he would often bring his work to the drawing room at night and write at the mahogany table as callers sat around the fire and put the world through [the Childerses'] hands. He had developed in himself such powers of concentration that he would soon be writing these oblivious of all else.' Gallagher went on to relate a story of the time Childers decided to devote an issue of the *Bulletin* to rebutting standard Castle criticism that the republicans did not wear uniform. First it was a question of finding the best opportunity for putting the republican side; then,

> 'Give me about twenty minutes,' Erskine said three days afterwards, and then sat down by the fire staring into it without moving, still in his raincoat just as he had come in. 'I'm ready now,' he said suddenly, and he dictated without pausing for the better part of an hour. When I had finished taking him in shorthand he said: 'Go back to the third paragraph where I said the names of the officers making up the court, change it to the officers composing the court. In the fifth paragraph change "certain requirements of Article 1 of the Hague Convention" to "certain requirements laid down by Article 1".' After that what he dictated was typed and no more alteration was necessary.[31]

It was a formidable talent 'the enemy' had taken on. Childers' efforts were soon to bear fruit.

IV

The bloody events following the death of MacSwiney, culminating in the Macroom incident, led to the imposition of martial law; this was followed by another ambush near Cork city, and in retaliation the Black and Tans looted and burned the town, causing more than three million pounds' worth of damage. (Childers' pamphlet, *Who Burnt Cork City?*, correctly apportioning the blame, appeared soon after.) On 5 January martial law was extended to the counties of Waterford, Clare, Kilkenny, and Roscommon. 'Rebels' taken in arms were to be shot; seven were, that February in Cork; the usual revolting reprisals followed. Increasingly, in England, it was beginning to be felt that enough was enough. The English liberal conscience, long uneasy, was stirred by Childers to no little effect; intellectuals such as H. G. Wells and Shaw fulminated against the government. They were the vanguard. Then the Archbishop of Canterbury protested. *Nation and Athenaeum* asked 'When is this going to end?'[32] *The Times* and the *Manchester Guardian* were not far behind. Asquith again denounced the 'hellish policy of reprisals'.[33]

Hampered though it was, on the one hand by the trouble elsewhere in the Empire, on the other by the sensitivities of a coalition government that included the arch-Unionist Bonar Law, the Cabinet was yet bound to react eventually. As early as November of 1919 Churchill had conceded that some of the consequences of the reprisal policy were 'discreditable'.[34] By the middle of December he was urging conciliation. He remarked in the Commons, 'Let the Irish people carry this debate into the field of fair discussions and they will instantly find that there will be a relief of all those harsh and lamentable conditions which are bringing misery on Ireland.'[35] By the end of the year Lloyd George, in Cabinet, was proposing a truce; Churchill supported him. Two months later Churchill exchanged the War Office for Joseph Chamberlain's old job of Colonial Secretary; here it fell to him to try to ease a building tension in relations with the United States, of which he felt the 'principal cause'[36] was Ireland. The pressure was beginning to tell. On 14 February 1921 Churchill wrote to his wife, 'I am feeling my way for a plan.'[37]

In some respects, the situation was now easier than it had been at the time of the last formal impasse, the Buckingham Palace Conference of July 1914. There Ulster, the chief obstacle to any sensible accommodation between an Empire which felt itself obliged to maintain its integrity and a colony that felt otherwise, had loomed large; by the spring of 1921, Ulster had become a less intransigent problem, thanks to its acceptance of the Better Government of Ireland Bill, enacted in December 1919. Elections to the separate Ulster parliament were held in May, with the voting overwhelmingly in favour of the Unionists. This was not a result particularly welcome to the third of the population who were Catholics, but it simplified the political position. In the South, the Dáil utilized the electoral machinery set up for the Dublin parliament, accepting the 128 constituencies in the twenty-six-county area that now constituted the South. The Protestant Trinity College, in Dublin, had four seats and returned Unionists; in the remaining 124 constituencies, Sinn Féin candidates were returned, forming the Second Dáil. While the British government was still faced with implacable republicanism, at least it did not have to reconcile it with equally implacable Unionism.

Childers had stood as one of a panel of five Sinn Féin candidates for Wicklow and Kildare, the campaign recalling memories of Devonport some ten years previously – now a lifetime away. Such were the times that the Sinn Féiners were unopposed, and his 'win' – if it could be so described in the circumstances – fulfilled another of Childers' ambitions. With it came recognition of his publicity work, when de Valera appointed him Minister for Publicity,[38] a Cabinet post. The President wrote, 'I am very glad that we shall now have you as a colleague in the Dáil. It will give you an opportunity of *directly* representing your own department.'[39]

It was just over two years since his arrival at Glendalough to convalesce from influenza; less than eighteen months since he had formally settled in Ireland, and taken Irish citizenship. Those were times which conjured up men with extraordinary qualities; a number on the Irish side, accorded the status of heroes, perhaps merited it – most obviously, de Valera, Griffith and Collins. Childers has been tellingly described as the 'strangest of all' these figures. And so he was, a slight, increasingly frail figure who had 'given up everything to his sense of justice'.[40] Not everyone finds it easy to understand Childers' sense of justice, and his defence of IRA tactics which were arguably as indefensible as those of the Crown can be puzzling. At the very least, however, he seems worthy of a measure of respect for the considerable courage and energy with which he pursued his hard-won convictions. As Basil Williams put it, after Childers' execution:

> We may think him wrong-headed and a fanatic, we may think of him as 'nourished on dreams', to quote a phrase of his own in what most of us believe to have been a saner and healthier outlook on the composition of rebels. But of one thing all those who know him well are convinced, that there was no particle of meanness or treachery in his nature; and whatever course of action he adopted – however we may deplore the judgement – it was based on the prompting of a conscience and sense of honour as sensitive and true as one may meet.[41]

V

There is no denying something defensive about Basil Williams' comments; in truth, all too soon Childers would be needing every friend he could muster.

The unfavourable reaction in England, as Childers' name became ever more clearly associated with those who wished to detach Ireland from the Empire, was as predictable as it was widespread, except among his close friends there. It was perhaps equally predictable that a number of the Irish should react in the same way. Before he committed himself and his family to Ireland in 1919, he had frequently been warned, by people like Horace Plunkett and George Russell, of the danger that his actions and motives might be misunderstood in Ireland. In some respects rightly, certainly bravely, he took the view that that would and should be the last thing to discourage him. In the end – even before the end – his position *was* open to misconstruction, and it *was* misconstrued. A simple patriotism was understandable; here, however, was a man very well known to have volunteered to fight for the Crown on two occasions, who had been decorated for his services, and who by courtesy remained Major Erskine Childers, DSC. If he was as committed to King and Castle as that suggested, why was he now very actively supporting those who might be seen as seeking the Empire's destruction? For Childers himself there was no paradox, compelled as he was by his constantly-developing notions of political liberty. At one level, these simply placed him at forefront of the liberal thinking of his day; for less subtle minds, the problem remained. What was this man, to all appearances the archetype of the English ruling classes – the very people from whom the republicans most wished to free themselves and their country – doing in Dublin in 1921? In such fevered times, it would have been contrary to human nature if there had not been those who both resented Childers' rapid rise in the republican hierarchy, and also suspected that he was not quite what he seemed.

It was of course greatly to Childers' advantage that he had won over the two most important republican leaders, de Valera and Collins. De Valera was by training a teacher, and the punctilious in Childers appealed to him, as did his increasingly unswerving intellectual advocacy of the republican cause. They had first met some time after de

Valera's return from America in the autumn of 1920, and now became close. Dry, academic and bespectacled, the two seemed closely matched, despite the disparity in size between the slight, frail Englishman and the lanky Irishman. Indeed, de Valera once remarked that if 'he could choose a person along whose lines of character he would like to model himself, that person would have been Childers'.[42] He described Childers as 'a prince amongst men',[43] and once wrote to Molly, 'Were I given the choice of the greatest blessing I could give our country, it would be that she might always be served by such loyal and unselfish, such able, courageous and laborious representatives as Mr Childers.'[44] Collins, of a less sophisticated background, had introduced Childers to de Valera; known as the 'big fellow', Collins seems to have been more charmed by the Childerses as a couple, by their refinement and their manners. Elizabeth Lazenby remarked of Collins that 'Many were the hours he had spent in Mrs Childers' sitting-room, captive to her spell . . . reading and studying the books she gave him, and gradually unfolding his strength and power beneath her magic influence.'[45] Collins had given Childers a small Spanish revolver at the time of the Connors affair in 1919, and Childers kept it always on his person – a considerable mark of affection which was to prove his death-warrant.

Estimates of Childers by other republican leaders were less favourable. Arthur Griffith, who like de Valera had been on the quayside at Howth, certainly thought Childers had his uses; it seemed to him less than wise, however, to admit a man he always saw as 'an Englishman' to the highest of republican counsels. Their early relationship had already cooled over what Griffith saw as Childers' pedantry in establishing the precise facts of Crown atrocities. And it was Griffith who later dubbed Childers 'a disgruntled Englishman'[46] fighting as much to dismantle the Empire as for the Irish cause. This was not true, but it was close enough to the facts to invite credence. More damning still was the verdict of Piaras Béaslaí, who later recorded:

> When Childers was appointed Dáil Director of Publicity, I was appointed Army Director of Publicity for the purpose of concentrating with him on the military side. All information with regard to the IRA on military matters passed to him through my hands. This brought me into close daily association with him and gave me a good opportunity

> of observing his character and abilities. In view of Collins' high opinion of his capacity, I was amazed at the impression of fussy, feverish futility he conveyed to me. He displayed the mind, outlook and ability of a capable British civil servant, but no adequate appreciation of the situation with which he was dealing. I formed the opinion, reluctantly, that he carried weight as an outsider, with an English-made reputation, which he could not have carried on his merits, had he been an Irishman in the movement for years, finding his own level.[47]

The term 'outsider', the phrase 'an Irishman in the movement for years', are pertinent, certainly, but enough in this appreciation reflects what we know of Childers from elsewhere for it not to be entirely discounted. And whether it is a justifiable estimate or not, its importance lies in the fact that it was made at all.

It might have been more convenient for Childers if those at Dublin Castle had shared Béaslaí's estimate of him. Unfortunately, much as many republicans felt Childers needed watching, so did the Castle, where the administration had been strengthened by the Chief Secretary for Ireland, Sir Hamar Greenwood, and by the energetic Assistant Under-Secretary, 'Andy' Cope.[48] Even had Childers' role at Howth not been widely (although not universally) known, as it now was, the Castle could scarcely miss the various letters and articles in the English press that had been appearing under his name from 1919 onwards. The Castle knew him, more generally, as a man well-connected in press circles both on the continent and in America, and knew very well of the part played by Bushy Park Road as republican press bureau and general post-office. When in April 1921 a Senator spoke on Capitol Hill in support of the resolution that 'the independence of Ireland ought to be recognised by the United States of America', all his evidence had been provided by Childers,[49] and the Castle would have assumed as much. It must all have been very galling for them. They did not just watch Childers: his first diary entry recording a Crown raid occurs on 9 March 1920: 'At 1.00 a.m. tank raid on house, officers violent, police polite. Search for arms. Left at 2.00 a.m.'[50] Thereafter official harassment was fairly regular, especially once it became known that republican leaders fraternized there.

An anecdote related by Robert Brennan conveys some of the atmosphere of these raids, and of Childers' very English response to them.

One night the young journalist was at Bushy Park Road, enjoying the Childerses' hospitality to the full by taking a bath, when Childers knocked on the door.

> 'There's a lorry outside,' Childers said through the door. 'Do you think they're after you?'
>
> 'More likely you.'
>
> 'I don't think so. Would you think of slipping on some clothes and getting out through the back?'
>
> 'They'll have it covered.'
>
> A thundering knock on the front door ended speculation. Childers went down and opened it.
>
> 'What's the meaning of this?' he asked in his posh voice.
>
> 'Who are you?' a loud English voice countered.
>
> 'I'm Major Erskine Childers. Who are you?'
>
> 'Can you tell us where we will find No. 8 Victoria Road?'
>
> 'I'm sorry, I can't.'
>
> 'You mean you won't.'
>
> 'I mean I'm sorry, I can't. Would you mind giving me your name and regiment? I intend making a complaint to the commander-in-charge about your conduct.'
>
> The officer mumbled something, backed out and drove away.[51]

Needless to say, this sort of thing was disturbing to the quiet, industrious, almost scholarly routine of Bushy Park Road.

Following Desmond Fitzgerald's arrest in February 1921, the Castle become more interested in Childers' role at the *Bulletin*, a role never, in the Castle's mind, quite sufficiently clear; their interest redoubled when Childers was elected to the Dáil in May. On the 9th of that month, the soldiers came again. Childers was at home with Molly, and Frank Gallagher was there. The two men were to be taken to the Castle, one of the Auxiliaries remarking 'You will know what to expect there.'[52] Bundled into separate lorries, they were warned they would be shot at once should one of the now commonplace ambushes of Crown vehicles take place during the journey; fortunately, they arrived unharmed at the Castle gates. Gallagher was then transferred to another barracks, while Childers was incarcerated in an underground *oubliette* close to Lower Castle Gate. Silence fell in the dark and grimy cell, and

Childers fell to pondering his fate. Interrogation was inevitable, torture possible, and death 'while trying to escape' just conceivable. Still, these were possibilities that had long existed, and which he had long elected to outface.

But his time was yet to come. Let him take up the story:

> To my immense astonishment I was called for in an hour, taken to an officers' sitting-room and given a cup of tea. After a long wait in another room, Arthur Cope came and told me I was to be released. I insisted that F.G. (who passed under another name) must be released too and this he agreed to and sent officers to get him out. The disgust of the officers at the whole business . . . was amusing, but Cope was adamant. While waiting news of Frank, Cope tackled me about Dominion Home Rule for fully an hour and a half and we went at it hammer and tongs . . . When the Colonel eventually reported that Frank had been released, I left the Castle myself, Cope effusive in his manner and actually carrying my valise out of the gate for me![53]

Childers' enemies read much into this incident, suggesting that his sudden release indicated collusion with the Castle. The contrary was the case. For months now, covert attempts had been being made to set up negotiations between the two sides, using various intermediaries, as Churchill felt his way towards a realization of his plan. At the time of Childers' arrest, these efforts seemed to be about to bear fruit; accordingly, whatever the views of the military in general, people in Cope's position appreciated that this was no time to arrest the likes of Childers. He was no turncoat; rather, he was an important figure on the Irish side. As Frank Gallagher himself observed, 'The political heads at the Castle felt that to hold him meant yet another kind of discredit to the whole regime.'[54]

In a sense, Childers contrived his own salvation.

In the course of the spring Archbishop Clune and Lord Derby had both attempted to act as peacemakers, and failed; General Smuts succeeded. Smuts had of course once fought against the Empire himself, and had long taken a serious view of the Irish situation, going so far as to remark that 'unless the Irish question is settled on the great principles which form the basis of this great Empire, this Empire must cease to exist.'[55] In June, in London for the first post-war Imperial

Conference, he made it his business to address the Irish issue, interviewing a number of those most closely involved. These included Horace Plunkett, and of course Lloyd George. He also saw Alexander Lindsay.[56]

'Sandy' Lindsay was an academic politician who had been in close correspondence with the Childerses since Easter. Between them the three had concocted a scheme for a settlement, which Lindsay presented to Smuts on 12 June. The result was encouraging; Lindsay wrote to Molly, 'It is very desirable indeed that he [Smuts] should see people like Mr Childers.'[57] By the 15th, the Childerses and Smuts appear to have been in direct communication.[58] On 25 June 1921 de Valera received from Lloyd George a note inviting him to a conference in London, its purpose 'to explore to the utmost the possibilities of a settlement'.[59] This was an olive branch. Then, on 5 July, Smuts arrived from London, as an emissary of Lloyd George, his purpose to explain the compromise that had ended hostilities in the Boer War to de Valera and his chosen men. 'We argued most fiercely all morning, all afternoon, until late at night,' recorded Smuts. 'And I found the men most difficult to convince were de Valera and Childers.'[60] A few days later, on 11 July, a formal truce was declared.

VI

The broader circumstances in which the parley came about are worth consideration.

The King's speech, made at the opening of the Ulster Parliament on 22 June, was the initial catalyst. 'I appeal to all Irishmen to pause, to stretch out the hand of forbearance and conciliation, to forgive and forget and to join in making for the land they love a new era of peace, contentment and goodwill,' he declared. 'May this historic gathering be the prelude of the day in which Irish people North and South, under one Parliament or two . . . shall work together in common love for Ireland.'[61] The speech, drafted by Smuts, 'moved public opinion throughout the British Isles'.[62] The military situation was also important. The precise balance between Crown and republican forces at the time was far from clear, but Collins later declared that the IRA was within three weeks of defeat; he was, however, in a position in which it was to his advantage to make such a claim, and other leading republicans later utterly refuted it. It was nevertheless true that the republicans were increasingly short of arms and ammunition, and that the Crown's own mobile forces had been quite successful in countering the republicans' flying column tactics. Even so, Churchill and Lloyd George could no longer feel they had 'murder by the throat'; on the contrary, it appeared that to ensure complete control of the situation would require a significant strengthening of the British military presence. By the beginning of the summer of 1921 there were already 80,000 troops in Ireland; Churchill, General Macready in Ireland and the Chief of General Staff, Sir Henry Wilson, reckoned that a *further* 100,000 would be necessary, as would the imposition of martial law throughout the south. Neither before nor after 22 June was this something which it was felt the British people would stomach.

That this was so was largely a result of the story of Ireland during these months, from the republican perspective, becoming widely disseminated, masterminded by Childers. From the beginning public opinion had been recognized by both sides as of major significance. The very first report of the Cabinet Committee on Ireland had noted its importance in Great Britain, still more in the Dominions and the United States of America.[63] Towards the end of the affair Lord Birkenhead, the British Attorney-General, commented that, so successful were the Sinn Féin propagandists, they 'not only induced persons all over the world who were evilly affected towards the British Empire to receive and even credit the charges that were made, but they actually induced large numbers of British people to take the view . . . that the balance of censure inclined in the direction of the Crown forces.'[64]

Quite what finally forced the government's hand cannot be isolated; a number of factors played a part, including the lack of any real military progress on the one hand, the pressure of public opinion both at home and abroad on the other. In this sense, it could almost be said that the truce was the joint victory of Childers and Collins. Arthur Griffith certainly later described Collins as 'the man who won the war';[65] equally, Michael McInerney noted that 'Most serious people . . . believed it was Childers' work as much as Michael Collins' that tipped the scale.'[66] Similarly, Roy Foster considers that 'public and political opinion broke the government's nerve while the IRA were still in the field.'[67] It was a very remarkable achievement. As Churchill later observed, 'No British Government in modern times has ever appeared to make so sudden and complete a reversal of policy.'[68] It was in many respects Childers' greatest work, employing the novel tool of propaganda in which he had become such a master – the most signal instance of his 'being useful'.

17
On the Breaking of Nations

1921

> 'Attacks me about *Riddle of the Sands.* Says I caused the European war and want to cause another.'
>
> Erskine Childers, 1921

I

As Churchill conceded afterwards, if the Irish had not won the war, they had at the very least won the truce. The question now was, could they win the peace? On their home ground, masters of their own terrain, the amateur soldiers of the republican army had shown themselves equal to the numerically superior Crown forces. In propaganda terms the Irish were outright winners. Now came a fresh challenge, in the subtle arts of formal negotiation. How would the Irish fare, relatively unversed in such skills as they were? The story is a curious one, in which Childers was to play a painfully controversial part.

The truce having been agreed, de Valera was invited by Lloyd George to London, 'to explore to the utmost the possibility of a settlement'. He was also asked to bring with him 'any colleagues whom [he] may select'.[1] Responding to a broad hint from de Valera, the British broadened his choice by arranging for a number of Sinn Féiners, including Arthur Griffith and Robert Barton, to be released from prison. In their respective capacities of Vice-President of the Dáil and Minister for Economic affairs, these two accompanied de Valera to London, as did the Minister for Home Affairs, Austin Stack, and the Minister for Publicity. For Childers it was a signal honour, and the party's reception in London must have been oddly reminiscent of that enjoyed by the CIV on their return from the Boer War. As Stack recalled, 'All the Irish in London seemed to be awaiting the train at Euston, and it was with difficulty that we reached the hotel.'[2]

This was 13 July. Over the next ten days de Valera met Lloyd George on four separate occasions, with a view to finding some common ground for a more formal process of negotiation to begin. It was also a time for the two leaders to size up one another. At first Lloyd George appeared to have the better of things. Lloyd George, noticing a lengthy document prepared for de Valera headed *Saorstat Éireann*, innocently enquired how that might be translated; on being told 'Free State', he asked, What was the Irish term for 'republic'? De Valera supposedly conceded there was none, prompting the reply, 'Must we not admit that the Celts never were republicans and had no native words for such an idea?'[3] Yet in subsequent meetings de Valera surely held his own, for as Lloyd George remarked, negotiating with him was 'like trying to pick up mercury with a fork'.[4] For his own part, de Valera remained unimpressed by Lloyd George's various attempts to cajole and flatter. At their first meeting the Prime Minister's ploy was to meditate

> on the contribution made by some of those who had sat in his present Prime Ministerial seat to the building-up that far-flung area marked in red. Pitt, Palmerston, Gladstone . . . He trolled out the names. He reflected on the amazing change that in these last fifty years had transformed the relationship of the Colonies to the Mother Country. An Imperial Conference was in daily session. He pointed to the chairs at the Cabinet table which the Dominion Premiers were accustomed to occupy. What, he could not help asking himself and his visitor, would Lord Palmerston have thought if he had been told that within seventy years of his death the representatives of the Colonies would be meeting here, *on equal terms*, the Prime Minister of the United Kingdom? He began enumerating the occupants of the chairs . . . Twice as he came to a particular chair he paused, then passed by it. He seemed to be expecting the question, who had sat there. But no question came, so at last perforce he returned to it. 'One chair remains vacant – waiting for Ireland . . . If she is ready to take her place . . . in the Council Chamber of the Commonwealth.[5]

It was an admirable performance to fall on deaf ears, yet here indeed was the rub. In the judicious terms used as a prelude to the formal treaty negotiations, the problem was to ascertain 'how the association of Ireland with the community of nations known as the British Empire may best be reconciled with Irish national aspirations'.[6] There was in Ireland a popular mandate for a republic, declared in January 1919, and for a republic the guerrilla war had been fought. Conversely, on the British side there was a requirement to avoid positively offending Ulster, to maintain the general integrity of the Empire, and to prevent anything which might encourage the concurrent nationalist movements in Egypt and India. If a settlement was to be achieved and a resumption of the war to be avoided, there would surely have to be concessions on both sides.

De Valera briefed his colleagues on the talks after each round had been completed. It had been decided that it should be the responsibility of the British to prepare formal written proposals, yet as the meetings progressed it became apparent to the Irish party that Lloyd George really had little to give. The Prime Minister wanted to hand de Valera the proposals on their fourth and last meeting; de Valera demurred, insisting that they should be produced beforehand, to enable the Irish to discuss them. Childers, staying, like the rest of the party, at the Grosvenor Hotel, noted: 'At 10 p.m., I and Bob being half-dressed, a messenger appeared and said in a hoarse whisper: "Sir James Craig and the Prime Minister." Tableau. Bob's face a study. Hasty dressing by him. I, who had not heard, maintained my *déshabille*. In came Sir Edward Grigg and Tom Jones (who said he was Secretary to the Prime Minister). Tableau. And much laughter all round. They brought Lloyd George's proposals and a message from the King.'[7]

Scarcely to the surprise of Childers and the rest of the Irish party, the draft did not make happy reading. The ideas constituted a qualified form of Dominion status. A complex and constantly evolving concept, at its simplest this meant offering Ireland the position of a country existing under the auspices of the Crown and with some significant limitations to its control of its own affairs. The specific caveats with regard to Ireland included the three crucial issues of trade, defence, and the status of Ulster, all of which were to be maintained largely as they then stood, under British control. While this was considerably more than had ever been proposed under Home Rule, it was by no means independence.

Following a certain amount of argument, the Irish returned to Dublin on 21 July to present the proposals to the rest of the Dáil ministers. Although they were in the end rejected, and rejected again in August when presented to a full session of the Dáil, opinion was nevertheless divided. Austin Stack's first response in London had been to find the ideas unacceptable; he was an unyielding republican. Barton, in a painfully prescient choice of words, then asked, 'Mr President, would it not be treason to the Republic to bear these terms back to Ireland?'[8] Griffith, on the other hand, when he heard them in Dublin, declared himself 'favourable to the proposals save as to Ulster'.[9] Much more surprisingly, Collins, the military genius of the whole republican movement, described the offer as 'a great step forward'.[10]

Childers was aghast. Yet he had been forewarned, as he later noted:

> It must have been about July 8th, when for the first time I heard words spoken which implied a possible weakening on the Republican issue. Collins' words especially struck me – something to the effect that it might possibly be necessary to pass through a Dominion phase and Mulcahy's rather pessimistic words about military prospects. But there was only a general discussion – no vote – there was uncompromising talk from several ministers . . . so that the painful impression temporarily passed from me. I think mainly from the reason that I could not yet seriously grasp the idea that an abandonment of the Republic was possible, least of all by a man such as Collins who was a unique hero to me.[11]

As Childers concluded, 'That there was cleavage was clearly apparent.' Equally clearly apparent was which side of it stood the man who had once, at length and with ardour, advocated Dominion status, now within reach, as the solution to the Irish question. For Childers, the government's activities during what had become known as the Black and Tan War had been the last straw. Despite retaining his affection for England, he was now an out-and-out republican. He had finally concluded that power held by one people over another ultimately corrupts. It is not entirely difficult to see why.

The stage was now set for the Treaty negotiations themselves, and for the subsequent split in both Sinn Féin and the republican army, causing that still more partisan civil war which 'created a caesura across Irish history, separating parties, interests and even families, and creating the rationale for political divisions that endured'[12] – a civil war which also saw Childers' repudiation, vilification, capture, trial, conviction, and execution by firing squad.

II

Following the initial rejection of the British proposals, there was a lengthy correspondence between Lloyd George and de Valera concerning the level of commitment to a given solution that the very act of attending any further conference would imply. Did Britain's involvement indicate recognition of Ireland's republican status? Did Ireland's signify her own acceptance of an altogether more modest status? Much of this material on the Irish side appears to have been drafted by Childers. It was eventually agreed that merely attending the talks committed neither side to anything, and a date early in October was set for a formal conference. It was hoped that this would at long last provide the final answer to the Irish question.

In view of what followed, it is worth noting here the peculiarities in the composition of the Irish party sent to London, and particularly the controversy over the inclusion of Childers. The group comprised Arthur Griffith as chairman, Collins as vice-chairman, Robert Barton as economics expert, and two lawyers. Éamon Duggan was a veteran of the Rising who had been court-martialled and sentenced to three years' imprisonment; on his release he acted for the next-of-kin of the hunger-striker Thomas Ashe, and had been a director of (republican) army intelligence. He was to be the liaison officer between London and Dublin; more to the point, he was Collins' man, and would follow his line throughout the negotiations. Gavan Duffy was Childers' old friend from Paris, short, bearded and stalwart, who had played a major part in drawing up the Dáil Declaration of Independence. These five were technically 'plenipotentiaries', envoys deputed with full powers to act at their own discretion, although in fact de Valera had instructed them to refer to Dublin before taking any irreversible step. The final member of the main party was Childers, who was chief secretary.

The nature of the job to be done made the inclusion of the lawyers more or less obligatory. Since the financial basis of the relationship between the two countries was always to be found lurking behind idealistic notions of freedom, the inclusion of Barton made sense too, although his estrangement from topical Sinn Féin thinking as a result of his imprisonment was later to prove a difficulty. Collins was an altogether odder choice. His success in masterminding republican army activity and exterminating British intelligence agents had made him a somewhat unpopular figure at Westminster, and he himself long resisted de Valera's call, claiming to be a soldier, not a statesman; in point of fact, as a negotiator he proved in many respects the pick of them all. Griffith, founder of Sinn Féin and vice-president of the party, was bound to go, even though verbal fluency was not his forté. Moreover, his intellectual commitment was to freedom under the Crown, rather than a full republic; if it was odd that he should lead the delegation, it was also odd that the senior hard-line republicans Stack and Cathal Brugha should be omitted; but they had refused to serve.

The most surprising absentee was of course de Valera, who had spied out the ground, probed British strengths and weaknesses, and shown himself in some respects the equal of Lloyd George. It is true that his absence – as he claimed – would in theory prevent unduly hasty decisions being taken in London. But to make up a team, and leave out the most talented player? Unlike Collins, de Valera remained on the less accommodating side of republicanism, and there he intended to stay – a stance rather easier to maintain in Dublin than in Downing Street, in that autumn of 1921. It is also worth remarking that there seems to have been surprisingly little discussion, let alone agreed common ground, with regard to what the five who went to London might, as negotiators, realistically achieve.

On Childers, very much his own personal choice, de Valera's view was that the Irish had 'no one to match him for knowledge of constitutional procedure and for general secretarial expertness'.[13] This seems entirely fair. It was of course significant, however, that he went as Secretary, not as a plenipotentiary. He would have no vote, and throughout the negotiations would be obliged to busy himself preparing papers on the British and Irish positions, trying to inform and influence the delegates but unable to act directly himself. He was known to be the least flexible towards the British of the whole party, and it may be that de Valera simply thought this intransigence in a full plenipotentiary would be a barrier to any settlement. On the other hand, he was probably closer to Childers, politically and personally, than to any of the other delegates, and may have perceived a usefulness therein.

But in reality, Childers' star by now was beginning to wane. The old Cabinet of which he had been a member was replaced in the summer of 1921 by a smaller one. Barton retained a seat as Minister for Economic Affairs, but the publicity post was excluded, and in any case the release of Desmond Fitzgerald from jail relieved Childers of the portfolio. Then there was Griffith: he objected to Childers' presence, even as Secretary. As Childers himself later wrote, 'Griffith had . . . always represented a moderate element . . . was never at heart a true Republican and had little sympathy with the militant party and the War of Independence.'[14] Childers being what he had become by the autumn of 1921, this set the two apart. At the same time, Griffith was suspicious of the motives of the 'disgruntled Englishman', and increasingly took Béaslaí's view of his 'fussy, feverish futility'. Before the end of the year, Griffith was to remark in the Dáil, 'I was Chairman of the Delegation of which Mr Childers, not with my approval, was appointed Secretary.'[15] De Valera had been insistent in a move which turned out to be an immediate prelude to Childers' tragedy.

The party left on the steamer for Holyhead on Friday, 7 October 1921, more than aware of its responsibilities, but with high hopes. One of the copy-typists Childers took with him recalled, 'For the first time since I met him, I saw Erskine Childers laughing, joking and carefree. He and his cousin Robert Barton were like two schoolboys exchanging tales of amusing adventures.'[16] Once again, the party was received like royalty at Euston, the crowds accompanying the delegates and their staff to Knightsbridge. One of the newspapers engagingly remarked upon the 'quaint humour really natural to the occasion in the cab full of cooks with their implements of office that brought up the rear.'[17] Childers wrote in his diary, 'Mobbed. Wonderful scene.'[18]

The Irish had rented two houses within a couple of hundred yards of each other, just off the northern end of Sloane Street. Collins's reputation demanded an entourage of bodyguards, and his party occupied 15 Cadogan Gardens; the other delegates were at 22 Hans Place. The weekend was spent settling into the offices they would use before a meeting on Monday, 10 October between the secretaries – Childers and his number two, John Chartres, on the Irish side, Sir Edward Grigg and Professor Tom Jones on the British – to settle protocol. The conference itself then began at Downing Street on 11 October.

To avoid obliging his team of negotiators to shake hands with the 'murder gang', Lloyd George adroitly introduced them across the broad Downing Street conference table. Facing the Irish – the secretaries sat slightly back from the table – were the Secretary for War, Sir Laming Worthington-Evans; the Lord Chief Justice, Sir Gordon Hewart; and the Chief Secretary for Ireland, Sir Hamar Greenwood. As Lord Longford observed in his seminal study of the treaty negotiations, so rich in political personalities was England at the time that any one of the other four could have played Prime Minister with distinction:[19] Austen Chamberlain (son of Joseph), the leader of the House; Lord Birkenhead, the Attorney General; Lloyd George himself; and Winston Churchill.

For Childers it must have been the oddest of experiences, to be sitting in such a place, for such a purpose, facing men such as these. And as he must have realized, on the events of the coming weeks hinged the success or failure of the cause to which he had now devoted his life.

III

The treaty proposals on the table were essentially those prepared by the British the previous July and rejected by the Dáil in August. They comprised the offer of Dominion status for Ireland, with its various qualifications. In a broad sense, the Irish *wanted* neither the qualifications nor the Dominion status: a predictable stand, perhaps, but one which Childers, over the course of the summer, had been one of the major intellectual influences in determining.[20] At the same time, what the Irish would be *prepared to accept* might be a different matter, particularly for Griffith and Collins. With these points in mind, one of the few tactics which the plenipotentiaries had agreed with de Valera was that Irish objections to the qualifications should be addressed at first; then – and only then – a distinct counter-proposal should be made. This would unveil the notion of 'external association', the Irish secret weapon.

'External association' was a half-way house between Dominion status and a full republic. As envisaged by de Valera, an 'external association' between Ireland and the Empire would give Ireland much the same level of freedom as that associated with Dominion status, with the crucial difference that Ireland would be neither a Dominion, nor within the Empire; there would be no formal allegiance to the Crown – no spoken oath – and Irishmen would not be considered British subjects. As Lord Longford puts it, it was a status 'shorn of the symbolism that was felt to humiliate'.[21] In his opening remarks at the conference, Arthur Griffith remarked that 'England's policy in the past has been to treat Ireland as a conquered and subject country. If there is a change in the policy of subordinating Ireland to English interest, then there appears to be a possibility of peace';[22] To de Valera, such an 'external association' would be the most acceptable proof of that change of heart. De Valera himself has been credited with the idea, but there is an interesting note from him to Childers, dated 15 June 1921, alluding to the paper drafted by Molly Childers and Alexander Lindsay which the latter had presented to General Smuts; that paper, embracing as it did the idea of a neutral Ireland within the Empire, was comparable to 'external association'. The note was written several weeks before the famous occasion on which de Valera drew his geometrical expression of 'external association' for Childers and Collins. De Valera had written to Childers that he thought the idea of Irish neutrality 'an interesting concept'.[23] In the end, though, however interesting de Valera found it, external association was a relatively complex idea which, if it was to be effectively pursued, had to be understood by, and have the commitment of, the full team of delegates. Neither appears to have been the case.

Whatever the position of the delegates, the agreed tactic was for this offer to remain veiled for the time being, only being put forward as part of the Irish counter-proposals to be outlined in due course. Certainly there were plenty of other matters to deal with. In a series of seven formal sessions over the two weeks that followed the opening of the conference, the negotiators touched upon all the qualifications the British Government wished to attach to Dominion status; they also discussed such matters as violations of the Truce, and a controversial telegram that de Valera had sent the Pope. The two most important issues, however, were Ulster, and defence. The Irish took the view that Ulster was an intrinsic part of Ireland, economically, socially and culturally, and as such had to be part and parcel of any general agreement regarding the island's relationship with the Empire. Whatever degree of sympathy the British delegates might or might not feel for this – both Chamberlain and Birkenhead were dyed-in-the-wool Unionists – they had of course to be sensitive to the perspective as seen from Ulster. In the first days of the conference the two sides gradually worked towards an agreement that the coercion of Ulster was untenable; she could not, and should not, be forced into any agreement. That having been established, a compromise of sorts was clearly required. So far, so good.

On defence, the British government's aim was to maintain bases – ports, and the new aerodromes – for the traditional purpose of defending its western seaboard – an issue which, in view of the success of the German U-boat campaign in the recent war, loomed large in British minds. The counter-argument, masterminded by Childers, was that whatever official status Ireland ultimately achieved, for Britain to retain bases there would effectively mean the continuance of military domination of Ireland by the Crown, thus reducing any form of autonomy to mere pretence. In Irish minds, this loomed as large.

A subcommittee was set up for the purpose of resolving this issue, led on the Irish side by Collins and Childers, on the British by Churchill. The first meeting was held on 13 October at the Colonial Office. Childers made a note of those present: 'Beatty, Churchill, Mick, me, Dalton'.[24] Expecting to find the British reserved, Childers found them to be 'not as stiff as we thought', but formality returned a few days later when he presented his own paper on the defence issue, in response to the British proposals. 'Memo presented,' Childers recorded. 'Great flutter. Long argument. Note of compromise at end.'[25] Churchill's conclusion was that the issues Childers raised were so fundamental, they would have to be considered by the main conference. They were duly brought forward on 21 October, just before the full Irish counter-proposals. 'I must say that the document was one of marked ability,' was Churchill's disarming opening salvo, 'but it was a reasoned and deliberate refusal of every article which we had made out for the defence of our security from the military and naval standpoints. Use of ports, aerodromes, facilities for recruiting, prohibition of an Irish Navy, all had been turned down. Instead the alternative was put up of a guaranteed Irish neutrality.' He went on to declare that the differences between the two sides highlighted by the memo 'lie at the root of the whole conference'.[26] In a sense, Childers had struck the gold: could a neutral Ireland be accommodated within the Empire? Apparently not.

Each side reached certain conclusions arising out of these various discussions, the nip-and-tuck and the position-taking of the first fortnight of the conference.

The British seem from the first to have suspected that there were divisions on the Irish side, and now felt them to have been confirmed. As Lloyd George remarked, 'The moderate section wanted a settlement whereas the gunmen did not.'[27] More accurately, the British had identified in Childers the least flexible member of the party, both generally, and on the central issue of Ireland's status within – or without – the Empire. He was credited by them with 'fanatical opposition to any Dominion settlement'.[28] As Churchill in particular saw it, it was Childers who 'pressed extreme counsels'.[29] They also saw that the Irish were procrastinating, avoiding addressing the main issues that divided the two sides. In these circumstances, British tactics were adroit. Having withdrawn from the conference of 21 October for a private consultation – in itself a stratagem – Lloyd George returned with some very specific requests with regard to the Irish counter-proposals, now due to be presented: he asked that they should define fully the plenipotentiaries' attitude on 'allegiance to the King, voluntary entry to the Empire, and the concession of defence facilities to secure British shores from attack'.[30] It was also arranged that a 'private conference' should be held between Griffith and Collins, Chamberlain and Lloyd George. The British purpose in this was partly to narrow the conference to its chief participants, but also to discount Childers, as the major obstacle to a settlement. Their agreement to the 'private conference' was an indication of the fact that Griffith and Collins had reached a similar conclusion. This was partly a consequence of the way Childers had handled the defence issue, but also stemmed from Collins' suspicion that he was sending de Valera private dispatches regarding the progress of the conference.[31]

The Irish delegation having been literally divided, the British could address themselves to the two members most enthusiastic for settlement. The first of the these smaller sessions was to be held following the main meeting on the afternoon of Monday, 24 November. For Childers it was not a happy development, and left him puzzled, hurt and suspicious. In his diary he noted, 'A great mystery was made about the meeting and a ridiculous communiqué published, saying that the main conference had been postponed for a "committee".'[32]

IV

It was now that the major issues began to be debated. To the British, of course, their own position seemed not unreasonable. As they saw it, the relationship of Ireland to the Empire was inextricably bound up with her recognition of the sovereignty of the Crown, and declaration of allegiance to it; for was not the Crown 'the symbol of all that keeps the nations of the Empire together. It is the keystone of the arch in law as well as in sentiment.'[33] Such issues were the essence of Empire, of an Empire they feared the Irish were intent to destroy.

When they saw the Irish counter-proposals, they were not reassured. Drafted chiefly by Childers, the proposals were intentionally ambiguous as to the form any association between England and Ireland should take. In the full meeting on Monday the 24th, Lloyd George questioned the Irish delegates about the meaning of the phrase, 'Ireland will consent to adhere for all purposes of agreed concern to the Commonwealth'. Assuming all other conditions were satisfied, he asked, 'does that mean . . . you are prepared to come inside the Empire as New Zealand, Canada?' Arthur Griffith's reply – 'That is not quite our idea of association'[34] – was hardly calculated to allay British concerns. On this central issue, the British seemed reluctant to give ground at all. De Valera, briefed on the substance of this meeting, commented:

'There can be no question of our asking the Irish people to enter into an arrangement which would make them subject to the Crown, or demand from them allegiance to the King. If war is the alternative, we can only face it . . .'[35] The pace was quickening.

Of the subsidiary issues, Ulster loomed large. Although both sides had accepted the need for compromise, they remained wary. The Irish in particular realized that if the conference were to fail, it was politically far more desirable that it should do so over Ulster's intransigent refusal to accept any form of Dominion status than over their own refusal to accept any form of association with the Crown. An important Unionist meeting in Liverpool was imminent, the annual Party Conference. With an eye to this, Lloyd George proposed as a compromise that Ulster should be part of any agreement reached between the two sides, but that she should have the opportunity of opting out after twelve months if she so wished; should she do so, a 'boundary commission' would then come into operation, to re-examine the line between the North and South. Ostensibly this would favour the latter, to the extent that in due course the Prime Minister was able to persuade the Irish to believe that Ulster would become economically unviable. After a good deal of wrangling among the Irish delegates, an appropriate form of words was drafted on 2 November. Subsequently, as the idea of the Boundary Commission came to take more concrete form, and as the day of the Party Conference approached, Lloyd George once again demanded reassurance from the Irish party that they would not oppose the Boundary Commission at a later date, on the ground that he would be risking his political career by proposing the compromise to the Unionists. Lloyd George suggested to Griffith that if he could give written assent to the British proposal on Ulster, the acquiescence could be obtained of Sir James Craig, the new leader of the Ulster Unionists, to an arrangement which would nominally retain the national integrity of the country.

Although Lloyd George's suggestion was presented to Griffith as a 'tactical' requirement for the meeting on the 17th November, it appears, with the benefit of hindsight, to have been rather more than this. Somewhat unguardedly, in a private meeting with Lloyd George on 12 November, Griffith assured Lloyd George that on this issue he would not repudiate him.[36] The consequence was the endorsement at the Liverpool meeting by Sir James Craig and the Unionists of the government's efforts, apparently in the belief that the impact of the Boundary Commission on the size of Ulster would be minimal. Other results, however, would follow.

More important was the British reaction to the Irish proposals, given to Childers on 16 November. There were some minor concessions, on defence and trade; the Ulster arrangements were as they had been discussed with Griffith, although his fellow delegates remained in ignorance of his personal assurances to Lloyd George. Significantly, Ireland was to remain within the Empire. The crux had thus been reached.

To this the Irish drafted in reply a 'Memorandum by the Irish Representatives', which combined 'recognition' of the King as head of an association of nations – Ireland being one – forming a British Commonwealth. Although the Memorandum had been prepared by Childers, Collins and Griffith were encouraged to think it was Robert Barton's handiwork. Another crux had been reached: tensions within the Irish party, latent from the beginning, had finally come to a head.

On the one hand were Collins, Griffith and Duggan, who increasingly felt that Dominion status was the best that might be extracted from the British. On the other were Barton, Duffy and above all Childers, who conceived that, in Barton's words, such a compromise constituted 'treason to the Republic'; they felt the Irish had made numerous concessions, the British few or none; they had lost confidence in Griffith. Childers returned very briefly to Dublin to alert de Valera to this fissure, but was unable to persuade him to act. Accordingly, while waiting for a response to the 'Memorandum', Childers busied himself in preparing, with his usual rigour, a document in which his views were detailed. He examined the proposals in the light of Ireland's full claim for, in his own words, a republic 'unfettered by any obligation or restriction whatsoever'. He concluded that 'out of the ten paragraphs of the current Irish proposals, Nos 1 and 7 are the only ones which do not make concessions from this position.'[37]

Fair and thorough though this assessment may have been, it was difficult for Griffith to take it as other than an assault on his chairmanship, and he went on to openly accuse Childers of trying to prevent a settlement. 'Attacks me about *Riddle of the Sands*,' noted Childers.

'Says I caused the European war and now want to cause another. I said I stood on the strategical case in both instances.'[38] Commenting on this squabble, Lord Longford wrote:

> Childers, the old Committee Clerk of the House of Commons, was prone to a formalism strange to Ireland and, in the eyes of Griffith, ridiculous. The story is told of how Childers, in the best Whitehall tradition, would stamp 'secret' on memoranda from, say, economic advisers in Dublin, and how Griffith could hardly bear the sight of the stamp. It has been said, and not by enemies of Griffith, that behind these trifling exasperations lay a genuine and growing suspicion that Childers was no honest friend of Ireland. Be that as it may, there is no doubt that Griffith saw in Childers, with his rigid limits on the verbal scope of the bargaining, an obstacle not much less menacing than the British themselves to a satisfactory settlement – that settlement to hopes of which Griffith had dedicated his life and surrendered a fortune, and which, once infinitely far off, seemed, but for Childers, certain to succeed.[39]

The conference that had begun so brightly for Childers was now turning into a nightmare. When he saw Basil Williams during a preliminary visit to London in July, Williams was shocked by Childers' physical and mental state;[40] now his behaviour at one or two of the formal sessions suggested a man beginning to buckle under the strain.[41] He wrote home to Molly, 'Oh for an hour even of talk with you!'[42]

Childers was by this time as emotionally attached to the ideal of a republic as the many who had risked their lives for it. Yet his commitment was not simply emotional. The British argument that the Irish should accept Dominion status and enjoy the same freedoms as the other dominions was fair enough in its way; but it was this very analogy he had taken issue with in *The Framework of Home Rule*. Now he argued that the considerable freedom enjoyed by Dominions like Canada was a consequence, not of the generosity of the legal framework that bound them to the Empire, but of mere custom and acquiescence on the part of England. In a memorandum prepared towards the end of November, he instanced:

In LAW: Canada is a subordinate dependency.
In FACT: Canada is, by the full admission of British statesmen, equal in status to Great Britain and as free as Great Britain.

In LAW: The British parliament can make laws for Canada.
In FACT: Canada alone can legislate for Canada.

In LAW: The British Government can veto Canadian Bills.
In FACT: It cannot.

And so on. It then followed that 'If the Irish accepted Dominion status they would be entrusting England through the Crown or Imperial Parliament with powers that legally entitled her to treat Ireland as a subordinate, but which it was hoped that England, following her conduct towards the Dominions, would forbearingly render nominal.'[43] The problem, as Childers saw it, was that all the evidence of history suggested that whatever British attitudes towards her other colonies and dominions might be, Ireland had long proved an exception to the general rule. As well as sentiment, therefore, there was an element of hard logic in Childers' position.

The disadvantage of taking this stance in the treaty negotiations was that it made no allowance for the Government's limited room for manoeuvre. Lloyd George had repeatedly stressed these limitations, and they were real enough. At home, particularly as the leader of a coalition government, Lloyd George had to balance Irish demands against the vociferous position of the Unionists, two of whom were among his fellow negotiators; abroad, he was having to cope with insurrection in Egypt and in India, both parts of Empire in which the Crown was, indeed, 'the keystone of the arch in law as well as sentiment'. As Churchill later put it, 'No act of British state policy in which I have been concerned aroused more violently conflicting sentiments than the Irish settlement. For a system of human government so vast and variously composed as the British Empire to compact with open rebellion in the peculiar form in which it was developed in Ireland was an event which might well have shaken to the foundations that authority upon which the peace and order of hundreds and millions of people of many races and communities depended.'[44]

So it was that Erskine Childers and Winston Churchill, their stories so curiously interwoven, their sentiments on Empire once so close, came to represent, that autumn in Downing Street, violently opposing notions as to the future management – indeed the very existence – of 'the mightiest and most beneficent Empire ever known in the history of mankind'.

V

The conference now had barely ten days to run, as it was most desirable that a settlement should be reached before the opening of the new Northern Ireland Parliament on 4 December. Much as the Irish had expected, the British greeted their 'Memorandum' in no very welcoming spirit: Lloyd George claimed that it evinced no progress from the position at the beginning of the conference. The Irish then briefly returned to Dublin, where on 25 November the Cabinet endorsed a limited recognition of Great Britain as 'accepted head of the Combination of Associated States'[45] – reflecting, of course, an association of Ireland with England *outside* the Empire. Informed of this, Lloyd George maintained that the position was impossible: 'Any British Government that attempted to propose to the British people the abrogation of the Crown would be smashed to atoms.'[46]

Then, suddenly, there was real progress. On the evening of Monday, 28 November Griffith was offered by Lloyd George the opportunity to add to any further draft treaty 'any phrase he liked' which would 'ensure that the position of the Crown in Ireland should be no more in practice than it was in Canada or in any other Dominion'.[47] Lord Longford comments that this was

> . . . a capital achievement. According to the promise given this day, Ireland in the Treaty receives not only the law of Canada, but in addition her practice and constitutional usage. If during the last ten years Childers has proved a false prophet and Ireland, so far from being denied constitutional advantages accruing to other Dominions, has actually led the way in Dominion constitutional advance, the credit must go to the splendid persistence of Griffith, and Childers himself.[48]

In view of the attraction Dominion status already held for perhaps the majority of the delegates by this time, surely this meant that an agreement would now be possible? – the various qualifications to Dominion status that still remained notwithstanding. On Thursday, 1 December the 'final' British proposals arrived at Hans Place; they had been modified, favourably to the Irish on the question of finance, in a meeting at the Treasury handled by Childers and Collins. On Saturday, the delegates returned again to Dublin for a final meeting before the signing of the Treaty, supposed to take place before 6 December. They were already careworn, and their journey was marred by a fatal collision which necessitated the return of their boat to Holyhead. Collins had reassured his fellow passengers, 'I have been in tighter corners than this';[49] Childers' diary says simply, 'I could not sleep a wink.'[50]

The question that faced the Irish Cabinet was whether the best possible terms had now been extracted from the British. In view of what had gone before, it was scarcely surprising that the delegates were divided; what was alarming was quite how divided they had become. Griffith was strongly in favour of acceptance, Collins and Duggan tacitly so. Robert Barton and Gavan Duffy pointed out that the terms gave neither full Dominion status, nor any real guarantees on Ulster or the results of the Boundary Commission; they also felt the British could be pushed further, especially on the question of allegiance to the Crown. Childers, no longer a Cabinet member, it should be remembered, and with no vote, still opposed any arrangement that fell so short of guaranteeing a full republic as the British proposals did, and was scathing about the defence provisions, which deprived Ireland of her own navy and effectively obliged her to co-operate with Britain in time of war.

When the Cabinet was alone, the matter became more heated. De Valera was for rejection on the basis that he 'could not subscribe to the Oath of Allegiance, nor could he sign any document which would give North-East Ulster power to vote itself out of the Irish state'.[51] Griffith took the view that the system of government provided for in the draft Treaty document constituted a republic in all but name. Finally Cathal Brugha, one of the firmest of the republicans, demanded,

'Don't you realize that if you sign this thing, you will split in Ireland from top to bottom?'[52]

In the end, it was decided that in its current form the document could not be signed, and the delegates were charged with a final attempt to persuade the British to revise the proposals. Whatever happened, they were to refer to Dublin before concluding anything. They were now sufficiently divided for Childers, Barton and Duffy to take the packet from Dublin's North Wall, the others from Kingstown. Back in London yet another document was duly prepared, but when it was discussed among the delegates there was disagreement over exactly what the Cabinet had enjoined.

As finally drafted for presentation, the paper reiterated the notion of external association so definitively repudiated by the British, stating that 'Ireland will agree to be associated with the British Commonwealth on all matters of common concern . . . and to recognize the Crown as head of that association.'[53] Griffith and Collins refused to countenance this drafting, and insisted that Barton and Duffy should present it themselves. But at the last moment Griffith yielded the point, and the three delegates arrived at Downing Street at four o'clock on Sunday, 4 December to meet Birkenhead, Chamberlain and Lloyd George. At the close of a lengthy and circular discussion Gavan Duffy all too directly exposed the Irish position. 'We should be closely associated with you in all large matters as the Dominions, and in the matter of Defence still more so; but our difficulty is to come into the Empire, looking at all that has happened in the past.'[54] Chamberlain rose to his feet, cried out 'That ends it', and the conversation was closed, with the British agreeing to send across final copies of their proposals, the Irish to reject them. In which case, responded Lloyd George, he would inform Sir James Craig that the negotiations had failed.[55]

This was another tactical manoeuvre on the part of Lloyd George. Far too astute not to realize the significance of Collins' absence, he at once made arrangements to see him. The two bed-rock issues remained Ulster and the Crown, and Lloyd George skilfully appeared to offer sufficient concessions on Ulster, specifically regarding the scope of the Boundary Commission, for Collins to see the possibility of reciprocating in the matter of allegiance to the Crown: if the 'essential unity' of the Irish state might be maintained, then allegiance – in practice,

Dominion status – might be acceptable: a *quid pro quo*. Following that meeting early on Monday, 5 December, negotiations were formally resumed; later that day the last conference began, and the final drama of the signing unfolded.

With the need to apprise Sir James Craig of the final result of the negotiations before the first session of the Ulster Parliament, and an increasingly real threat of a resumption of hostilities in Ireland if the conference failed, the pressure was on. 'After two months of futilities and rigmarole,' wrote Churchill, 'unutterably wearied Ministers faced the Irish delegates themselves in actual desperation, and knowing well that death stood at their elbows.'[56] Lloyd George at once attacked on the Ulster issue. The Irish strategy – that if negotiations were to break down, they should do so at this point, so that the blame might reasonably be laid on the failure of Ulster to accept any sort of Home Rule that might eventually apply to them – has already been noted. Against this, Lloyd George had two cards to play: his extraction from Griffith, before the Party Conference of 17 November, of a promise 'not to let him down' on the Ulster issue; and the ambiguity with which he had represented, to the Unionists on the one hand and to Sinn Féin on the other, the real scope of the Boundary Commission. On the issue of the Oath of Allegiance, a form of words more acceptable to Irish dignity was agreed; on defence and the proscription of an Irish Navy, Churchill remained obdurate. The British then withdrew, to pave the way for Lloyd George's most brilliant piece of legerdemain.

First of all, Churchill returned to make the concession that after five years Ireland might take a share in her own coastal defence. Then Lloyd George himself appeared. Having previously implicitly reminded Griffith of his promise, he now produced the document to which he said he had understood Griffith to have agreed, embodying a Boundary Commission revision of the Northern Ireland boundary, should Ulster opt out of the proposed all-Ireland Parliament – the document he had used to placate Sir James Craig. Lloyd George now directly reminded Griffith of his pledge. Griffith, a man of the highest personal honour, said simply, 'I have never let a man down in my life, and I never will.'[57] Thus Griffith ended all possibility of breaking on Ulster, leaving the Irish with the unpalatable option of breaking on the Crown – since

Lloyd George, in another masterpiece of timing, now offered a further concession: not a limited freedom in trading arrangements, but complete fiscal autonomy.

Time was running out. The courier who was to take the message to Sir James Craig would now not be able to make the ordinary boat-train to Belfast. With time of the essence, Lloyd George had contrived to face the Irish delegates with the simplest and starkest of choices. The Prime Minister, producing two letters, held one in either hand:

> I have to communicate with Sir James Craig tonight. Here are the alternative letters which I have prepared, one enclosing Articles of Agreement reached by His Majesty's Government and yourselves, and the other saying that the Sinn Féin representatives refuse to come within the Empire. If I send this letter it is war, and war within three days. Which letter am I to send? Whichever letter you choose travels by special train to Holyhead, and by destroyer to Belfast. The train is waiting with steam up at Euston, [the messenger] is ready. If he is to reach Sir James Craig in time we must know your answer by 10 p.m. You can have until then, but no longer, to decide whether you will give peace or war to your country.[58]

It was the performance of a lifetime, and, perhaps inevitably, the Irish were ensnared. Churchill recorded the delegation's reactions:

> Mr Griffith said, speaking in his soft voice, and with his modest manner, 'I will give the answer of the Irish Delegates at nine tonight; but, Mr Prime Minister, I personally will sign this agreement and recommend it to my countrymen.' 'Do I understand, Mr Griffith,' said Mr Lloyd George, 'that though everyone else refuse, you will nevertheless agree to sign?' 'Yes, that is so, Mr Prime Minister,' replied this quiet little man of great heart and great purpose . . . Michael Collins rose, looking as though he was going to shoot someone, preferably himself. In all my life I never saw so much passion and suffering in restraint.[59]

VI

The five delegates and Childers then assembled in Hans Place 'and the last tragic wrangle began between the six men chosen by Ireland to represent her in her greatest crisis, all worthy in character and attainment of their position, all ready to die for her, but all now overtired, over-strained, and hopelessly at variance.'[60] They had been painted into a corner by Lloyd George. He had placed tremendous pressure on them to accede, making them believe that no postponement of the answer to Craig was possible, no time available for reference to de Valera in Dublin – and that a terrible war would follow, for which they, collectively and individually, would be responsible, if they did not all agree at once, and agree moreover to recommend the proposals to the Dáil. On every one of these points the Prime Minister was massaging the truth, in varying degrees; but then, he *was* Prime Minister, and he *was* Lloyd George.

Griffith had already indicated his willingness to sign; Collins did so on the way back to Hans Place, and Duggan followed suit. This left Robert Barton and Gavan Duffy in an inconceivably difficult position. If they held out, on them alone would lie the responsibility for the resumption of war. 'Final discussion,' noted Childers. 'A.G. spoke almost passionately for signing. It seems the other side insist all delegates shall sign and recommend Treaty to Dáil. Monstrous document. M.C. said nothing. Bob refused to sign, and G.D. Then long and hot argument – all about war and committing our young men to die for nothing. What could G.D. get better? etc., etc. G.D. murmured quietly, Bob shaken.'[61] Ten o'clock passed, ten-thirty, then eleven.

In Downing Street, expectations were low. Chamberlain and Churchill began to wonder if the Irish would return at all. 'The day had been one of unrelieved strain,' wrote Chamberlain. 'The tension reached its height during the long wait for the return of the Irish Delegation in the evening. But there is a limit to human endurance. The reaction came. I recall as we waited, our talk was of the merriest, and the room rang with laughter. Finally, news came from Hans Place. The delegates were on their way. When they entered it was clear from their faces that they had come to a great decision after a prolonged struggle. As before, they were superficially very calm and quiet. There was a long pause.'[62]

Barton had been the king-pin. He was torn between two irreconcilable imperatives, the threat of war on the one hand, on the other his oath to the Republic, 'the most sacred bond on earth'. Three times Duggan, Griffith and Collins made to leave for Downing Street. Three times Barton recalled them. Then at last it was agreed that he might talk privately with Childers. 'I said it was principle,' recorded Childers, 'and I felt Molly was with us. Suddenly he said: "Well, I suppose I must sign." '[63] The mention of Molly marked the last great turning-point in Childers' life, and a turning-point in Irish history. Childers commented in his diary: 'Privately . . . RCB said that my allusion to Molly's support for refusal to sign last night made him sign – deciding element – because his home reminded him of thousands of homes to be ruined. Strange reason! But chief reason seems to have been his belief that war was really imminent and inevitable . . .'[64] And so it was over.

'There was a long pause,' recounted Chamberlain, 'or seemed to be: then Mr Griffith said: "Mr Prime Minister, the delegation is willing to sign the agreements." '[65]

So ended seven hundred years of Anglo-Irish history, ended by an agreement whose division of the country in to North and South stands to this day.

The 'Articles of Agreement for a Treaty' conferring Dominion status upon 'The Irish Free State' were finally signed at 2.20 a.m. on 6 December 1921. The delegates and the British negotiators then shook hands. Childers waited outside during those 'inexpressibly miserable hours'; unable to concentrate on a biography of Lincoln, he found some distraction in re-reading *The Riddle of the Sands* and discussing it with the British courier. At last the great doors swung open, and Lloyd George's eyes, as he emerged in his triumph, fell upon (as he later wrote)

> a man who had used all the resources of an ingenious and well-trained mind, backed by tenacious will, to wreck every endeavour to reach agreement, Mr Erskine Childers. At every crucial point in the negotiations he played a sinister part. When we walked out of the room where we had sat for hours together, worn with toil and anxious labour, but

> all happy that our great task of reconciliation had been achieved, we met with Mr Erskine Childers outside, sullen with disappointment and compressed wrath at what he conceived to be the surrender of the principle he fought for.[66]

This of course was Lloyd George's own view, and not a very generous one. Lord Longford's is more judicious: '[The] Irish Delegates had met with wills as strong, intelligences as subtle, and diplomacy more experienced than theirs. Threats, too, more potent.'[67] Of the Irish party, Childers' intelligence was not the least able, nor his will the least strong, nor his diplomacy the least experienced. Despite his problems with Griffith, as Secretary he had contributed as much as any of the delegates, other than Griffith himself and Collins, to the inclusion of such liberties as were embodied in the final agreement, particularly in the matter of defence and the issue of Ireland's real, as opposed to legal, status as a Dominion. Had he been a delegate himself, he would surely have achieved more, despite the little the British had to give. With Barton and Gavan Duffy as fellow delegates, would he have outfaced Duggan, Collins and Griffith? Surely not. But had there been any sensible measure of agreement between the delegates, conceivably the six together might have extracted from the Crown something closer to de Valera's 'external association', if assuredly not acceptance of that revolutionary concept itself.

What would have been the effect of this? As Michael Hopkinson has remarked, 'the Treaty-signing was the decisive event which led to the civil war. No document could have more effectively brought out into the open divisions in the philosophy and leadership of the Sinn Féin movement. If it had offered a little more or a little less, it might well have unified opinion for or against it.'[68] Now, Childers' was the most articulate, forceful and intelligent voice of the political movement for self-determination that then dominated Ireland. With the benefit of hindsight, it could be argued that in the autumn of 1921 any form of republic was beyond Ireland's reach, and that she should have reconciled herself to political reality and accepted the first terms offered; in these circumstances, and given his known views, Childers should not have been sent to London at all. Alternatively, a concerted and united attempt should have been made to preserve the essence of a republic; in this case, Childers should have gone as a delegate. In either circumstance, it seems just possible that the subsequent splits, in the Cabinet, the Dáil, Sinn Féin, the republican armies, and the country – indeed, the civil war itself – might have been averted.

But the terms of the Treaty were as they were, and the following morning Childers awoke 'desperately dreary and lonely'.[69] His world seemed in ruins. For him, it was not the end of the beginning; it was the beginning of the end.

18
Nemesis

1922

'I'll never understand this country.'

Erskine Childers, 1922

I

A year later Childers was dead, 'shot at dawn', as Lloyd George put it, 'for rebellion against the liberties he had helped to win.'[1] Perhaps it could not have ended otherwise.

De Valera had all along maintained a position somewhat aloof from the realities of the negotiations in Downing Street. On the morning of Tuesday, 6 December he awoke in Limerick to rumours that an agreement had been reached in London, terms and conditions unknown. He travelled up to Dublin that day, and learned the details of the Treaty from Éamon Duggan, newly arrived from London. He was appalled. While the negotiators were still on their way back from London, he consulted those Cabinet members available. One suggested that the 'delegates should be arrested as traitors immediately on their return',[2] but it was agreed that a full meeting of the Cabinet should be called to hear what the negotiators had to say for themselves – or, as the press release put it, to 'consider the circumstances under which the plenipotentiaries had signed the agreement in London'.[3] Desmond Fitzgerald was once again handling publicity; when given the draft press release, he remarked, 'This might be altered, Mr President. It reads as if you were opposed to the settlement.' 'And that is the way

I intend it to read,' replied de Valera. 'Publish it as it is.'[4] So opened the last and the saddest phase of the struggle for Irish freedom.

Considering his stature and the part he had played in the treaty negotiations, it was scarcely surprising that Childers should also have been asked to attend the Cabinet meeting. It lasted all of Thursday, 8 December, and well into the night, covering both the terms of the Treaty itself and the circumstances of the signing, in particular the delegates' failure to consult Dublin. The signatories felt, at the least, obliged to defend the document, and to recommend it, as they had undertaken, to the Dáil; Griffith and Collins were more positive advocates. The outcome was that de Valera led the minority of the Cabinet in voting against recommending the Treaty to the assembly. The split had come.

The next step was for the Treaty to be formally debated in the Dáil; here, of course, as a TD, Childers could play a fuller part.

It was inevitable that the Dáil should have been already divided. Since 1919 its members had been grouped into moderate and more militant elements. The aim of the original Sinn Féin, as established by Griffith, was to achieve its ends by constitutional methods; it had envisaged independence, but under the aegis of the Crown. Once Sinn Féin had become a significant political force, its infiltration by those more ambitious for the country, and less regulated in their methods, began. The centre of gravity of the organization was shifted decisively by the events of 1916, and by the end of 1921 the nuances of the Irish political scene had become even more complicated. Among both militants and moderates who were closely in touch with those they were supposed to represent, the war-weariness of the whole country seemed the primary consideration. For more than three years Ireland and its people had been living under an intolerable strain. If it was not a question of peace at any price, it was at least fairly clear that there was little will among the electorate for prolonging the struggle. Allied to this group were those who might be termed the realists among those originally of militant allegiances; these were the most sensitive to Lloyd George's threat of 'immediate and terrible war', believing that the resumption of the war was pointless in military terms. The leaders of the Supreme Council of the Irish Republican Brotherhood, including

Michael Collins, are generally believed to have been among these 'realists'.

There remained, at least within the Dáil, a number who were altogether less prepared to give up the Republic. In a letter to the press on 10 December, following the split Cabinet meeting, de Valera claimed that 'the terms of the agreement are in violent conflict with the wishes of the majority of the Nation as expressed freely in successive elections during the last three years'.[5] While this phrasing was technically true of the elections themselves, it was misleading in the sense that majority sentiment by December 1921 appears to have been definitely, although not overwhelmingly, in favour of the settlement. As Austin Stack later conceded, 'The British and Irish press carried the people off their feet in favour of the "Treaty and Peace".'[6] Yet there were still idealists; men like Robert Barton, who regarded his oath to the Republic as 'the most sacred bond on earth'; men like the Galway republican army leader Liam Mellows, who spoke of the Republic as 'a living tangible thing. Something for which men gave their lives, for which men were hanged, for which men are in gaol, for which the people suffered and for which men are still prepared to give their lives.'[7] It was people like this to whom the Treaty really did amount – in Barton's phrase – to treason to the Republic. Needless to say, Childers was among them, as was Molly. Of Childers, Desmond Fitzgerald later observed that, 'He admired the heroism that had been so marked a feature of the recent struggle. He affirmed his principles as a religious faith. Compromise meant recantation and apostasy.'[8]

There were other reasons for the two sides to disagree. As Robert Kee has pointed out, some of the divisions were surely a consequence of 'the removal of the need for what had often been unnatural unanimity'.[9] Between 1919 and 1921 the various strands that made up Sinn Féin had been unanimous at least in their opposition to the presence of every manifestation of the Crown: with that unifying bugbear now on the point of withdrawal, it was perhaps not surprising that the party should turn upon the loci of dissatisfaction within itself. Perhaps, too, it was only natural that, as quarrels broke out, so much animus should be directed against the man who, whatever his protestations to the contrary, would always seem the sole remaining Englishman in their midst.

The Dáil debate was distinguished more by its length than by the brilliance of its speeches; various public and private sessions occupied the assembly from 14 December to 7 January, with an adjournment for Christmas. The debate also quickly became bitter and rancorous. The whole of the first session was devoted to a disagreeable but inconclusive examination of the failure of the plenipotentiaries to consult Dublin before signing the Treaty. The next session was private. Here de Valera, leading those opposing the Treaty, introduced a coherent alternative to the Treaty, a proposal which in due course came to be known as Document No. 2. This, over which de Valera and Childers together had burned much midnight oil, was essentially an elaboration of the 'external association' proposals. But it was as intellectual in its approach and its demands on its auditors as the original idea, so made little headway and was temporarily withdrawn. All the republican leaders spoke at some length during the public session on 19 December: de Valera, Griffith, Collins – and Childers, whose speech was received without enthusiasm. He examined the Treaty in detail and at length; he talked of the 'honourable' notion of external association, and how the defence terms which gave the British bases in the country left Ireland vulnerable to British authority in times of emergency. Finally, he inverted Parnell's famous dictum. 'This treaty is a step backward,' he declared, 'and I, for my part, would be inclined to say he would be a bold man who would dare set a boundary to the backward march of a nation which of its own free will has deliberately relinquished its own independence.'[10] The indifference of his audience notwithstanding, Childers had very thoroughly enumerated the disadvantages of the Treaty. Indeed, as F. S. L. Lyons observed, 'With this speech, one of the ablest delivered on either side, the case against the Treaty had been presented in all its most important aspects . . . Childers so to say wound up for the opposition.'[11]

For the pro-Treaty faction, a young lawyer named Kevin O'Higgins advocated the Treaty as the 'sole way of avoiding bloodshed',[12] and there had been powerful speeches from Griffith, and from Collins, who best summarized the way the Treaty was increasingly seen by the moderates: 'In my opinion it gives us freedom, not the ultimate freedom that all nations aspire and develop to, but the freedom to achieve it.'[13] Thereafter, however, the quality of the addresses and debate diminished. As Dorothy Macardle put it:

> Every circumstance that could cloud vision and distort judgement was present. Ancestral passions, reaction and exhaustion, hatred of England, fear of responsibility, respect for the patriot dead, loathing of war, fear of the taunt of 'traitor', fear of yielding to that fear, personal loyalties, all were at work and all were expressing themselves in the form of reasoned advocacy for this or that clause. Party spirit, for the first time, split the Dáil into two factions, violently antagonistic to one another.[14]

Childers himself could hardly avoid the divisions. At one point, Collins was found by Robert Barton, pleading with him: 'The two men stood facing one another – the big broad-faced country lad with the heavy jowl and the hanging lock of hair; the little English officer with the skeleton head and the haggard face, "sicklied o'er with the pale cast of thought". "Does this mean that we're going to part?" Collins asked. "I'm afraid so." Collins crushed his fists into his eyes, and all at once Barton saw the flood of tears as he tossed his head in misery.'[15] Friends, comrades – a whole nation was being torn apart.

When the vote in the Dáil was finally taken on 7 January, those against the Treaty numbered 57, those in favour 64. De Valera at once resigned as President, and Griffith took his place. The Treaty having been approved by the Dáil, the task ahead was to implement its terms, setting up the state – the Irish Free State, as it was to be known – outlined by the agreement. 'Within the next three months,' Griffith declared, 'we are going to have the heaviest task ever thrown on to the shoulders of Irishmen.'[16] Childers, belligerent to the end, rose to his feet and ironically enquired what policies Griffith intended to pursue. He was widely barracked; as Béaslaí commented,

> There was something particularly irritating in the spectacle of this English ex-officer, who had spent his life in the service of England and English Imperialism, heckling and baiting the devoted Griffith, with his lifelong record of unselfish slaving in the cause of Ireland – answering Griffith's moving appeal with carping criticism. Griffith, usually so stolid and unemotional, lost his patience. He rose, like a sleeping lion roused, and declared – 'Before this proceeds any further I want to say that President de Valera made a statement – a generous Irishman's statement – and I replied. I will not reply to any Englishman in this

> Dáil.' 'What has my nationality got to do with it?' asked the ultra-rational Erskine Childers. Banging the table furiously, Griffith repeated, 'I will not reply to any damned Englishman in this assembly!'[17]

The ignorance and misunderstanding of Childers displayed by Béaslaí was all too widespread among the members of the Dáil. For its subject, Nemesis was at hand.

II

In some respects, the deliberations of the Dáil were neither here nor there. Such direct contemporary evidence as we have suggests that the narrow advantage enjoyed by the pro-Treaty faction on that January day was a serious under-reflection of popular support for the Treaty. Yet popular support was not entirely the point. The way things were in Ireland in early 1922, the will of the people was of less significance than the will of armed men to impose whatever they thought fit. Moreover, the extent to which the republican army was under any form of political control was debatable. As Kee has observed, 'The IRA had never been very respectful of its nominal allegiance to Dáil Éireann and had often been remarkably independent even of its own head-quarters.'[18]

On 16 January 1922, in a ceremony of particular symbolism for the country, the Lord Lieutenant handed over Dublin Castle to Michael Collins, representing the new Free State; at the same time, the evacuation of British troops began. As was natural enough, Crown forces throughout the Free State handed over to the republican army. It was, by this time, equally natural that some of these army groups should have been pro-Treaty, others fiercely republican. Within weeks, the die-hard republicans began to organize themselves into a force separate from their former comrades. Adherents of the Treaty were known as 'Free Staters', their opponents as 'Republicans' – a capital 'R' – or 'Irregulars'. The IRA headquarters in Dublin remained largely under Collins' sway, supporting the nascent Free State. But many of the other groups took the view of Liam Lynch: 'We have declared for an Irish Republic and will not live under any other law.'[19] Among them was a young medical student, a veteran of the Black and Tan War, who came to be a close friend of the Childerses. This was Ernie O'Malley, who on 26 February led a raid on the RIC barracks at Clonmel in County Tipperary. Thus, tentatively, began the civil war.

A month later, the Republicans in the army held a convention at which the authority of the Dáil was rejected in favour of the old republic. Their leader, Rory O'Connor, when asked if the country was to have a military dictatorship, replied, 'You can take it that way if you like.'[20] He appears to have done so: on 14 April he seized the Four Courts on the Liffey quays, and there established a rival republican force. The sporadic incidents that had punctuated the new year since February – a murder here, an explosion there – multiplied, both in the North and the South.

Needless to say, the propaganda perspective was not neglected, and from the outset Childers was intimately involved. The Republican splinter-group politicians, headed by de Valera, established the newspaper *An Phoblacht no h-Éireann* – 'The Republic of Ireland'. From the beginning Childers was its mainstay, soon its editor. He published the paper once or twice a week, often in circumstances which made the production of the *Irish Bulletin* seem easy in retrospect. He was now in his fifty-third year and, with de Valera, the intellectual backbone of the Republicans; the pressure on Childers had never been greater. An American journalist who sought him out at Bushy Park Road recalled: 'The photographs I have seen of Erskine Childers have little prepared me for the shock . . . Thin almost to the point of emaciation, and looks ill and unhappy almost to the point of death. I can only liken his face to a mask, to which the eyes alone give life. Restless they show him, and haunted, as if he is driven by inner soul-consuming time. However courteous, he is aloof . . . One emotion only lightens the intensity of his eyes – his very real devotion to his wife.'[21] Like his father before him, Childers seemed to be working himself to death.

The seizure of the Four Courts, although something O'Connor had discussed with Childers, nevertheless lacked the formal political endorsement of de Valera. With or without such endorsement, it was not something Griffith and Collins might be supposed to welcome. Behind them was Churchill, whose job as Colonial Secretary gave him direct responsibility for Ireland. Soon the continuing unrest began to infuriate him; in a note to the Cabinet he observed that 'the Irish have a genius for conspiracy, not government. The Government is feeble, apologetic, expostulatory; the conspirators active, audacious, and utterly shameless.'[22]

The truth was, of course, that Collins, as a root-and-branch republican army man himself, was not likely to lead the way in advocating the use of force to dislodge the 'Irregulars'. Even as late as May 1922 he retained a hope, particularly as a general election was approaching, that some sort of peaceful constitutional settlement might be achieved. The particular purpose of the election, held on 16 June, was to seek endorsement of the Treaty by the electorate and thereby legally establish the government of the Free State, hitherto of 'Provisional' status. Of 128 members of the new Dáil, 94 were in favour of the Treaty. Along with a number of others who had voted against the Treaty that January, Childers was rejected by his Wicklow constituents; indeed, he came bottom of the poll. It was another blow. As the results clearly destroyed the republican mandate, the activities of Childers and others in continuing their struggle after this rejection may seem less defensible. Joseph M. Curran observes: 'It did not matter that Childers was mistaken in his assessment of the Treaty, or that he differed from the great majority of his countrymen in this view. It mattered very much that he refused to allow the people to decide their own political future.'[23]

Before the last of the election results had been published, the final fuse of civil war had been lit with the assassination in London of Sir Henry Wilson. A distinguished professional soldier, he had recently become adviser on law and order to the Belfast Unionists, and was assumed to be responsible for the persecution of Catholics there. The British government, not unreasonably supposing the blame for Wilson's death to lie with the Republicans, now demanded that Collins and Griffith should clear the Four Courts. Collins at first played for time; then, on the morning of 28 June, he sent O'Connor an ultimatum to surrender. There was no response, and at seven minutes past four the Free State forces opened fire, using two artillery pieces borrowed from the few remaining Crown troops. After two days O'Connor and most of his followers surrendered. Another Rubicon had been crossed.

Now the civil war began in earnest. Its material and economic impact was to be the equal of the war against the Crown forces, its effect on the national psyche infinitely greater. As Kevin O'Higgins, soon to play a terrible part in Childers' nemesis, was to declare:

> We had an opportunity of building up a worthy State that would attract and, in time, absorb and assimilate [the Unionist] elements. We preferred the patriotic way. We preferred to burn our own houses, blow up our own bridges, rob our own banks, saddle ourselves with millions of debt for the maintenance of an Army and for the payment of compensation for the recreations of our youth. Generally we preferred to practise upon ourselves worse iniquities than the British had practised on us since Cromwell and Mountjoy, and now we wonder why the Orangemen are not hopping like so many fleas across the Border in their anxiety to come within our fold and jurisdiction.[24]

It was as great a tragedy for Ireland as the Famine.

III

In such circumstances, Childers could not long expect to survive. As early as the previous November, we are told,[25] Arthur Griffith had begun to feel there was something odd in the intransigence of Childers' republicanism. The 'damned Englishman' episode indicated a hardening of the new President's attitude, and in the Dáil in April he made the extraordinary accusation that Childers had 'spent his life in England's secret service'.[26]

Later, when Childers created an opportunity to repudiate the charge, he noted that Griffith's implication was that his 'position and connection here [the Dáil] were in some way dishonourable; that in opposing the Treaty as I have opposed it I was acting not only in English interests but in some disreputable way, I suppose, as some secret agent of England.'[27] For a man such as Griffith to have made such an accusation is indicative of what O'Higgins, rather later, described as the 'weird composite of idealism, neurosis, negation, and criminality [that] is apt to be thrown to the surface even in the best-regulated revolution.'[28] As anyone who has followed Childers' intellectual odyssey will understand, there was not and could not be a grain of truth in the charge. Yet there it was. And as Childers was all too clearly to be numbered among the leading Republicans, all too clearly the driving force of its propaganda effort, special attention from the Free State forces was something he might well expect. When he was editing the *Bulletin* he had been provided with a secret room in a house in Rathgar; now no such facilities were available. To have remained at Bushy Park Road would have been madness, and by the time of the Four Courts attack he was effectively on the run, and would remain so until his arrest by Free Staters some four months later. Anguished by the separation from Molly, his diary for the period, subjected to Molly's later censorship, gives a flavour of what his life had become:

> *Wed. June 28.* Heard Four Courts attack – got out first stop press edition of *Phoblacht*. Slept at ——.
>
> *Thurs. June 29.* Daily or bi-daily of *Phoblacht*. Slept as before.
>
> *Friday June 30.* Moved to ——. Four Courts fall. Slept at Wood Press. Many wounded, streets full of snipers.
>
> *Sat July 1.* Moved to ——.
>
> *July 3.* Wood Press raided.
>
> *July 5–7.* O'Connell Street surrender. Cathal Brugha shot. No.12 raided. Bob caught. House watched. Constant alarm.[29]

Stained, fragmentary, and in places burnt, it is like the document rescued from the fire at Norderney.

Ernie O'Malley pictures Childers at about this time, walking 'through streets heavy with rifle and machine-gun fire, seemingly unconscious of danger, gravely preoccupied with his work, his light macintosh coat a conspicuous mark.'[30] Soon, he left Dublin with the other Republican leaders, for the Republican stronghold in the south-west. His official position was the modest one of a staff captain in the Southern Brigade of the IRA, but in practice his role was to publish a southern edition of *An Phoblacht*, called *Republican War News*. He was to return to Dublin only for his trial; Molly, now barely mobile, remained there. To her he wrote, 'I shall probably not be able to communicate. Oh my darling, my heart is so full. I am yours, yours, for ever, the child of your spirit . . . your comrade, lover, husband.'[31] Molly was concerned for her husband's welfare. 'I ask you to be very careful to avoid reckless self-giving,' she wrote. 'There is a danger, I think. I want the self-giving for both of us to be reckoned and made as powerful factors as can be made . . . Eat as a duty, get all the sleep you can . . . O my beloved husband, in all that you go through you do know that I am with you – if it is to be to crucifixion – then I will suffer Calvary by your side and share the cross with you.'[32]

Much now depended on the country's leaders. As an institution, the Free State was too young to have gained any respect; such authority as it possessed was vested in such figures as Griffith, Collins, the Free State general Richard Mulcahy, and the rising stars of William Cosgrave and Kevin O'Higgins. Griffith himself was not an easy man, but his courage, the following he commanded, the success with which he had led the more moderate among the republicans, all boded well for Ireland's future; but for some time he had not been well. Like all the Treaty delegates, he had been under an enormous strain, and early in August he went into a nursing-home to recuperate. There he died, from a massive cerebral haemorrhage, on 12 August. There is little doubt that his death changed the course of Irish history. In his obituary of Griffith in *War News*, Childers described him as 'the greatest intellectual force stimulating the tremendous national revival'.[33] This was the man who had accused Childers of treason.

If this were not enough, within days Childers would be writing the obituary of another of his former friends.

'I've been in tighter spots,' Collins had cheerily remarked to his fellow-passengers in the course of the accident which befell the ship returning the Treaty delegates to Ireland. After the Dáil split, he was in the tightest ever. Here was a man who, whatever reservations there might be as to his leadership of 'the murder gang', was a colossus of the freedom movement, the 'big fellow', the hero of Ireland; on the very brink of what he had come to regard as the most successful possible outcome for his country, he was forced by circumstances entirely beyond his control to wage a bitter war against those who had, quite literally, fought at his side against the British. 'I am really and truly having an awful time,'[34] he wrote in January to his fiancée – and he was. He was also increasingly resigned to his own death. On a visit to London in April he told Churchill, 'I shall not last long; my life is forfeit.'[35]

Characteristically, Collins had thrown himself into work, assuming overall command of the Free State army. On 11 August the army took Cork, the only city in Republican hands. Preparations for a tour of the area were interrupted by Griffith's funeral, but afterwards Collins set out in an open Rolls-Royce. It was an opportunity to see and be seen, despite the obvious risks attached. His intentions were not advertised, but word of his presence soon got around. As it happened, de Valera, Childers and other 'top-ranking figures on the Republican side'[36] were also in the area at the time, and it remains the belief in some quarters that Collins was intending, or hoping, to arrange some sort of a parley with them. But all that happened was an ambush at Bealnamblath, on a lonely stretch of road between Macroom and Bandon. To escape would have been easy, but Collins being Collins, he elected to fight, and at some stage in the skirmish he was shot in the head. With perhaps the greatest of her leaders died the greatest hopes of Ireland.

There too, in a sense, died Erskine Childers; as one of Collins' biographers commented, 'Of all the tragedies of the Civil War, that which came upon that strangely consorted friendship is perhaps the most moving, for only Collins of the Free Staters really understood Childers' sincere devotion to Ireland, even while he hated its negation of the evolutionary processes he himself believed in. Certainly, had Collins lived, he would have saved Childers to serve his espoused country in more comprehending days, as Childers himself found only cause for mourning in the killing of Collins.'[37] In *War News* Childers wrote of his friend's 'buoyant energy, his organising powers, immense industry, acute and subtle intelligence, charm and gift of oratory, which he flung without stint into the Republican cause for five years'.[38]

Griffith and Collins were replaced as leaders by men already marked out by Churchill as of uncommon quality, and who certainly took the firm grip on power that they felt necessary if the infant state was to survive. William Cosgrave was the new President; in the vital post of Home Affairs was the man who had replied to Childers' anti-Treaty speech in the Dáil, Kevin O'Higgins.

'The life of the nation is menaced,' O'Higgins now told the Dáil, 'menaced politically, it is menaced economically, it is menaced morally.' And he went on to describe Childers as 'the able Englishman who is leading those who are opposed to this Government [and who keeps] steadily, callously, and ghoulishly on his career of striking at the heart of this Nation, striking deadly, or what he hopes are deadly, blows at the economic life of the nation.' He finished with a warning: 'I don't think any of us hold human life cheap, but when, and if, a situation arises in the country when you must balance human life against the life of the nation, that presents a different problem.'[39] For Childers the knives – or rather the guns – were now out. To Molly he wrote on 19 August from the wilds of Munster, where he was struggling to gather material for, print, and distribute *War News*, 'Conditions here are very difficult.'[40]

Quite how the Free State politicians managed to persuade themselves – or at least, why they put it about – that Childers was the military as opposed to one of the intellectual leaders of the Republicans, is in itself an interesting question. In a broad sense there was of course a great tradition of blaming Englishmen for Irish troubles – to an extent, a tradition quite justifiable. More specifically, the view of Childers as a military leader was certainly Griffith's legacy; as his biographer writes of the leader's last days, 'There was something else that was affecting the solidity that was Arthur Griffith. An individual had come to dominate his outlook, a man who he conceived to be behind every move that threatened the establishment of the democratic state that he, Arthur Griffith, had planned and worked for all his life. That man was Erskine Childers.'[41] Nor was it likely that Griffith's death would lessen a sentiment well disseminated among his Free State colleagues, not the least of whom was Desmond Fitzgerald.

There is also Childers' reputation as both military man and military strategist to be considered: in both Ireland and England, this was substantial. Begun at the time of his service in the Boer War and with *In the Ranks of the CIV*, it had been augmented by *The Riddle of the Sands*; then came *The Times History of the South African War* and its fine chapters on guerrilla tactics, to be followed by *War and the Arme Blanche* and *The German Influence on British Cavalry*; then Howth, followed by his service – often as an Intelligence Officer – in the Great War, and his DSC. One might say that in reality his reputation was greater than was justified by the known facts, and that his war record was very much one of individual acts of daring and courage. But as a propagandist himself, Childers would have known that the *sine qua non* was not fact, but belief. Around him had gathered the aura of legend. As to his being 'an Englishman', that too was a moot point – but in the terrible matter of *seeming*, the issue was clear. Childers was now being helped on *War News* by two young journalists, Frank O'Connor and Sean Hendrick. It was O'Connor who noted that 'Apart from his accent, which would have identified him anywhere, there was something peculiarly English about him; something that nowadays reminds me of some old parson or public-school teacher I have known, conscientious to a fault, and overburdened with minor cares.'[42] From a propaganda point of view, it was infinitely preferable that the Free State should blame the Englishman in their midst rather than pillory de Valera, an acknowledged hero of the Rising.

As a point of simple fact, the memoirs and memories of those who knew Childers indicate that he took no part at all in the military activity of those sad last days. Moreover, among such Republican papers as have survived and are available, there is no record of his involvement in military activity. The Free State newspapers certainly reported him as leading various raids, but Childers' activities were purely those of a propagandist. As an historian of the Irish Army remarks, 'Childers . . . had been ridiculously demonised by the pro-Treatyites: every blown-up culvert was attributed to his evil genius. The idea of an Englishman interfering in Irish affairs maddened them. The truth was that de Valera and Childers had been ostracised by the scornful Republican generals. They were given no military standing whatsoever.'[43]

From a Free State point of view it was now clear that, having created an ogre, they must proceed to destroy it – especially as there were rumours that Childers might replace de Valera as the Republican political leader.[44] Accordingly, the Free State Army was given emergency powers to set up its own courts to try those found in illegal possession of explosives, ammunition or firearms; on conviction, one of the penalties was death.

By September Childers was unwell, and leading what must have been an almost unbearably stressful life. The difficulties of producing *War*

News while on the run, using a portable printing press trailed around in a pony and trap, were very considerable; those of distributing it were even more so. It was useful work, true, but in what, following the fall of Cork, seemed an increasingly lost cause: time and again, he would find packaged bundles of the paper, uncollected, unread, in the dusty corner of a barn. He had of course been living under immense pressure ever since his return to Ireland, and especially since the Treaty negotiations of the previous year. Two of the Treaty negotiators were already dead. His sciatic leg was giving him trouble, and he also had a persistent cough. He must himself have wondered whether the cough was tubercular; tuberculosis had killed both his parents, and was soon to kill his companion of the Howth run, Mary Spring Rice.

There are many anecdotes of encounters with Childers at this time. All stress his physical frailty, his dedication to the struggle, and his utter selflessness over the smaller things in life. In addition to fellow-journalists, he was now accompanied by a friend of the Bartons: David Robinson was another figure of Ascendancy background who had fought for the British during the war, and subsequently joined the IRA. He was one of the many who remained loyal to Childers and inspired by him in his last days. Writing to Molly, Robinson remarked, 'Erskine and I are going to a show tonight, but only as spectators . . . I need hardly say very few of us have either his mania for work, his powers of concentration, or his capacity to accomplish things . . . everyone loves him, especially the people in the cottages who vie with each other wherever he goes to do him a kindness and make him as comfortable as possible . . .'[45] It was on one such occasion that Childers was moved to remark, 'I'll never understand this country. I thought I was going off to bloody combat, and instead I found myself in Mick Sullivan's feather bed in Kilnamartyr.'[46] It was a comment that could be said to have a wider application.

In the end, the problems of producing the paper overcame him. For a meticulous man like Childers, to produce accurate copy without accurate information, even for propaganda purposes, was to produce bricks without straw. In an office in Dublin he might manage to get hold of the factual information he needed, even during a civil war; to do so when he was being forced from pillar to post by the advance of the Free State troops was another matter. After the evacuation of Cork, his press was established in an empty barracks near Macroom; then it was shifted to a two-roomed cottage at Ballyvourney; then west towards Kealkill. The loss of a vital part of the press machinery spelled the end. Childers informed the Southern Brigade of his decision to give up the publicity side, and offered himself to them in any other capacity. They were horrified. 'That wouldn't do at all,' he was told. 'My God, if the Free State troops down in Dunwanway heard you were with us they wouldn't give us any peace, night or day.'[47]

But what of de Valera? He had been having a scarcely better time than Childers, on the run and scarcely in control of the military, his life's hopes apparently gone. By way of disguise he had even been obliged to grow a beard. By the middle of October, however, he had finally achieved some sort of tentative backing from the Republican army for an underground government, of which he would be the head; he sent word to Childers that he should return to Dublin to help him set up an administration. This was an opportunity, and one which would also give Childers the chance to put together his papers on the Treaty negotiations, with a view to publication.

On 25 October, in the company of David Robinson, Childers set off. The country through which they travelled was largely in Free State hands, and they were obliged to pass from safe house to safe house, entirely avoiding towns. At first on ramshackle bicycles, then on foot, it was a journey reminiscent of a Buchan hero. Their clothes threadbare, the weather wintry, they trekked through Waterford and Wexford to Wicklow, sometimes sleeping under the stars. On 30 October, on the nineteenth anniversary of their engagement, he managed to send Molly a scrap of paper from his notebook. It read simply, 'I would like to ask you to be with me always.'[48] On 3 November 1922 they reached Glendalough, of which Childers had so many happy memories. It was home.

Glendalough was home, but not necessarily a 'safe house': Free State troops were in the area. Discretion was the fugitives' watchword, and they kept to the house itself as far as possible during the ensuing days; Childers began to put his Treaty papers in order. But any number of people came and went, as a matter of course, on estate business, and Robinson thought the place dangerous. Nevertheless, after a week the

Free Staters moved off, and the coast seemed clear. Then, suddenly, in the early morning of 10 November, came the thunderous knock on the door that presaged a raid. Someone had informed. The Free Staters had returned.

Childers was in his bedroom off the long gallery on the second floor of the house. Emerging at the commotion, he drew his pistol – Michael Collins' pistol – just as three of the troops approached up the stairs, rifles levelled. Childers cocked his gun, but before he could fire a family servant, rushing up the stairs, threw herself in front of the troops, crying: 'You'll not shoot Mr Childers!'[49] Then he was seized from behind.

Together, he and Robinson were taken, first by cart to Wicklow gaol, then to Portobello Barracks in Dublin, where Childers was badly beaten. The following day, Churchill declared in a speech in Dundee, 'I have seen with satisfaction that the mischief-making, murderous renegade Erskine Childers has been captured. No man has done more harm or shown more genuine malice or endeavoured to bring a greater curse upon the common people of Ireland than this strange being, actuated by a deadly and malignant hatred for the land of his birth.'[50] Even if one takes account of the extent to which Churchill may himself have been led astray by the Free State propaganda, such remarks were less than just from a man normally so perspicacious. To Molly, Childers wrote, 'Beloved, they have taken me.'[51]

IV

Childers was to be tried by one of the new military courts set up by Cosgrave and O'Higgins in an attempt to bring the Republicans into line. The charge was 'that he, on the 10th day of November, 1922, without proper authority, was in possession of an automatic pistol when apprehended by a party of National forces'.[52] He languished in various barracks for a week, then was brought to trial.

In view of his activities over the previous ten months, indeed over the preceding four years, his line of defence was predictable: 'Captain Childers [his rank in the Republican army] does not recognise the legality of the Provisional Government and consequently does not recognise the legality of the Court,' his counsel declared.[53] To have recognized either government or court would have been to repudiate the ideal which had become the climax of his life's work.

Childers did, however, take the opportunity to repudiate some of the wilder charges made against him, initially by Griffith. 'I have constantly been called an Englishman who, having betrayed his country, came to Ireland to betray and destroy Ireland, a double traitor. Alternatively, I have suffered the vile charge or innuendo that instead of betraying England I have been acting as a spy or *agent provocateur* in England's interest'; on the contrary, he told the court. He recounted his experiences of the Boer War, and how these first seeded in him a belief in self-determination for small nations. He talked of the circumstances that turned him from a Unionist into a Home Ruler, then of his disillusion with the Asquith government of 1914 in its kow-towing to Ulster, and his consequent adventure at Howth. Regarding the Great War, he spelled out how he was misled 'by the idea of a war for small nations' – and how others had been misled by the term 'Intelligence' for the aerial reconnaissance work for which he was decorated.

Finally, Childers related his disillusionment with the Irish Convention of 1917, his subsequent enlistment in the republican cause, and his absolute conviction of its righteousness. 'The slow growth of moral and intellectual conviction had brought me to where I stood, and it was and is impossible and unthinkable to go back. I was bound by honour, conscience and principle to oppose the Treaty by speech, writing and action, and, when it came to the disastrous point, in war.' In the language of what had become his religion, he had fought, he said, and worked 'for a sacred principle, the loyalty of a nation to its declared Independence and repudiation of any voluntary surrender to conquest and inclusion in the British Empire. That is the faith of my comrades, my leaders and myself. Some day we shall be justified when the Nation forgets its weakness and reverts to the ancient and holy tradition which we are preserving in our struggle, and may God hasten the day of reunion amongst us all under the honoured flag of the Republic.'[54]

It was on the whole an accurate summary of the strange path that had led Childers to that court, in that dreary room. In the wider sense, as a defence it was unimpeachable; but as a defence against the simple charge on which he had been arraigned, it was scarcely effective. To that, there was no defence.

The intention of the Free State government was clear: it had selected Childers as the ideal scapegoat for the Republicans' activities, and it pursued its intentions remorselessly. Once Childers had been captured, only one outcome was possible. To date, the Emergency Act under which Childers was being tried had run for only a month, and no one had been executed for being in unauthorized possession of guns, ammunition or explosives; yet on the very day of Childers' trial, O'Higgins ordered the execution of four young Irregulars caught with revolvers. A precedent, apparently, had been set.

On the evening of the day the sentence of execution on the four was carried out, O'Higgins was sharply questioned in the Dáil. He defended the action in a famous but curiously jumbled exposition: 'If they took, as their first case, a man who was outstandingly active and wicked in his activities, the unfortunate dupes throughout the country might say that he was killed because he was a leader, because he was an Englishman, or because he combined with others to commit rape.'[55] The implication was clear: Childers was the leader of the executed men, and he too must be executed. O'Higgins, as he spoke before the Dáil, was careless – in a matter that was still *sub judice* – of any influence that his words might have on the Dáil, on the public, in particular on the court; careless of the fact that no evidence of 'outstandingly wicked activities' on the part of Childers was produced (nor has it ever been, subsequently); careless of Childers' work over the previous four years; careless of the fact that Childers had done the young state some service. As O'Higgins' biographer concedes, 'Childers did arouse deadly hatred, but one can only regret that . . . a great Irishman did not give him the benefit of that reticence which the common law demands for the most wretched criminal before his trial.'[56]

On the first day of the trial, Friday, 17 November, no verdict was reached. Childers' defence counsel, Michael Comyn, wished to prepare for the worst by seeking a writ of *habeas corpus*, but to this Childers was only brought to agree when it became apparent that it might be a possible way of saving the lives of a further eight men since arraigned under the same Emergency Act. He was ready to take the responsibility for his own life, in upholding his own sense of honour by his repudiation of the legality of the court; but in recognition of the court, implicit in the application for the writ of *habeas corpus*, lay the only hope of commutation of sentence for the eight Irregulars. To Molly he wrote from his cell: 'I think of those four lads and eight unknown . . . oh, I hope it is understood that my honour is unsullied, that I refused to act alone and that by direction – orders – I have acted for the eight as well, as it was by direction in the Black and Tan war in capital cases. There was no possibility of a test save on my specific case.'[57] On the following Monday Comyn's application was delivered to the Master of the Rolls, Sir Charles O'Connor.

In the meantime, the court delivered its verdict. At five o'clock that afternoon, November 20, the door of Childers' cell was unlocked, and he was informed of it. He wrote to Molly:

> Beloved wife, I am told that I am to be shot tomorrow at 7.00. I am fully prepared. I think it best so, viewing it from the biggest standpoint, and perhaps you will agree. To have followed those other brave lads is a great thing for a great cause. I have belief in the beneficent shaping of our destiny – yours and mine – and I believe God means this for the best: for us, Ireland and humanity. So in the midst of anguish at leaving you, and in mortal solicitude for you, beloved of my heart, I triumph and know you triumph with me. It is such a simple thing, too, a soldier's death, what millions risk and incur, what so many in our cause face and suffer daily.[58]

The President of the Immortals had yet to finish his sport with Childers. In a refinement of torture, five hours later he was told that his execution had been postponed, pending the Master's ruling on Comyn's application. At the same time, a great campaign was being waged by his friends to save him. De Valera publicly blamed England for using Ireland to kill 'a man whose crime was that he had worn himself out in the service of Ireland, and that he had remained incorruptible when many became corrupt.' Douglas Hyde, later himself to become President, wrote to Cosgrave: 'I would most respectfully beg that his great services during the Black and Tan terror be remembered. I had the opportunity of observing how very much his writings at that time impressed the British people. I hope very much that owing to his past services the extreme penalty may not be enacted.' Mary Spring

Rice's father, Lord Monteagle, wrote: 'I beg to renew my appeal on behalf of Childers. General Collins told me three days before his death that Childers being an Englishman might well be deported, and having regard to his past services to Ireland, especially in propaganda, venture to urge commutation.' W. B. Yeats's brother Jack, the painter, wrote: 'I urge you to hold your hand and not to execute Erskine Childers, I write to you in the name of humanity and in the name of sober judgement.' From California, the delegates of the Convention to Recognise the Republic cabled: 'We would look upon the killing of Erskine Childers or any other republican prisoner of war as murder and hold your Free State junta responsible.'[59]

On Thursday 23 November the Master of the Rolls refused the application for a writ of *habeas corpus* on the ground that, as a state of war existed, his court could not, 'for any purpose, or under any circumstances, control the military authority'.[60] Comyn immediately filed an appeal. But Cosgrave and O'Higgins had had enough: rumours of an attempt to rescue Childers were in the air, and the prisoner was moved from barracks to barracks as a preventive measure; the appeal might succeed. Orders went out that Childers was to be shot the following morning, Friday, 24 November 1922. At seven o'clock, in his cell at Beggars Bush Barracks, the prisoner was informed of his fate.

19
No Greater Love
24 November 1922

> 'Now I am going. Coming to you, heart's beloved, sweetheart, comrade wife, I shall fall asleep in your arms, God above blessing us – all four of us.'
>
> Erskine Childers, 24 November 1922

I

Childers faced death with absolute equanimity and indomitable courage. In a sense he welcomed death. Alive, it was clear that he could now do no more for the cause; his life was the last contribution that he could make to Irish freedom: 'Living I was weighted with a load of prejudice, unjust but so heavy that it may be I was even harming our cause,' he wrote to Molly. 'Dead I shall have a better chance of being understood and of helping the cause.'[1]

He asked to see a Catholic friend, Father Albert. This was refused. Eventually he saw Edward Waller, the Protestant clergyman with whom, so many years previously, he had tramped the Wicklow hills. He was allowed, too, to see his elder son, now himself an avowed Republican. Childers made him promise never to use his name to political advantage, and to shake hands with each person who figured in his own death – including Cosgrave and O'Higgins. From a man such as this, the guard wanted souvenirs. They were given: books and signatures, all Childers had. Very briefly he saw Molly. Others were present. To her he wrote: 'I have had nineteen years of happiness with you. No man could claim so great and precious a blessing as that. But for you I should have foundered; and died, a younger possibly, possibly older, but unhappy man, a dwarfed soul, not understanding love, the secret of all, not grasping life like a man. You redeemed me.'[2] He asked to spend that final night alone, and to see a last sunrise. The latter was granted.

The morning of his execution he rose, and wrote a line to Molly. He was escorted to the barracks yard. There, in a gesture many of his friends and comrades later recalled as entirely typical of him, he shook hands with every member of the firing squad. Marched to the wall by the officer in charge, he was saluted, and left alone to face the guns. No mask or blindfold concealed the scene from his eyes – the grey granite square, the firing squad, the rifles. To the squad he called, 'Take a step or two forwards, lads. It will be easier that way.'[3] The officer lowered the white flag, signalling the men to put pressure on their triggers; he dropped it, the sign to fire.

It was finished.

By intuition, Molly knew her husband was dead. To Basil Williams and his wife she cabled: 'He sent you both his love, was serene, contented fulfilled.'[4] His last words, written on that grey morning, were: 'Now I am going. Coming to you, heart's beloved, sweetheart, comrade wife, I shall fall asleep in your arms, God above blessing us – all four of us. Erskine.'[5]

20
The Picture of Erskine Childers

31 July 1961

Treason doth never prosper: what's the reason?
For if it prosper, none dare call it treason.
Sir John Harington

On 31 July 1961, there occurred an event of such character as quite to define the spirit of those happier times, marking as it did the first public acknowledgement by the Irish state of Erskine Childers' contribution to the creation of modern Ireland. Forty-seven years after her first arrival, *Asgard* came a second time to Howth. There to meet her was a tall elderly man, now virtually blind, dressed in top hat and tails. He was the country's President, Éamon de Valera. With him was one of his cabinet ministers, who in 1973 would succeed him as President: Childers' elder son, Erskine Hamilton, who had indeed sought out and forgiven the perpetrators of his father's death. At Glendalough Molly, now a frail octogenarian, was kept abreast of events. The *Asgard*, rejuvenated, was to be used as a sail training ship by the State. She was greeted by de Valera as the 'harbinger of liberty'[1] – the very words with which she had last been met at Howth.

Politically, de Valera's country was no longer part of Great Britain. By the spring of 1923 the military position of the Republicans had become hopeless, and under de Valera's direction – more or less – they had laid down their arms. For most politicians it would have been the end; for de Valera, there followed nine years of struggle. Then, in 1932, at the heart of a new party of republican aspect, Fianna Fáil, he became 'head of the government of a state against which he had fought in arms, and against which he had fought passionately by every word'.[2] In 1937 he successfully introduced a new constitution cleansed of all reference to the Crown and the oath of allegiance, the matters over which the Treaty of 1921 had so nearly broken down; cleansed too of 'Irish Free State', embodying rather the alternatives 'Ireland' and 'Eire'. Practically and politically, this culminated in the country being able to maintain its neutrality during the Second World War, which the genius of Churchill enabled Britain to survive. There followed in 1948 the Republic of Ireland Bill and, on Easter Monday 1949, the formal inauguration of the Republic.

Once, Britain's response to such events would have been 'immediate and terrible war'. But by 1937, to Westminster, Ireland was no longer the problem she had once been. In any case, the problem had never been Ireland alone, but Ireland in the larger context of Empire; and by 1937 the Empire, to most intents and purposes, was no more. A series of Imperial Conferences held between 1926 and 1930, culminating in the Statute of Westminster, had given to all the Dominions that very equality of status with Britain to which Ireland – the South – had particularly aspired. Indeed, the Statute of Westminster effectively embodied that concept of 'external association' formulated by de Valera and Childers in 'Document No. 2': it had been an idea ahead of its time. At the same time, the term 'Empire' fell out of use, to be replaced by a phrase first officially used in Article 4 of the Anglo-Irish Treaty, the 'British Commonwealth of Nations'. As the old concept of Empire dwindled, so too, slowly, did Great Britain's position as the dominant world power. To the west America, to the east a renascent Germany, began to assume the mantle of grandeur and power that once was Britain's own. The Twenties and Thirties in England were not the times of great feats, great discoveries, great challenges or great men that the era of Disraeli, Gladstone and the Empress of India, Queen Victoria, had been.

Childers' reputation, once so shining, was lamentably slow to recover from the circumstances of his death. The press, largely pro-Treaty, took the line that the execution was a regrettable necessity; *The Times* held the view that 'the only means for the Free State to establish its authority is to make that authority real.'[3] It was Molly, needless to say, who made of his memory a shrine. In the long years following his death, her faith in her husband remained undimmed. Like him, she became among the staunchest advocates of Republicanism, as did their sons, particularly the elder. Outside the family, Basil Williams began the attempt to set the record straight, with his fine and touching memoir written in 1925; but as late as 1941 he was told that 'The name of Erskine Childers is, I am afraid, under a cloud in many quarters, even in Ireland.'[4] Churchill, on the other hand, had recanted by then; he wrote of Childers that he was 'a great patriot and statesman, with whom, however, I had disagreed on everything.'[5] John Buchan declared that 'No revolution ever produced a nobler or purer spirit.'[6] And in his study of the Anglo-Irish Treaty, Lord Longford observed that Childers had been 'misunderstood and misrepresented as no man in recent history', continuing:

> If ever it is possible to prophesy mundane immortality for a man who has held no high-sounding office, nor given his name to any epoch-making invention, the figure of Erskine Childers seems certain to stand out always more clearly as we move onwards into the future. For, with all his wanderings, his was a continuing journey, governed by no passing influence, guided to no ephemeral end. He lived and laboured, and he fought and died, under the shadow of the eternal.[7]

And, gradually, Erskine Childers does indeed emerge from the calumny of his execution; over him, death has had no dominion. 'He wrote only one novel,' wrote Geoffrey Household, 'and that is immortal.'[8] So it is; *The Riddle of the Sands* will surely be enjoyed for as long as the English language is understood.

As timeless, too, are some of the values which his life embodied. In so much, Childers was a pioneer. Born in a foreign country, where things were differently done, his achievement was to question the received wisdom of his age. The creed of his day was 'Empire', a creed inherently incompatible with the growing self-consciousness of the time, the growing desire for responsibility on the part of individuals and nations alike, the growing aspiration towards liberty. Not only was Childers among the first to understand this, he was also one of the first to realize that their move towards self-determination was as much in the interest of Great Britain herself as it was of her colonies and dominions. Not only did he see this, but he was prepared to sacrifice everything for that which he conceived to be the greater good of the countries and the peoples that he loved; and however it may have been regarded at the time, there are many today who will agree with his conception of that greater good. In Lord Longford's words, he was 'perfectly prepared to place his slight figure across the onward march of an Empire'.[9] Yet Childers could truly say, as he did in one of his last letters, that he 'died loving England, and passionately praying that she may change completely and finally towards Ireland'.[10] To his wife he wrote that but for her he should have died 'a dwarfed soul, not understanding love, the secret of all, not grasping life like a man. You redeemed me'.[11] His own self-imposed task was the redemption of the British Empire through the medium of Ireland.

Childers was not of course a reasonable man. His early losses seem to have given him an independence of mind that detractors would call self-righteousness. Later this searching intellect, this 'creed of his own conscience', was reinforced by a like-minded and devoted wife, a catalyst of his thinking, a helpmeet and friend. The consequence was what Childers himself called the 'slow growth of moral and intellectual conviction' that led him from the Unionism of his youth to the Republicanism of his last few years. He then relentlessly applied the political logic at which he had arrived to the country of his mother's birth, a country whose religious and cultural diversity made any rigidity of idea or form awkward, to say the least, whatever its logic. Whether he was right to do so is a question, but hardly one with a simple answer. Would the spiritual and material well-being of the people of Ireland have been better or worse served by her remaining fully within the Empire? Would they have been better served by a country united rather than partitioned? Were the material and the spiritual needs in any case at odds? Readers will have their own views.

Childers certainly had his, but for him views alone were insufficient; for him, thought had to be translated into action; the word was merely father to the deed. Infuriated by what he and many others saw as Asquith's fatal weakness in giving in to Carson and the Ulster Volunteers, he took the law into his own hands and ran guns into Howth. After the war he became an apologist for a political direction with an unmistakable mandate from the people – at least, from some of the people, for some of the time – but whose methods of violence many would (and did) question. He became a confrère of gunmen, and a pioneering propagandist of such energy and talent that it might be taken for genius. Few of us are obliged to face moral dilemmas such as those of which Childers was all too vividly aware. He made his decision. If ever there was a man who justified the phrase, 'the courage of his convictions', it was Erskine Childers.

It was not the recipe for a comfortable life. It was not even, necessarily, the blueprint for a good one. Many who admire his work in exposing the undoubted iniquities of British rule at the time have reservations about the way in which he continued the struggle after republicanism had been rejected by the majority of the Irish people. Still, as Shaw once said, the reasonable man adapts himself to the world: the unreasonable one persists in trying to adapt the world to himself. Therefore all progress depends on the unreasonable man.[12] Childers was an unreasonable man, and he certainly sacrificed himself for liberties, far from commonplace in his own age, which we now take largely for granted.

In Ireland Childers was for too long a prophet without honour; in some circles, indeed, a prophet absolutely dishonoured. But when, on the return of *Asgard* in 1961, President de Valera talked of her as the 'harbinger of liberty', the role of Erskine Childers was publicly acknowledged by his friend. It is a strange part that Childers can now be seen to have played in the history of Britain, but one of a piece with that played by his novel, *A Record of Secret Service Recently Achieved*. It was the part of the 'clarion warning', of a man ahead of his times, the harbinger of liberty, the seer.

Notes

Provided below are sources for all the more important or controversial facts in the text. It has seemed sensible to use abbreviations minimally. REC is Robert Erskine Childers, MAC Mary Alden Childers, TCD Trinity College, Dublin; to avoid misreading or confusion, Trinity College, Cambridge is used in its full form. Many of the references are to correspondence between Erskine and Molly Childers. The originals are generally, but not invariably, legibly dated.

CHAPTER 1: THE GATHERING STORM

1. Morris, *Heaven's Command.*
2. Morris, *Pax Britannica.*
3. Ensor, *England 1870–1914.*
4. Strachey, *Queen Victoria.*
5. Longford, *Victoria RI.*
6. Strachey, *Eminent Victorians* (London, 1918).
7. Matthew Arnold, 'Dover Beach', 1867.
8. Strachey, *Queen Victoria.*
9. REC to Flora Priestley, 5 January 1901; Childers Papers, TCD.
10. Morris, *Pax Britannica.*
11. Erskine Childers, *Military Rule in Ireland* (Dublin, 1920).
12. Erskine Childers, *The Riddle of the Sands* (London, 1903).
13. Morris, *Pax Britannica.*
14. Childers, *Riddle of the Sands.*

CHAPTER 2: THE GOLDEN MORNING

1. REC to Flora Priestley, 5 January 1901; Childers Papers, TCD.
2. Boyle, *Riddle of Erskine Childers.*
3. REC to Basil Williams, 12 June 1902; Childers Papers, Trinity College, Cambridge.

4. Drummond, *The Riddle.*
5. In this letter to Williams (REC to Basil Williams, 12 June 1902; Childers Papers, Trinity College, Cambridge) Childers remarks that he has yet to submit the book to his prospective publisher, Reginald Smith. It follows that the introduction of the romantic interest *preceded* Smith's requests to revise the book. The correspondence with Smith has not survived.

   There is then a letter written by Dulcibella Childers to her brother on the occasion of his engagement (Dulcibella Childers to REC, 27 November 1903; Childers Papers, TCD). Here she declares, 'Perk, my romantic soul was stirred at the idea of your driving for hours together after dinner. Do you remember how piteous were my appeals that you should write a "*love*-story" – and you declared you knew nothing about it and were incapable and now – oh how sweet Molly must be!' From this we may perhaps infer that, subsequent to the book's inception, it was Dulcibella's inspiration rather than Smith's that brought about the creation of Fräulein Dollmann. Contrary to some assertions, the Fräulein does appear in the original MS of the book, to be seen in Trinity College, Dublin.
6. REC to Basil Williams, 25 February 1903; Childers Papers, Trinity College, Cambridge.
7. REC to Basil Williams, 1 May 1903; loc. cit.
8. Boyle, *Riddle of Erskine Childers.*
9. Wilkinson, *Zeal of the Convert.*
10. Childers, *Riddle of the Sands.*
11. A collection of reviews of *The Riddle of the Sands*; Childers Papers, Trinity College, Cambridge.
12. John Buchan, in *John O'London's Weekly* (London, 1926).
13. Drummond, *The Riddle.*
14. Boyle, *Riddle of Erskine Childers.*
15. REC to Basil Williams, 14 October 1903; Childers Papers, Trinity College, Cambridge.
16. REC to Basil Williams, 14 January 1903; loc. cit.
17. Wilkinson, *Zeal of the Convert.*
18. op. cit.
19. REC to Basil Williams, 14 October 1903; Childers Papers, Trinity College, Cambridge.
20. REC to Dulcibella Childers, December 1903; Childers Papers, TCD.
21. REC to MAC, 30 October 1922; loc. cit.
22. MAC to Agnes Barton, 13 December 1903; loc. cit.

23. REC to Basil Williams, 14 November 1903; Childers Papers, Trinity College, Cambridge.

CHAPTER 3: NATIVE IMPULSES, STUCCO CRUSTS

1. Kee, *The Green Flag.*
2. *Dictionary of National Biography.*
3. George Farrington and Thomas Roberts, *Journal of a Voyage Around the Fens* (privately printed, 1868).
4. Strachey, *Queen Victoria.*
5. Rudyard Kipling, 'Recessional', 1897.
6. André Maurois, *Disraeli* (Paris, 1927).
7. *Dictionary of National Biography.*
8. Boyle, *Riddle of Erskine Childers.*
9. REC to Flora Priestley, 4 August 1903; Childers Papers, TCD.
10. Ralph Waldo Emerson, 'Self-Reliance', in *Essays* (1841). Equally pertinent to Childers was Emerson's dictum from the same essay: 'To believe your own thought, to believe that what is true for you in your own private heart is true for all men – that is genius.'
11. Private papers in the possession of Mrs Diana Stewart.
12. Robert Barton, 'Early Recollections of REC'; Childers Papers, TCD.
13. Brennan, *Allegiance.*
14. Porter, *The Lion's Share.*
15. Strachey, *Eminent Victorians.*
16. Churchill, *My Early Life.*
17. MAC, notes for a biography of REC; Childers Papers, TCD.
18. Ivor Lloyd-Jones, 'Erskine Childers, An Appreciation' in *The Haileyburian.*
19. Boyle, *Riddle of Erskine Childers.*
20. Robert Barton, 'Early Recollections of REC'; Childers Papers, TCD.
21. Boyle, *Riddle of Erskine Childers.*
22. John N. Young, opening chapters of a biography of REC; Childers Papers, TCD.
23. REC to Dulcibella Childers, October 1889; Childers Papers, TCD.
24. Robert Barton, 'Early Recollections of REC'; Childers Papers, TCD.
25. Marsh, *A Number of People.*
26. REC to Charles Barton, April 1890; Childers Papers, TCD.
27. So-called because one of its properties was a glass case enclosing two stuffed magpies perching on a stump. Speeches were addressed to His Majesty the Bird.

28. John N. Young, opening chapters of a biography of REC; Childers Papers, TCD.
29. REC to Basil Williams, September 1908; Childers Papers, Trinity College, Cambridge.
30. The final examinations taken by undergraduates at Cambridge University.
31. Marsh, *A Number of People*.
32. REC to Charles Barton, 14 March 1890; Childers Papers, TCD.
33. Boyle, *Riddle of Erskine Childers*.
34. C. L. Ferguson, *A History of the Magpie and Stump Debating Society* (Cambridge, 1931).
35. Evelyn Waugh, *Decline and Fall* (London, 1928).
36. Marsh, *A Number of People*.
37. Childers, *Riddle of the Sands*.
38. REC to Dulcibella Childers, 13 October 1889; Childers Papers, TCD.

CHAPTER 4: A DOUBLE LIFE

1. Letter to the author from the archivist of the Inner Temple, 7 July 1995.
2. REC to Walter Runciman, 22 October 1893; Childers Papers, TCD.
3. W. R. McKay, *Clerks in the House of Commons* (HMSO, 1989).
4. Hassall, *Biography of Edward Marsh*.
5. REC to Constance Childers, 11 November 1890; Childers Papers, TCD.
6. REC to Walter Runciman, October 1884; loc. cit.
7. Queen Victoria to Lord Lansdowne on 12 August 1892; variously cited.
8. Boyle, *Riddle of Erskine Childers*.
9. Massie, *Dreadnought*.
10. Variously quoted, notably by Massie in *Dreadnought*.
11. Ensor, *England 1870–1914*.
12. op. cit.
13. Thomas Burke, 'London in my Time', quoted in Leonora Collins (ed.), *London in the Nineties* (London, 1950).
14. Childers, *Riddle of the Sands*.
15. REC to Basil Williams, 31 January 1902; Childers Papers, Trinity College, Cambridge.
16. Williams, *Childers, A Sketch*.
17. op. cit.
18. Boyle, *Riddle of Erskine Childers*.
19. Popham, *A Thirst for the Sea*.
20. op. cit.

21. Williams, *Childers, A Sketch.*
22. Popham, *A Thirst for the Sea.*
23. REC to Walter Runciman, October 1897; Childers Papers, TCD.
24. Popham, *A Thirst for the Sea.*
25. Drummond, *The Riddle.*
26. Childers, *Riddle of the Sands.*
27. op. cit.
28. Hassall, *Biography of Edward Marsh.*
29. REC to his sisters, October 1898; Childers Papers, TCD.
30. John N. Young, opening chapters of a biography of REC; Childers papers, TCD.

CHAPTER 5: IMPERIAL GUARD

1. Porter, *The Lion's Share.*
2. Buchan, *Memory Hold-the-Door.*
3. REC to Basil Williams, 14 October 1903; Childers Papers, Trinity College, Cambridge.
4. Childers, *Riddle of the Sands.*
5. F. H. Hinsley (ed.), *The New Cambridge Modern History*, Vol. XI (Cambridge, 1962).
6. Ensor, *England 1870–1914.*
7. REC to Walter Runciman, 9 January 1896; Childers Papers, TCD.
8. Ensor, *England 1870–1914.*
9. Morris, *Heaven's Command.*
10. Longford, *Victoria RI.*
11. Morris, *Pax Britannica.*
12. Kipling, 'Recessional', 1897.
13. Boyle, *Riddle of Erskine Childers.*
14. op. cit.
15. op. cit.
16. Popham, *A Thirst for the Sea.*
17. REC to Dulcibella Childers, 31 October 1899; Childers Papers, TCD.
18. Boyle, *Riddle of Erskine Childers.*
19. REC to Dulcibella Childers, 2 January 1900; Childers Papers, TCD.
20. REC to Dulcibella and Sybil Childers, 5 January 1900; loc, cit.
21. REC to Basil Williams, 23 January 1901; Childers Papers, Trinity College, Cambridge.
22. Erskine Childers, *In the Ranks of the CIV* (London, 1900).
23. Rudyard Kipling, 'Bobs', 1898.

24. Childers, *In the Ranks of the CIV.*
25. James Boswell, *The Life of Samuel Johnson* (London, 1791).
26. Williams, *Childers, A Sketch.*
27. In a letter to *The Times* in March 1901, Childers wrote of General De Wet as 'not only a gallant soldier but a humane and honourable gentleman': Wilkinson, *Zeal of the Convert.*
28. Childers, *In the Ranks of the CIV.*
29. Williams, *Childers, A Sketch.*
30. Childers, *In the Ranks of the CIV.*

CHAPTER 6: THE RIDDLE OF THE SANDS

1. *Dictionary of National Biography.*
2. Childers, *In the Ranks of the CIV.*
3. op. cit.
4. Lloyd-Jones, 'Erskine Childers, An Appreciation'.
5. REC to Flora Priestley, 5 January 1901; Childers Papers, TCD.
6. Magnus, *Edward VII.*
7. REC to Basil Williams, 5 January 1901; Childers Papers, Trinity College, Cambridge.
8. Gilbert, *Churchill.*
9. Dennis was a fellow member of the Savile Club.
10. Williams, *Childers, A Sketch.*
11. Popham, *A Thirst for the Sea.*
12. The allusion is to Childers' letter to *The Times* of March 1901 (see note 27, Chapter 5). The letter to Williams is quoted by Boyle.
13. REC to Basil Williams, 25 February 1902; Childers Papers, Trinity College, Cambridge.
14. REC to Basil Williams, 29 August 1902; loc. cit.
15. REC to Basil Williams, 25 February 1903; loc. cit.
16. Massie, *Dreadnought.*
17. Childers, *Riddle of the Sands.*
18. I. F. Clarke, 'The Shape of Wars to Come', in *History Today*, February 1965.
19. The title of the concluding chapter of *Riddle of the Sands.*
20. REC to Basil Williams, 12 June 1902; Childers Papers, Trinity College, Cambridge.
21. Childers, *Riddle of the Sands.*
22. op. cit.
23. op. cit.

24. John Buchan, in *John O'London's Weekly* (London, 1927).
25. Childers, *Riddle of the Sands.*
26. op. cit.
27. Dulcibella Childers to REC, 27 November 1903; Childers Papers, TCD.
28. Childers, *Riddle of the Sands.*
29. Churchill, *My Early Life.*
30. Childers, *Riddle of the Sands.*
31. op. cit.
32. Lloyd-Jones, 'Erskine Childers, An Appreciation'.
33. Boyle, *Riddle of Erskine Childers.*
34. Drummond, *The Riddle.*
35. *Dictionary of National Biography.*
36. John Bennet Carruthers was elected to the Savile on 30 May 1904, describing himself as a 'naturalist from Ceylon'. Childers and he may well have been acquainted before either joined the club.
37. Childers, *The Riddle of the Sands.*
38. op. cit.
39. Roy Foster, 'A Patriot for Whom? A Very English Gentleman', in *History Today*, 1988.

CHAPTER 7: MOLLY

1. *Dictionary of National Biography*; Leo Amery was the father of the Conservative MP Julian Amery.
2. Landreth, *Mind and Heart of Mary Childers.*
3. op. cit.
4. REC to Dulcibella Childers, 27 November 1903; Childers Papers, TCD.
5. Landreth, *Mind and Heart of Molly Childers.*
6. Private papers in the possession of Mrs Diana Stewart.
7. Constant Coquelin (b. 1841) was also well known in London.
8. Molly's letters home to her parents, undated but about 1895; Childers Papers, TCD.
9. Gilbert, *Churchill.*
10. REC to Agnes Barton, 13 November 1903; Childers Papers, TCD.
11. MAC to REC, 29 March 1919; loc. cit.
12. *Boston Globe*; Childers Papers, Trinity College, Cambridge.
13. REC to Mrs Hamilton Osgood, 11 January 1904; Childers Papers, TCD.
14. REC to his sisters, February 1904; loc. cit.

CHAPTER 8: A TERRIFYING HAPPINESS

1. MAC, notes for a biography of REC; Childers Papers, TCD.
2. loc. cit.
3. *New York Times*, 1 January 1964; loc. cit.
4. Williams, *Childers, A Sketch.*
5. Boyle, *Riddle of Erskine Childers.*
6. REC to Mrs Charles Childers, 5 January 1906; Childers Papers, TCD.
7. E. M. Forster, *Howards End* (London, 1910).
8. Wilkinson, *Zeal of the Convert.*
9. Churchill, *My Early Life.*
10. Massie, *Dreadnought.*
11. REC to Dr Hamilton Osgood, June 1904; Childers Papers, TCD.
12. Landreth, *Mind and Heart of Molly Childers.*
13. REC to MAC, December 1906; Childers Papers, TCD.
14. MAC to REC, December 1905; loc. cit.
15. REC to Mrs Charles Childers, 5 January 1906; loc. cit.
16. Private papers in the possession of Mrs Diana Stewart.
17. REC to Mrs Hamilton Osgood, 2 April 1904; Childers Papers, TCD.
18. REC to Mrs Hamilton Osgood, May 1904; loc. cit.
19. MAC to Dr Hamilton Osgood, 17 August 1906; loc. cit.
20. Popham, *A Thirst for the Sea.*
21. MAC to Dr and Mrs Hamilton Osgood, 19 September 1906; Childers Papers, TCD.
22. MAC, notes for a biography of REC; Childers Papers, TCD.
23. Popham, *A Thirst for the Sea.*
24. 1931 edition of *The Riddle of the Sands.*
25. Collection of reviews in Childers Papers, Trinity College, Cambridge.
26. REC to Flora Priestley, 4 May 1903; Childers Papers, TCD.
27. Williams, *Childers, A Sketch.*
28. REC to Gretchen Fiske Warren, 18 June 1904; Childers Papers, TCD.
29. Drummond, *The Riddle.*
30. op. cit.
31. Collection of reviews in Childers Papers, Trinity College, Cambridge.
32. Erskine Childers, *The Times History of the War in South Africa*, Vol. 5 (London, 1907).
33. Collection of reviews in Childers Papers, Trinity College, Cambridge.
34. Williams, *Childers, A Sketch.*
35. MAC to Dr and Mrs Hamilton Osgood, 13 September 1906; Childers Papers, TCD.

36. Popham, *A Thirst for the Sea.*
37. Papers on the Sunday Tramps, Childers Papers, TCD.
38. loc. cit.
39. Boyle, *Riddle of Erskine Childers.*
40. REC to MAC, 14 December 1907; Childers Papers, Trinity College, Cambridge.
41. REC to MAC, March 1908; loc. cit.
42. MAC, notes for a biography of REC; Childers Papers, TCD.

CHAPTER 9: 'THIS GREAT TURNING-POINT IN OUR LIVES'

1. Ensor, *England 1870–1914.*
2. op. cit.
3. Taylor, *England 1914–1945.*
4. Ensor, *England 1870–1914.*
5. David Fitzpatrick, 'Ireland since 1870', *The Oxford History of Ireland* (Oxford, 1989).
6. Gilbert, *Churchill.*
7. Douglas Hyde (1860–1947) was a scholar who wrote the first modern play in Gaelic. He was a senator of the Irish Free State between 1925 and 1926, and became President of the Republic in 1938.
8. Eoin MacNeill (1867–1945) was a scholar who became intimately involved in the struggle for independence. In 1916 he was Chief-of-Staff of the Irish Volunteers, later becoming Minister of Finance in the first Dáil, and in 1924 a member of the Boundary Commission appointed to redraw the line between Northern and Southern Ireland.
9. Augustine Birrell, *Things Past Redress* (London, 1937).
10. Horace Plunkett (1854–1932) combined membership of the Ascendancy with a keen interest in social and political reform. Tom Jones observed, 'No man worked harder for his country, forgave so much, or was so shamefully treated.' Jones, Childers' opposite number in the Treaty negotiations, might justly have said the same of Childers.
11. REC to Basil Williams, September 1908; Childers Papers, Trinity College, Cambridge.
12. Churchill, *English-speaking Peoples.*
13. MAC, notes for a biography of REC; Childers Papers, TCD.
14. Childers, *Riddle of the Sands.*
15. Ensor, *England 1870–1914.*
16. Churchill, *My Early Life.*

17. Erskine Childers, *The German Influence on British Cavalry* (London, 1911).
18. REC to MAC, September 1909; Childers Papers, Trinity College, Cambridge.
19. REC to MAC, 21 September 1909; loc. cit.
20. Introduction to Childers, *War and the Arme Blanche* (London, 1910).
21. Collection of reviews in Childers Papers, Trinity College, Cambridge.
22. loc. cit.
23. loc. cit.
24. Childers, *War and the Arme Blanche.*
25. Williams, *Childers, A Sketch.*
26. Morris, *Heaven's Command.*
27. Ensor, *England 1870–1914.*
28. op. cit.
29. Erskine Childers, *The Framework of Home Rule* (London, 1911).
30. REC to William Le Fanu, December 1909; Childers Papers, Trinity College, Cambridge.
31. Ensor, *England 1870–1914.*
32. REC to Sumner Pearmain, 24 May 1910; Childers Papers, Trinity College, Cambridge.
33. Ensor, *England 1870–1914.*
34. REC to MAC, December 1910; Childers Papers, Trinity College, Cambridge.
35. REC to MAC, 28 November 1910; loc. cit.
36. REC to MAC, December 1910; loc. cit.
37. REC to MAC, 13 December 1910; loc. cit.
38. loc. cit.
39. *United Services Magazine*, May 1910; loc. cit.
40. REC to MAC, 14 December 1910; loc. cit.
41. REC to Mrs Hamilton Osgood, 7 December 1910; loc. cit.
42. Ironically, this phrase was coined by Winston Churchill's father, Lord Randolph.
43. Ensor, *England 1870–1914.*
44. Boyle, *Riddle of Erskine Childers.*
45. REC to MAC, March 1911; Childers Papers, Trinity College, Cambridge.
46. REC to MAC, March 1911 (another letter); loc. cit.
47. George Russell was a member of Plunkett's Irish Agricultural Organization Society from its early days. Subsequently Plunkett's secretary, he was a poet and painter of genuine talent.
48. REC to MAC, March 1911; Childers Papers, Trinity College, Cambridge.

49. Boyle, *Riddle of Erskine Childers.*
50. Collection of reviews of *Framework,* Childers Papers, TCD.
51. loc. cit.
52. loc. cit.
53. loc. cit.
54. loc. cit.
55. loc. cit.
56. loc. cit.
57. loc. cit.
58. Childers, *Framework of Home Rule.*
59. REC to Constance Childers, December 1911; Childers Papers, TCD.
60. REC to MAC, March 1912; Childers Papers, Trinity College, Cambridge.

CHAPTER 10: THE LIBERAL CANDIDATE

1. REC to MAC, May 1912; Childers Papers, Trinity College, Cambridge.
2. Ensor, *England 1870–1914.*
3. op. cit.
4. op. cit.
5. REC to MAC, January 1913; Childers Papers, TCD.
6. Williams, *Childers, A Sketch.*
7. Boyle, *Riddle of Erskine Childers.*
8. Gilbert, *Churchill.*
9. Ensor, *England 1870–1914.*
10. Leslie, *Memoirs of . . . Shephard.*
11. op. cit.
12. Wilkinson, *Zeal of the Convert.*
13. REC to Flora Priestley, 14 August 1913; Childers Papers, TCD.
14. MAC, notes for a biography of REC; loc. cit.
15. Drummond, *The Riddle.*
16. Popham, *A Thirst for the Sea.*
17. Boyle, *Riddle of Erskine Childers.*
18. Popham, *A Thirst for the Sea.*
19. Childers, *Riddle of the Sands.*
20. REC to Constance Childers, 20 August 1913; Childers Papers, Trinity College, Cambridge.
21. Popham, *A Thirst for the Sea.*
22. Boyle, *Riddle of the Sands.*
23. op. cit.
24. op. cit.

25. *Dictionary of National Biography*, as is the preceding quotation.
26. REC to MAC, 25 September 1913; Childers Papers TCD.
27. Boyle, *Riddle of the Sands.*
28. MAC to REC, 27 September 1913; Childers Papers, TCD.
29. Barton Papers, National Archives, Dublin.
30. REC to Flora Priestley, 24 November 1913; Childers Papers, TCD.
31. Ensor, *England 1870–1914.*
32. REC to Alice Stopford Green, 7 November 1914; loc. cit.
33. *Dictionary of National Biography.*
34. Gilbert, *Churchill.*
35. As success has many fathers, several people have been put forward as the inspiration of the committee. The credentials of Darrell Figgis are generally regarded as less tenable than those of Mary Spring Rice.
36. Williams, *Childers, A Sketch.*

CHAPTER II: THE ROUSING OF MR GORDON

1. REC to MAC, 22 May 1914; Childers Papers, TCD.
2. op. cit.
3. Boyle, *Riddle of Erskine Childers.*
4. REC to MAC, 21 June 1914; Childers Papers, TCD.
5. Mary Spring Rice's diary of the voyage; loc. cit.
6. loc. cit.
7. loc. cit.
8. loc. cit.
9. loc. cit.
10. loc. cit.
11. Description by MAC, in de Valera papers; Killiney.
12. MAC to Alice Stopford Green, July 1914; Childers Papers, TCD.
13. MAC to Alice Stopford Green, July 1914 (another letter); loc. cit.
14. Mary Spring Rice's diary; loc. cit.
15. Martin, *Howth Gun-running.*
16. Description by MAC, in de Valera papers; Killiney.
17. Mary Spring Rice's diary; Childers Papers, TCD.
18. By The O'Rahilly, a leading Volunteer, and among the instigators in Ireland of the plot.
19. Martin, *Howth Gun-running.*
20. MAC, notes for a biography of REC; Childers Papers, TCD.
21. Gilbert, *Churchill.*
22. Churchill, *The World Crisis.*

23. Gilbert, *Churchill.*
24. REC to Harry Chester, 8 October, 1914; Childers Papers, TCD.
25. G. M. Trevelyan, *English Social History.*
26. REC to Dulcibella Childers, 2 January 1900; Childers Papers, TCD.
27. Variously quoted.
28. Gilbert, *Churchill.*
29. Boyle, *Riddle of Erskine Childers.*
30. op. cit.
31. op. cit.
32. Childers war diary, 17 August 1914; Imperial War Museum.
33. Williams, *Childers, a Sketch.*

CHAPTER 12: AN INCALCULABLE EXPERIMENT

1. Churchill, *My Early Life.*
2. Walter Raleigh, *The War in the Air* (Oxford, 1922).
3. Gilbert, *Churchill.*
4. Childers war diary, 12 September 1914; Imperial War Museum.
5. loc. cit., 21 August 1914.
6. A comment attributed to Tyrwhitt's colleague at Harwich, Roger Keyes; see Cecil Aspinall-Oglander, *Roger Keyes* (London, 1951).
7. Temple Patterson, *Tyrwhitt.*
8. Childers war diary, 11 September 1914; Imperial War Museum.
9. REC to MAC, 10 March 1916; Childers Papers, TCD.
10. REC to Grètchen Fiske Warren, 30 July 1915; loc. cit.
11. Childers war diary, 6 September 1914; Imperial War Museum.
12. REC to MAC, 7 September 1914; Childers papers, TCD.
13. Childers war diary, 26 August 1914; Imperial War Museum.
14. Arthur J. Marder, *From Dreadnought to Scapa Flow* (Oxford, 1965).
15. Buchan, *The King's Grace.*
16. Churchill, *The World Crisis.*
17. E. F. B. Charlton remained in this post until early 1917, despite what some supposed to be his inefficiency: in the eyes of Admiral of the Fleet Sir John Fisher, he was 'Quite unfit for so immense a job . . . he ought to have been blown from a gun' (Marder, *Dreadnought to Scapa Flow*).
18. Temple Patterson, *Tyrwhitt.*
19. Childers Diary, 9 September 1914; Imperial War Museum.
20. REC to Mrs Hamilton Osgood, 13 September 1914; Childers Papers, TCD.
21. Childers war diary, 2 November 1914; Imperial War Museum.

22. loc. cit., 25 October 1914.
23. loc. cit., 24 October 1914.
24. Churchill, *The World Crisis.*
25. Childers war diary, 18 November 1914; Imperial War Museum; the two following quotations are from the same source.
26. loc. cit., 24 December 1914.
27. loc. cit., 25 December 1914.
28. loc. cit.
29. The entrance to a harbour is conventionally known as the roads.
30. Childers war diary, 27 December 1914; Imperial War Museum.
31. Churchill, *The Aftermath.*
32. *Ben My Chree* is Manx for 'Lady of my Heart'.
33. Buchan, *The King's Grace.*
34. Churchill, *The World Crisis.*
35. Boyle, *Riddle of Erskine Childers.*
36. Churchill, *The World Crisis.*
37. op. cit.
38. op. cit.
39. *A Short History of the Royal Air Force* (Air Ministry, 1929).
40. Like Tyrwhitt, Keyes (1872–1945) was one of the leading naval commanders of the war, in his time as well-known as Admiral Beatty. He made his name masterminding the blockade of Zeebrugge.
41. Admiral Sir Roger Keyes, *The Naval Memoirs of Admiral of the Fleet, Sir Roger Keyes* (London, 1934).
42. According to some accounts, the ship had been previously disabled.
43. Julian S. Corbett, *Naval Operations* (London, 1923).
44. Childers war diary, December 1915; Imperial War Museum.
45. loc. cit.
46. loc. cit.
47. Boyle, *Riddle of Erskine Childers.*
48. Sykes, *From Many Angles.*
49. REC to MAC, 19 February 1916; Childers Papers, TCD.
50. Childers war diary, 10 March 1916; Imperial War Museum.
51. loc. cit.
52. loc. cit.

CHAPTER 13: NEUROTICS, DREAMERS, AND THE CLAIMS OF A REPUBLIC

1. Boyle, *Riddle of Erskine Childers.*
2. Key, *The Green Flag.*
3. Jenkins, *Asquith.*
4. REC to Mrs Hamilton Osgood, 8 September 1917; Childers Papers, TCD.
5. See Denis Gwynn, *Sunday Press*, 22 April 1955; loc. cit.
6. Williams, *Childers, A Sketch.*

CHAPTER 14: THE IRISH AIRMAN

1. Barry Domvile spent the whole war with the Harwich force, working closely with Tyrwhitt, and eventually became an Admiral. Later he became well-known for his pro-German views.
2. Temple Patterson, *Tyrwhitt.*
3. Childers press cuttings, Childers Papers, TCD.
4. REC to MAC, 2 October 1916; loc. cit.
5. REC to MAC, 26 July 1916; loc. cit.
6. REC to Mrs Hamilton Osgood, October 1916; loc. cit.
7. Temple Patterson, *Tyrwhitt.*
8. REC to MAC, 22 November 1916; Childers Papers, TCD.
9. REC to MAC, 27 December 1916; loc. cit.
10. REC to MAC, 1 January 1917; loc. cit.
11. REC to MAC, 17 February 1917; loc. cit.
12. Childers war diary, 8 April 1916; Imperial War Museum.
13. REC to MAC, 10 April 1917; Childers Papers, TCD.
14. Childers war diary, 10 April 1917; Imperial War Museum.
15. loc. cit., 19 April 1917.
16. loc. cit., 5 May 1917.
17. Boyle, *Riddle of Erskine Childers.*
18. REC to MAC, 5 July 1917; Childers Papers, TCD.
19. Childers war diary, 6 July 1917; Imperial War Museum.
20. loc. cit., 27 July 1917.
21. Leslie, *Memoirs of . . . Shephard.*
22. Taylor, *England 1914–1945.*
23. REC to MAC, 5 July 1917; Childers papers, TCD.
24. Edward MacLysaght was one of those unusual figures of the period

who – like Robert Barton – were landowners on a significant scale, yet sympathized with Sinn Féin.

25. Boyle, *Riddle of Erskine Childers.*
26. REC to Mrs Hamilton Osgood, 8 September 1917; Childers Papers, TCD.
27. REC to Constance Childers, 14 October 1917; loc. cit.
28. McDowell, *Irish Convention*; Lady Diana Manners later became the wife of (Alfred) Duff Cooper, and was a close friend of Evelyn Waugh.
29. Boyle, *Riddle of Erskine Childers.*
30. Childers war diary, 2 November 1917; Imperial War Museum.
31. REC to Mrs Hamilton Osgood, 20 November 1917; Childers Papers, TCD.
32. Kee, *The Green Flag.*
33. Childers war diary, October 1917; Imperial War Museum.
34. Boyle, *Riddle of Erskine Childers.*
35. REC to Mrs Hamilton Osgood, 22 December 1917; Childers Papers, TCD.
36. REC to Constance Childers, 29 January 1918; loc. cit.
37. Taylor, *The First World War.*
38. op. cit.
39. Boyle, *Riddle of Erskine Childers.*
40. op. cit.
41. MAC to Lady Shephard, January 1918; Childers Papers, TCD.
42. Childers war diary, 17 February 1918; Imperial War Museum.
43. Boyle, *Riddle of Erskine Childers.*
44. McDowell, *Irish Convention.*
45. Childers war diary, 10 April 1918; Imperial War Museum.
46. Trevelyan, *English Social History.*
47. Tierney, *Modern Ireland.*
48. Childers' defence at his trial; Childers Papers, TCD.
49. Sykes, *From Many Angles.*
50. Like Churchill, a man whose life touched Childers' at several curious points. One of the successful generals of the Boer War, Smuts subsequently became more sympathetic to the Empire. His meeting with Childers helped bring about the truce in the Black and Tan war.
51. Taylor, *England 1914–1945.*
52. REC to MAC, April 1918; Childers Papers, TCD.
53. loc. cit.
54. Childers war diary, 24 April 1918; Imperial War Museum.
55. REC to MAC, 9 September 1918; Childers Papers, TCD.

56. Childers Diary, September 1918; Imperial War Museum.
57. loc. cit.
58. loc. cit.
59. loc. cit.
60. loc. cit., 10 November 1918.
61. REC to MAC, 11 November 1918; Childers Papers, TCD.
62. Buchan, *The King's Grace.*
63. REC to MAC, 11 Novemebr 1918; Childers Papers, TCD.

CHAPTER 15: SORCERER'S APPRENTICE

1. Boyle, *Riddle of Erskine Childers.*
2. REC to MAC, 23 March 1919; Childers Papers, TCD.
3. Churchill, *The World Crisis.*
4. REC to MAC, 27 March 1919; Childers Papers, TCD.
5. MAC to REC, 29 March 1919; loc. cit.
6. loc. cit.
7. loc. cit.
8. MAC, notes for a biography of REC; loc. cit.
9. Brennan, *Allegiance.*
10. Childers Diary, 3 July–3 August 1919; Childers Papers, TCD.
11. Desmond Fitzgerald, father of the Irish politician Dr Garret Fitzgerald.
12. Brennan, *Allegiance.*
13. Childers Diary, 15–24 June 1919; Childers Papers, TCD. The suit for damages was ultimately successful.
14. Michael Collins (1890–1922) was born in County Cork and fought in the Easter Rising, subsequently masterminding the intelligence network that helped win the Black and Tan war; the most naturally gifted of the Irish leaders.
15. De Valera Papers; Killiney.
16. Childers Diary, 3 July–3 August 1919; Childers Papers, TCD.
17. loc. cit.
18. loc. cit.
19. REC to MAC, July 1919; loc. cit.
20. Mitchell, *Revolutionary Government in Ireland.*
21. Childers Diary, 3 July–3 August 1919; Childers Papers, TCD.
22. Macardle, *The Irish Republic.*
23. REC to MAC, 23 July 1919; Childers Papers, TCD.
24. REC to MAC, 27 February 1917; loc. cit.
25. Churchill, *The World Crisis.*

26. REC to MAC, 26 July 1919; Childers Papers, TCD.
27. Williams, *Childers, A Sketch.*
28. Childers Diary, 6 August – 17 September 1919; Childers Papers, TCD.
29. MAC, notes for a biography of REC; loc. cit.
30. This is excellently covered by Lord Longford in *Peace by Ordeal.*
31. REC to MAC, September 1919; Childers Papers, TCD.
32. Wedgwood Benn (later Viscount Stansgate): father of the Labour MP Tony Benn.
33. Childers, 'Might and Right in Ireland' (Dublin, 1920).
34. REC to MAC, December 1919; Childers Papers, TCD.
35. Williams, *Childers, A Sketch.*
36. McInerney, *Riddle of Erskine Childers.*
37. Jenkins, *Asquith.*
38. Taylor, *England 1914–1945.*
39. Childers, *Military Rule in Ireland.*
40. REC to Basil Williams, 12 June 1902; Childers Papers, Trinity College, Cambridge.
41. *Freeman's Journal*, July 1920; Childers Papers, TCD.
42. *Who's Who in Ireland.*
43. Childers Diary, 24 February 1920; Childers Papers, TCD.
44. Molly was made CBE in recognition of her war work with the Belgian refugees.
45. Foster, *Modern Ireland.*
46. Childers Diary, 4 March 1920; Childers Papers, TCD.

CHAPTER 16: THE NECESSARY MURDER

1. Tierney, *Modern Ireland since 1850.*
2. Gilbert, *Churchill.*
3. Owen, *Tempestuous Journey.*
4. Gilbert, *Churchill.*
5. loc. cit.
6. Kee, *The Green Flag.*
7. Owen, *Tempestuous Journey.*
8. Kee, *The Green Flag.*
9. Childers Diary, 31 July 1920; Childers Papers, TCD.
10. The White Cross was a charitable fund set up to compensate Irish victims of the Black and Tan war. Its main source of funds was the United States, and its executive committee included Collins, Griffith and Childers.
11. Sir Hamar Greenwood told the Commons on 22 February 1921 that

Erskine Childers was 'an extreme friend of the Republic, whose house was a rendezvous, and with that of another person, a clearing house of correspondence between heads of the Irish Republican Army'; War of Independence press cuttings, Childers Papers, TCD.

12. Wilkinson, *Zeal of the Convert.*
13. REC to Basil Williams, 14 October 1903; Childers Papers, Trinity College, Cambridge.
14. REC to Dulcibella Childers, 2 January 1900; Childers Papers, TCD.
15. REC to Mrs Hamilton Osgood, October 1916; loc. cit.
16. Ryan, *Remembering Sion.*
17. Childers, *Military Rule in Ireland.*
18. Boyle, *Riddle of Erskine Childers.*
19. Ryan, *Remembering Sion.*
20. Kee, *The Green Flag.*
21. op. cit.
22. op. cit.
23. De Valera papers; Killiney.
24. Frank Gallagher later wrote, as David Hogan, *Four Glorious Years* (Dublin, 1971).
25. Brennan, *Allegiance.*
26. Wilkinson, *Zeal of the Convert.*
27. Macardle, *The Irish Republic.*
28. Foster, *Modern Ireland.*
29. Mitchell, *Revolutionary Government in Ireland.*
30. loc. cit.
31. Hogan, *Four Glorious Years.*
32. Wilkinson, *Zeal of the Convert.*
33. loc. cit.
34. Gilbert, *Churchill.*
35. loc. cit.
36. loc. cit.
37. loc. cit.
38. A controversial appointment; Padraic Colum in his biography of Griffith noted the Vice-Chairman's comment, 'Parnell would not have it!'
39. De Valera to REC, 16 May 1921; de Valera Papers; Killiney.
40. O'Faoláin, *De Valera.*
41. Williams, *Childers, A Sketch.*
42. Longford and O'Neill, *Éamon de Valera.*
43. op. cit.
44. De Valera to MAC, 11 November 1922; Childers Papers, TCD.

45. Lazenby, *Ireland, A Catspaw.*
46. Boyle, *Riddle of Erskine Childers.*
47. Béaslaí, *Michael Collins*; on the other hand, Arthur Mitchell (*Revolutionary Government in Ireland*) notes that Béaslaí's contemporary comments on Childers were 'most favourable'.
48. Arthur Cope, known as 'Andy', was a former customs officer who established underground contacts with the Republicans.
49. Boyle, *Riddle of Erskine Childers.*
50. Childers Diary, 9 March 1920; Childers Papers, TCD.
51. Brennan, *Allegiance.*
52. Wilkinson, *Zeal of the Convert.*
53. Childers Diary, 9 May 1921; Childers Papers, TCD.
54. Hogan, *Four Glorious Years.*
55. Curran, *Birth of Irish Free State.*
56. 'Sandy' Lindsay (1879–1952) became a national figure after the Second World War; an academic politician, his prominence was 'more by virtue of his moral fervour than his contribution to scholarship' (*DNB*).
57. Alexander Lindsay to MAC, 12 June 1921; Childers Papers, TCD.
58. MAC to Lindsay, 15 June 1921; loc. cit.
59. Taylor, *England 1914–1945.*
60. Millin, *Smuts*; see also Colum, *Arthur Griffith.*
61. Taylor, *England 1914–1945.*
62. loc. cit.
63. Boyce, *Englishmen and Irish Troubles.*
64. op. cit.
65. *Dáil: Report on Treaty Debate.*
66. McInerney, *Riddle of Erskine Childers.*
67. Foster, *Modern Ireland.*
68. Churchill, *The Aftermath.*

CHAPTER 17: ON THE BREAKING OF NATIONS

1. Macardle, *Irish Republic.*
2. Longford, *Peace by Ordeal.*
3. op. cit.
4. op. cit.
5. op. cit.
6. Childers Treaty negotiations papers; Childers Papers, TCD.
7. Childers Diary, October 1921; copy held with de Valera Papers, Killiney.
8. Longford, *Peace by Ordeal.*

9. op. cit.
10. op. cit.
11. Boyle, *Riddle of Erskine Childers.*
12. Foster, *Modern Ireland.*
13. Longford, *Peace by Ordeal.*
14. Boyle, *Riddle of Erskine Childers.*
15. *Dáil: Report on Treaty Debate.*
16. Wilkinson, *Zeal of the Convert.*
17. Longford, *Peace by Ordeal.*
18. Childers Diary, 7 October 1921; Childers Papers, TCD.
19. Longford, *Peace by Ordeal.*
20. Childers had prepared various critiques of the British Treaty proposals, for the Cabinet.
21. Longford, *Peace by Ordeal.*
22. op. cit.
23. De Valera to REC, 15 June 1921; Childers Papers, TCD.
24. Childers Diary, 13 October 1921; Killiney.
25. loc. cit., 18 October 1921.
26. Childers Papers on the Treaty negotiations; Childers Papers, TCD.
27. Owen, *Tempestuous Journey.*
28. Longford, *Peace by Ordeal.*
29. Churchill, *The Aftermath.*
30. Longford, *Peace by Ordeal.*
31. See Ryle Dwyer, *Michael Collins*, and Jones, *Whitehall Diary III.*
32. Childers Diary, 24 October 1921; Killiney.
33. Longford, *Peace by Ordeal.*
34. op. cit.
35. Macardle, *The Irish Republic.*
36. Longford, *Peace by Ordeal.*
37. Childers Papers on the Treaty negotiations; Childers Papers, TCD.
38. Childers Diary, 21 November 1921; Killiney.
39. Longford, *Peace by Ordeal.*
40. Williams, *Childers, A Sketch*, in which Williams writes that Childers 'physically . . . was almost a wreck [and] his mind [had] a hectic brightness, with almost all his old sense of humour and of proportion vanished'; yet other friends and colleagues challenged this view.
41. Boyle, *Riddle of Erskine Childers*; Wilkinson, *Zeal of the Convert.*
42. REC to MAC, 6 November 1921; Childers Papers, TCD.
43. Childers, Papers on the Treaty negotiations; loc. cit.
44. Churchill, *The Aftermath.*

45. Macardle, *Irish Republic.*
46. Longford, *Peace by Ordeal.*
47. op. cit.
48. op. cit.
49. O'Connor, *The Big Fellow.*
50. Childers Diary, 3 December 1921; Killiney.
51. Longford, *Peace by Ordeal.*
52. op. cit.
53. op. cit.
54. op. cit.
55. op. cit.
56. Winston Churchill, *The Aftermath.*
57. Longford, *Peace by Ordeal* (but variously quoted/misquoted).
58. op. cit.
59. Churchill, *The Aftermath.*
60. Longford, *Peace by Ordeal.*
61. Childers Diary, 5 December 1921; Killiney.
62. Longford, *Peace by Ordeal.*
63. Childers Diary, 5 December 1921; Killiney.
64. Childers Diary, 6 December 1921; Childers Papers, TCD.
65. Longford, *Peace by Ordeal.*
66. Lloyd George in *The Daily Telegraph*, 23 December 1922.
67. Longford, *Peace by Ordeal.*
68. Hopkinson, *Green Against Green.*
69. Childers Diary, 6 December 1921; Killiney.

CHAPTER 18: NEMESIS

1. Lloyd George, *The Daily Telegraph*, 23 December 1922.
2. Longford, *Peace by Ordeal.*
3. op. cit.
4. op. cit.
5. Macardle, *Irish Republic.*
6. Kee, *Green Flag*, as is the next quotation.
7. op. cit.
8. Desmond Fitzgerald, 'The Anglo-Irish Treaty', in *Studies* (Vol. XXIV, 1935).
9. Kee, *Green Flag.*
10. *Dáil: Report on Treaty Debate.*
11. Lyons, *Ireland since the Famine.*

12. *Dáil: Report on Treaty Debate.*
13. op. cit.
14. Macardle, *Irish Republic.*
15. O'Connor, *The Big Fellow.*
16. *Dáil: Report on Treaty Debate.*
17. op. cit.
18. Kee, *The Green Flag.*
19. Tierney, *Modern Ireland since 1850.*
20. Hopkinson, *Green Against Green.*
21. Wilkinson, *Zeal of the Convert.*
22. Gilbert, *Churchill.*
23. Curran, *Birth of the Irish Free State.*
24. Kee, *The Green Flag.*
25. Longford, *Peace by Ordeal.*
26. op. cit.
27. Papers on Childers trial and execution; Childers Papers, TCD.
28. Kee, *The Green Flag.*
29. Childers Diary, 28 June–3 November 1922; Childers Papers, TCD.
30. O'Malley, *The Singing Flame.*
31. REC to MAC, 13 July 1922; Childers Papers, TCD.
32. MAC to REC, 14 July 1922; loc. cit.
33. Wilkinson, *Zeal of the Convert.*
34. Kee, *The Green Flag.*
35. Churchill, *The Aftermath.*
36. Coogan, *Michael Collins.*
37. Forester, *Collins: The Lost Leader.*
38. Wilkinson, *Zeal of the Convert.*
39. Boyle, *Riddle of Erskine Childers.*
40. REC to MAC, 19 August 1922; Childers Papers, TCD.
41. Colum, *Arthur Griffith.*
42. O'Connor, *An Only Child.*
43. Duggan, *History of the Irish Army.*
44. Hopkinson, *Green against Green.*
45. David Robinson to MAC, August 1922; Childers papers, TCD.
46. O'Connor, *An Only Child.*
47. Boyle, *Riddle of Erskine Childers.*
48. REC to MAC, 30 October 1922; Childers Papers, TCD.
49. Boyle, *Riddle of Erskine Childers.* The servant has since been identified as Catherine Mee.
50. Wilkinson, *Zeal of the Convert.*

51. REC to MAC, 11 November 1922; Childers Papers, TCD.
52. Papers on Childers trial and execution; loc. cit.
53. loc. cit.
54. loc. cit.
55. Hopkinson, *Green against Green.*
56. White, *Kevin O'Higgins.*
57. REC to MAC, 20 November 1922; Childers Papers, TCD.
58. loc. cit.
58. Wilkinson, *Zeal of the Convert.*
60. Papers on Childers trial and execution; Childers Papers, TCD.

CHAPTER 19: NO GREATER LOVE

1. REC to MAC, 20 November 1922; Childers Papers, TCD.
2. loc. cit.
3. Boyle, *Riddle of Erskine Childers.*
4. MAC to Basil Williams, 24 November 1922, Papers on Childers trial and execution; Childers Papers, TCD.
5. REC to MAC, 24 November 1922; loc. cit.

CHAPTER 20: THE PICTURE OF ERSKINE CHILDERS

1. The O'Rahilly's remark: Martin, *Howth Gun-running.*
2. O'Faoláin, *De Valera.*
3. *The Times*, 25 November 1922.
4. James A. Whelan to Basil Williams, 10 December 1941; Childers Papers, Trinity College, Cambridge.
5. McInerney, *Riddle of Erskine Childers.*
6. Buchan, *The King's Grace.*
7. Longford, *Peace by Ordeal.*
8. Geoffrey Household's Introduction to the 1978 Penguin edition of *The Riddle of the Sands.*
9. Longford, *Peace by Ordeal.*
10. REC to MAC, 20 November 1922, Childers Papers TCD.
11. loc. cit.
12. George Bernard Shaw, *Reason.*

Sources

PRIMARY SOURCES

The primary source for a life on Childers lies in the Childers Papers in Trinity College, Dublin. This is an extensive, not to say exhaustive, archive, carefully catalogued and professionally managed. It contains Childers' own voluminous personal and public correspondence, together with that of his wife and several other associated figures. There is a highly valuable but far smaller collection of Childers papers at Trinity College, Cambridge, and his war diary is to be found at the Imperial War Museum. I have also consulted papers in:

The archives of the National Library of Dublin
The archives of University College, Dublin
Franciscan Archives, Killiney, County Dublin (de Valera papers)
Army Archives, Dublin
National Archives, Dublin
Public Record Office, Kew
National Maritime Museum, Greenwich
Private papers in the possession of John Murray
Private papers of Lord Monteagle, relating to the Howth gun-running
Private papers of Mrs Diana Stewart, relating to her grandfather
Private papers of Dr Rory Childers, relating to his grandfather

SELECT BIBLIOGRAPHY

Secondary sources for the life of Childers are now very various; any reader will wish to roam its bibliography, but I list below the works I have found most helpful. The Notes include references to a number of articles concerning Childers, and I would also suggest the newspapers of the period, most obviously the *Irish Bulletin* and *An Phoblacht noh-Éireann.*

Tom Barry, *Guerrilla Days in Ireland* (Tralee, 1962)

Pairas Béaslaí, *Michael Collins and the Making of the New Ireland* (London, 1926)

Richard Bennett, *The Black and Tans* (London, 1970)
Paul Bew, *Ideology in the Irish Question* (Oxford, 1994)
D. G. Boyce, *Englishmen and Irish Troubles* (London, 1972)
Andrew Boyle, *The Riddle of Erskine Childers* (London, 1977)
Brian Bond, *War and Society in Europe, 1870–1970* (London, 1984)
Dan Breen, *My Fight for Irish Freedom* (Dublin, 1926)
Robert Brennan, *Allegiance* (Dublin, 1950)
Mary C. Bromage, *De Valera* (London, 1956)
—— *Churchill and Ireland* (Indiana, 1964)
John Buchan, *The King's Grace* (London, 1935)
—— *Memory-hold-the-Door* (London, 1940)
Padraic Colum, *Arthur Griffith* (Dublin, 1959)
Winston Churchill, *The World Crisis* (4 vols., 1923–9)
—— *The Aftermath* (London, 1929)
—— *My Early Life* (London, 1930)
—— *History of the English-speaking Peoples* (4 vols., 1956–8)
Tim Pat Coogan, *The IRA* (London, 1970)
—— *Michael Collins* (London, 1990)
—— *De Valera* (London, 1993)
Tom Cox, *Damned Englishman* (New York, 1975)
Lt Colonel Spencer Childers, *Life and Correspondence of the Rt Hon Hugh Culling Eardley Childers* (London, 1901)
Joseph M. Curran, *The Birth of the Irish Free State, 1921–1923* (Alabama, 1980)
Dáil Éireann, Official Report: Debate on the Treaty Between Great Britain and Ireland signed in London on 6 December 1921
Liam Deasy, *Brother against Brother* (Dublin, 1982)
Maldwin Drummond, *The Riddle* (London, 1987)
Charles Duff, *Six Days to Shake an Empire* (London, 1966)
John D. Duggan, *A History of the Irish Army* (Dublin, 1991)
T. Ryle Dwyer, *Michael Collins and the Treaty* (Dublin, 1981)
R. C. K. Ensor, *England 1870–1914* (Oxford, 1936)
St John Ervine, *Craigavon, Ulsterman* (London, 1949)
Darrell Figgis, *Recollections of the Irish War* (London, 1927)
Margery Forester, *Michael Collins: the Lost Leader* (London, 1972)
R. F. Foster, *Modern Ireland* (London, 1988)
Frank Gallagher (David Hogan), *Four Glorious Years* (Dublin, 1953)
Martin Gilbert, *Churchill, A Life* (London, 1991)
Desmond Greaves, *Liam Mellowes and the Irish Revolution* (London, 1971)
Denis Gwynn, *John Redmond* (London, 1932)

O. J. Hale, *Publicity and Diplomacy, 1890–1914* (Oxford, 1940)
Christopher J. Hassall, *A Biography of Edward Marsh* (London, 1959)
Bulmer Hobson, *Ireland Yesterday and Today* (Tralee, 1983)
David Hogan (Frank Gallagher), *Four Glorious Years* (Dublin, 1953)
Michael Hopkinson, *Green against Green* (Dublin, 1988)
Brian Inglis, *Roger Casement* (London, 1973)
Roy Jenkins, *Asquith* (London, 1964)
Tom Jones, *Whitehall Diary III* (London, 1971)
Robert Kee, *The Green Flag* (London, 1972)
Paul Kennedy, *The Rise and Fall of British Naval Mastery* (Basingstoke, 1983)
Clifford King, *The Orange and the Green* (London, 1965)
Frank Kitson, *Low Intensity Operations* (London, 1971)
Helen Landreth, *The Mind and Heart of Mary Childers* (privately printed, 1965)
Elizabeth Lazenby, *Ireland, A Catspaw* (London, 1968)
J. J. Lee, *Ireland 1912–1985, Politics and Society* (Cambridge, 1989)
Shane Leslie, *Memoirs of Brigadier-General Gordon Shephard* (privately printed, London, 1924)
Longford, Earl of, and T. P. O'Neill, *Éamon de Valera* (London, 1970)
Elizabeth Longford, *Victoria RI* (London, 1964)
F. S. L. Lyons, *Ireland since the Famine* (London, 1971)
Dorothy Macardle, *The Irish Republic* (Dublin, 1937)
Philip Magnus, *Edward VII* (London, 1964)
Edward Marsh, *A Number of People* (London, 1939)
F. X. Martin (ed.), *The Howth Gun-running* (Dublin, 1964)
Robert K. Massie, *Dreadnought* (London, 1992)
R. B. McDowell, *The Irish Convention, 1917–1918* (London, 1970)
Michael McInerney, *The Riddle of Erskine Childers* (Dublin, 1971)
André Maurois, *Disraeli* (Paris, 1927)
Peter Mead, *The Eye in the Air* (London, 1983)
Gary S. Messinger, *British Propaganda and the State during the First War* (Manchester and New York, 1992)
Sarah Millin, *General Smuts* (London, 1976)
Arthur Mitchell, *Revolutionary Government in Ireland* (Dublin, 1994)
James Morris, *Heaven's Command* (London, 1968)
—— *Pax Britannica* (London, 1968)
Frank O'Connor, *An Only Child* (London, 1961)
—— *The Big Fellow (Michael Collins and the Irish Revolution)*, (Dublin, 1969)
Ulrick O'Connor, *A Terrible Beauty is Born* (London, 1975)
Sean O'Faoláin, *De Valera* (London, 1939)

Ernie O'Malley, *The Singing Flame* (Dublin, 1978)
—— *On Another Man's Wound* (Dublin, 1979)
T. P. O'Neill and the Earl of Longford, *Éamon de Valera* (Dublin, 1970)
Frank Owen, *Tempestuous Journey: Lloyd George, his Life and Times* (London, 1954)
T. P. O'Neill and the Earl of Longford, *Éamon de Valera* (Dublin, 1970)
Frank Pakenham (Lord Longford), *Peace by Ordeal* (London, 1935)
Thomas Pakenham, *The Boer War* (London, 1979)
A. Temple Patterson, *Tyrwhitt of the Harwich Force* (London, 1973)
Hugh and Diana Popham, *Thirst for the Sea* (London, 1979)
Bernard Porter, *The Lion's Share* (London, 1975)
J. B. Priestley, *The Edwardians* (London, 1970)
Charles Roetter, *Psychological Warfare* (London, 1974)
Desmond Ryan, *Remembering Sion* (London, 1934)
Geoffrey Shakespeare, *Let Candles be Brought In* (London, 1949)
Norman Stone, *Europe Transformed, 1878–1979* (London, 1983)
Lytton Strachey, *Eminent Victorians* (London, 1918)
—— *Queen Victoria* (London, 1921)
Major-General Sir Frederick Sykes, *From Many Angles* (London, 1942)
A. J. P. Taylor, *The First World War* (London, 1961)
—— *England 1914–1945* (Oxford, 1965)
Rex Taylor, *Michael Collins* (London, 1961)
Mark Tierney, *Modern Ireland since 1850* (Dublin, 1972)
G. M. Trevelyan, *English Social History* (New York, 1942)
Alan J. Ward, *Ireland and Anglo-American Relations* (London, 1969)
Nigel West, *MI6: British Intelligence Service Operations, 1909–1945* (London, 1983)
Terence de Vere White, *Kevin O'Higgins* (London, 1948)
Burke Wilkinson, *The Zeal of the Convert* (Gerrards Cross, 1978)
Basil Williams, *Erskine Childers, A Sketch* (privately printed, 1926)
Desmond Williams (ed.), *The Irish Struggle, 1916–1922*
Calton Younger, *Ireland's Civil War* (London, 1968)
—— *A State of Disunion* (London, 1972)

Index

Abbreviations: REC refers to (Robert) Erskine Childers; *RS* to *The Riddle of the Sands*.

Index

Index

Index

Index

Index

Index

Index